AMY'S BREAD

AMY'S BREAD
updated and revised

Amy Scherber & Toy Kim Dupree

Photography by Aimée Herring

WILEY

John Wiley & Sons, Inc.

This book is printed on acid-free paper. ∞

Photography copyright © 2010 by Aimée Herring
Prop styling by Laurent Laborie and Lauren Hunter
Book design by Cassandra J. Pappas

Published by John Wiley & Sons, Inc., Hoboken, New Jersey
Published simultaneously in Canada

For general information on our other products and services or for technical support, please contact our Customer Care Department within the United States at (800) 762-2974, outside the United States at (317) 572-3993, or fax (317) 572-4002.

Wiley also publishes its books in a variety of electronic formats. Some content that appears in print may not be available in electronic books. For more information about Wiley products, visit our Web site at www.wiley.com.

Library of Congress Cataloging-in-Publication Data:

Scherber, Amy.
  Amy's Bread / Amy Scherber and Toy Kim Dupree ; photography by Aimée Herring. —Updated and revised.
    p. cm.
  Includes index.
  ISBN 978-0-470-17075-5 (cloth)
  1. Bread. 2. Amy's Bread (Bakery) I. Dupree, Toy Kim. II. Amy's Bread (Bakery) III. Title.
  TX769.S396 2010   2009004206

Printed in China

10 9 8 7 6 5 4 3 2 1

To my Grandmother Florence,
who taught me to put a little bit of love
into everything I make.
A. J. S.

For my Mother,
who started me on my culinary adventures
with my first cookbook when I was
seven years old.
T. K. D.

Contents

Acknowledgments ix

Preface xi

INTRODUCTION 1

ESSENTIALS FOR MAKING GOOD BREAD 12

TECHNIQUES: OUR SECRETS AND TIPS 23

THE MAGIC OF MAKING BREAD RISE 48

SIMPLE BREADS TO GET YOU STARTED 70

BREADS MADE WITH WHOLE WHEAT FLOUR 99

SOURDOUGH BREADS 120

BREADS MADE WITH RYE FLOUR 147

FULL-FLAVORED BREADS 166

GOLDEN SEMOLINA BREADS 190

BAKERY FAVORITES: PIZZA AND FOCACCIA 201

SANDWICHES 211

BRIOCHE AND SWEET SPECIALTY BREADS 230

ADDITIONAL TECHNIQUES AND INFORMATION FOR AVID BAKERS 250

Glossary 266

Mail-Order Sources 269

Index 270

Acknowledgments

FIRST WE WISH TO THANK the staff at the bakery who work every day to make beautiful bread. Their dedication has helped us to earn our reputation for producing bread of the finest quality.

We are grateful to our editor, Justin Schwartz, for his enthusiasm and willingness to take this out-of-print book and give it new life. He's made it possible for us to once again share our recipes and our passion with others who love baking bread. Thanks also to the rest of our team at John Wiley & Sons, Inc.—senior production editor Alda Trabucchi, cover designer Suzanne Sunwoo, and promotional team of Gypsy Lovett and Carrie Bachman—as well as copy editor Suzanne Fass and book designer Cassandra Pappas.

A huge thank you goes to our agent Sharon Bowers for her boundless energy and support, and also to Angela Miller at the Miller Agency for believing in this project.

To our photographer, Aimée Herring, once again we feel blessed to be on the receiving end of your amazing ability to create a three-dimensional experience for a two-dimensional environment. Thanks also to Laurent Laborie, our talented prop stylist, and our favorite photographer's assistant, Katie Hawthorne.

Toy would like to say *grazie* to her dear friend and neighbor Tina Higgins for being such a willing guinea pig for the results of her recipe testing. She would also like to thank all of the bakers in the daytime pastry kitchen for doing an amazing job of holding down the fort while their executive pastry chef was at home working on this manuscript at the same time that their pastry chef was out on maternity leave!

And finally, Amy would like to thank her parents, Pat and Tony Scherber, her siblings, Sally Hopkinson and John Scherber, and her son and husband, Harry and Troy Rohne, who have encouraged her all along the way.

Preface

MAKING BREAD IS one of the simplest pleasures we know. This nurturing food is a staple of the diet in many cultures. Friends and customers have often told us that bread making is a "noble profession" because it is a way to serve people—to give pleasure, energy, and sustenance to those who eat it. Bread goes to the very roots of life and its ingredients are the most elemental. Rain, sunshine, and healthy soil to grow the wheat; human hands to harvest, mill, and turn the grain to flour; water captured in reservoirs, which moistens the flour; yeast, which occurs naturally around us in fermenting fruits and starches; and salt from the earth and sea are the basic ingredients. These, along with the warmth of the baker's hands, his or her strength, skill, and passion, and a fiery hearth, are all that are needed to make this simple yet incredible food.

Besides this glorious image of "earth to table," we like to make bread because it is always changing, and thus it challenges our skills, intuition, and senses. Does the dough feel right, smell right, and taste right? Is it wet or dry, warm or cool? How is the weather, how is the flour, and how is the oven? The same ingredients, mixed the same way every day, yield slightly different results in the hands of each baker. Some people may find this frustrating, but to be a good baker you must be calm, intuitive, and patient. You must use all of your senses to be aware of the dough, the environment, and your own mood. The challenge and the tasty, tangible reward make bread baking a great pleasure to experience—and to share.

—AMY SCHERBER AND TOY KIM DUPREE

INTRODUCTION

THE STORY OF THE BAKERY

Opening Amy's Bread was the fulfillment of a lifelong dream. I was raised in Minnesota on my mother's home-cooked meals and my grandmother's freshly baked bread, cookies, and homemade pies, and the kitchen has always been one of my favorite places. Both of my parents grew up on dairy farms, and big family meals were an important part of their lives.

My professional food career began modestly. Working as a waitress in a pie shop during high school and college, I served plenty of cream pies, fruit pies, and grilled burgers to hungry customers. I polished my skills as a dishwasher, food server, and waitress in the college cafeteria. One summer during college I worked as a private cook and baker for a family. After graduating from college with degrees in economics and psychology, I helped launch an innovative local restaurant.

At that point I thought I should pursue a "real" career, so I made a break for New York City and the business world, where I worked in a marketing agency for three years. Although presentations, client meetings, and promotional plans had their interesting moments, I was confined to a desk in an office cubicle, and I longed to work with food again.

With the idea of opening a restaurant one day, I went to the New York Restaurant School for culinary training. Afterward I worked for two years as a cook at Bouley, one of New York's most highly acclaimed restaurants. That was a tremendous learning

experience, and it was there that I discovered my true passion: bread making. To understand more about the bread-making process, I traveled to France, which has a strong tradition of baking good bread. I worked at boulangeries in three different towns, spending a month at each one. In these bakeries I learned about the production of baguettes and beautiful regional specialties. When I returned to New York, I was brimming with ideas and excitement about opening my own bakery. For the next two years, I worked as a bread baker at Mondrian restaurant with chef Tom Colicchio, and through trial and error developed my recipes and refined my techniques. Then I felt ready to launch my own business. Little did I know I had a lot left to learn.

It was at Mondrian that I met Toy, who was working as an apprentice in the pastry kitchen. She too had changed careers, from computer software development to baking, and she had also studied at the New York Restaurant School. When I broke my hand in a biking accident, Toy came to my rescue, shaping hundreds of loaves and rolls for the restaurant for no pay, in exchange for bread baking experience. With her skill, enthusiasm, and willingness to take on any challenge, I knew her contribution to the bakery would be invaluable. She has worked at Amy's Bread since we opened in June 1992, and the bakery thrives because of her dedication to quality.

Finding the perfect space for the bakery was my first mission. An old store-front on Ninth Avenue, in the heart of the neighborhood still fondly referred to as Hell's Kitchen, beckoned to me—and the location and the look of the old shop have become an important part of the bakery's identity. The area had been known for its food markets since the early 1900s. Our building had housed a fish market since it was constructed in 1896 and had been owned by the same landlord for forty years. He was proud of the area's history and had tried to maintain the feel of the neighborhood by keeping the old wood storefront, with its carved trim and bay window, the last of its kind on Ninth Avenue. The dilapidated ground floor space, with its high ceilings and decorative moldings, seemed the perfect place for a new Old World bread shop.

With the help and support of my parents, friends, and a gifted carpenter, the tiny 650-square-foot bakery took shape. We did all of the renovations ourselves:

We patched, plastered, painted, and in the process exposed a beautiful brick wall that had been hidden behind wood slats and horsehair plaster. We shored up the drooping bay window, gave it a fresh coat of turquoise paint, and replaced the tattered cloth on the old rollout awning with turquoise and white striped fabric. A wooden counter with trompe l'oeil painting, wooden shelves to hold the bread, a tin ceiling, and antique floor tiles were installed in our tiny retail space. The store was reborn, looking as it could have nearly a century before.

After the renovation, my staff of six dedicated employees, five women and one man, helped finish getting the bakery ready. We scrubbed used equipment and set up the shelves in the retail store. I taught them my bread recipes and techniques. Then, with little idea of what was to come, we opened our doors.

The first year was the hardest, and we had some difficult times. We learned to handle dough in brutally hot weather with no air conditioning, to keep going day after day on only a few hours of sleep, and to get by without money when our wholesale customers didn't pay us. Our space was so small and narrow that we could hardly wheel the racks of dough through it. But the hard early days made us enjoy the good days, when our only problem was too much demand. Sometimes we sold the bread so quickly nothing would be left by noon!

We also learned that a baker's work is never done. The dough keeps rising and must be controlled from beginning to end. The bakery operates twenty-four hours a day, seven days a week. Our wholesale customers want bread every day, and on holidays they double their orders. There is no shutting down for a two-week vacation. People expect their daily bread—every day!

Within the first ten months I realized we would need more space, so I borrowed more money and rented the adjoining ground floor space to make a larger kitchen. It didn't take long to fill that side of the bakery with equipment,

dough, and people, and by year four, we were really ready to expand. At that time I was lucky enough to meet the visionary developer and landlord Irwin Cohen, who had a dream of renovating a large old building in far west Chelsea, the former Nabisco factory, which he would make into an innovative food market. It would have all small, family-run food businesses, and each tenant would have a large space to produce their wholesale products, and a retail store. Both sides of the hall would be lined with glass so people could watch workers preparing food, and since I would be one of the first tenants, I could pick out whatever space I wanted. The place was to be called Chelsea Market. The minute I stepped into the vast empty building filled with dumpsters, open loading docks, arched ceilings, and tons of beautiful brick walls, I knew that was just where we belonged. Within weeks I signed a lease and we began building our new 7,500-square-foot bakery—what seemed like a huge space at that time. I was able to lay out the bakery in a very practical way so the bread could be carefully controlled from mixing through baking. We designed a separate air-conditioned mixing room where all the doughs would begin. Then the tubs of dough would move to an air-conditioned shaping room in front of the big windows, where kids and adults could watch the process of dividing and forming all the loaves. Finally, through the next doorway we would build a huge oven room where all our ovens could be seen through the window, and where we would have room to let the dough rise and the loaves cool, and finally to pack them into their brown satchel bags for wholesale deliveries. We kept all the original walls and ceilings in order to maintain the integrity of the building.

We were also able make a beautiful retail space that was softer than the other brick-and-cement-block shops in the market. I wanted to carry on the atmosphere of our first location with wheat-colored walls, warm lighting, antique floor tiles, and an antique display counter. I had a talented French blacksmith make us a lovely bread rack, created space on the long counter for sweets and sandwiches, and added lots of tables and chairs and an espresso machine. And voilà! We became a retail bakery/café.

Over the years the Chelsea Market has taken on a life of its own. It is filled with business people who work upstairs, neighborhood people doing their daily food shopping, tourists looking for Food Network stars (one of several TV networks in the building), and little children just learning to walk with their nannies. It's a warm, friendly place, bustling with activity day and night. We are very proud to have been one of the first tenants to sign on, and to realize the future potential of such a wonderful neighborhood market.

In the autumn of 2004 we were offered another amazing opportunity: the chance to open a third retail store right next to the famous Murray's Cheese in Greenwich Village. Murray's is one of the premier cheese stores in the United States, and we knew that being able to offer our bread to the cheese-loving shoppers in the neighborhood was a winning combination. Our customers in the Village needed a place to get their coffee, sweets, sandwiches, and bread, and we are very pleased to be part of such a strong neighborhood community.

Entering the bakery, the first thing you notice is a wonderful aroma. In any of our three retail cafés, the smell of toasty bread, freshly brewed coffee, just-from-the-oven sweets, and sandwiches toasting on our grill tempt you to try something from our wide array of products. You might see the shadow of the words "FRESH BREAD" cast on the wall by the afternoon sunshine as it passes through the large bay window in our original location. The antique light fixtures, black-and-white mosaic tile floor, and long wooden counter piled high with a multitude of baked goods give the bakery a feeling of warmth and intimacy. In each location the counter is filled with baskets of dinner rolls, bread twists, and focaccia, and stacks and stacks of freshly baked cookies. The bread shelves behind the counter are lined with dozens of golden brown loaves: semolina with golden raisins and fennel, black olive, organic whole wheat with walnuts, fresh rosemary bread, rustic Italian. Baskets lined with colorful cloths are brimming with freshly baked biscuits, Irish soda bread, sticky buns, muffins, croissants, and almond brioche toast. A big basket of rustic-looking oat scones beckons, but stacks of rich brownies, cashew bars, and dream bars vie for your attention. Then your eyes light on a loaf of organic miche, a deep brown round of bread with a floured top that has been scored with a square cut. The crust is slightly glossy

BIG CRUSTY LOAVES

Big crusty rounds of organic miche are coming out of the oven. Their color is almost that of dark walnut furniture, or roasted coffee beans. The crusts are hard and cracked. Ridges have formed where the loaves have been scored and have burst open from the intense oven heat. Each loaf smells like dark buckwheat honey and wonderful, hot whole wheat toast. They crackle and snap when they are removed from the oven, singing as their crusts shrink slightly in the cool, dry air. These large four-pound loaves feel heavy and dense, but have a certain lightness from being baked at the peak of fermentation. Their hard crusts protect a moist, chewy crumb. The reward of seeing these fresh-baked loaves is the reason we are bakers. We hope that you will experience this pleasure, too. It is these rustic loaves that fuel our memories and our imaginations and make us feel proud of the tradition we carry on.

and cracked along the scoring, and the loaf looks hearty and robust. Today you select the organic miche and resist the other temptations. You'll try something else next time—you know you'll be back.

HOW WE CREATE YOUR DAILY BREAD

The day begins at 5:00 A.M. with the mixing of the dough. Our largest mixer is filled with flour, water, sourdough starter, salt, and a pinch of yeast. Before long, a mass of creamy, glossy dough, smelling of robust wheat, is slapping and snapping as it is pulled and stretched by the fork kneader. After mixing, the dough is lifted from the bowl and cut by hand, placed into dough tubs to rest and rise slowly at a cool temperature, and then divided into portions to be shaped later in the day. With four large dough mixers kneading dough all morning, there are many rolling racks and hundreds of tubs of rising dough waiting to be divided and formed by our team of shapers who arrive at noon. While the mixing is in progress a team of baguette makers and organic bakers are busy shaping hundreds of baguettes, dinner rolls, and rustic or-

ganic loaves that are baked and delivered to restaurants around the city for their lunch and dinner service. At midday the radio is turned up to broadcast a Latin beat, coffee is brewed, and ten people surround the smooth wooden worktable to start shaping. With this much hand power, it doesn't take long to fill the racks with hundreds of loaves of every shape and size, from boules and ficelles to logs and batards, and hundreds of dozens of rolls as well. Skilled hands gently mold the loaves, piece by piece, being careful to seal the breads tightly while leaving some of the open air pockets intact—a feat a machine could never achieve. The bread is left to rise again and then is placed in a 50°F retarding walk-in refrigerator, where it will ferment and rise slowly until it is ready to be baked later during the day and night. The air in the retarder is moist, cool, and intoxicating with the smells of sourdough, wheat, and fennel.

The pace slows slightly, but then the night crew begins to arrive: first the organic mixer and baker, then the baguette mixer and assistant, the pack person, and then another dozen bakers and packers who fill out the team. Up goes the volume of the radio—this time we hear rock, heavy metal, or reggae— and up goes the pace. The room becomes warm and steamy as batch after batch of dough is loaded into the stone-hearth ovens. It's a thrill to watch through the oven windows as the intense heat transforms the slack loaves into plump domes. When the crust has reached a deep, rich dark brown, the loaves are pulled from the oven with a long wooden paddle called a peel, and placed on a rack to cool. Soon we share our favorite moment of the day: We hear the song of the crackling, snapping crust as the hot bread hits the cooler air of the room. The loaves look gorgeous with their glossy dark crusts decorated with stripes of flour and flared cuts, and they smell delicious.

After the bread has cooled, it is packed into brown paper bags for wholesale deliveries to some of the finest stores and restaurants in the city. Many drivers stop throughout the early morning to pick up the satchel bags of fresh bread. At 7:30 A.M. we open our three retail cafés for our neighborhood customers to the tune of classical music, jazz, and popular standards. By then most of the bread is baked, cooled, and stacked on the shelves, ready to be tasted and enjoyed. Meanwhile, we have already begun the whole process all over again!

THE PHILOSOPHY OF THE BAKERY

Our philosophy of work life is to enjoy the way we spend our days—life is too short to be miserable while you work. Many of us have changed professions because we love making bread—and baking in general—and have made our passion our career. We are proud of what we do, and our pride shows in the beautiful bread and sweets we make each day. In fact, part of our mission statement is to create and maintain a profitable bakery and cafés that nourish the bodies, minds, and spirits of the communities we serve—our neighborhood retail customers, our wholesale customers, and our bakery employees, by:

- making carefully handcrafted foods that taste as good as they look.
- providing service that makes you smile.
- maintaining a professional and congenial workplace that encourages stability and growth for our employees.
- using ingredients and procedures that sustain the health of the planet.

When we first opened we had no idea how long our employees would work with us at the bakery or how much they would enjoy our congenial workplace.

But over the past seventeen years, many of our bakers and managers have stayed for such a long time that they are now part of our "bakery family." It's not unusual to celebrate the tenth, thirteenth, or fifteenth anniversary of many of our employees who put their pride, love, and attention to detail into the bread they make every day.

With this book, we hope to show you the honest pleasure that comes from putting your heart into what you make. We believe so strongly in this important ingredient that we will mention it again and again. Think of the foods most dear to you—most often they were made by someone who put love, and even passion, into the preparation. Your grandmother's pie, your father's bacon and eggs, your best friend's chocolate chip cookies—all were lovingly made. These food memories carry with them a powerful emotion. With practice, some of our recipes can become your specialties as you begin to put more of yourself into the preparation. Your perseverance will pay off in beautiful baked goods that give great pleasure to you and to those who eat them.

At the bakery, every loaf of bread is formed by hand, and we believe that using hands rather than machines really makes a difference. In most of our recipes we recommend that you knead the dough by hand. You will learn more about the dough than you would if you let a machine knead it, and you'll have more fun getting your hands into the action. Our hand-formed loaves and rolls have a better crumb, with more irregular holes, than machine-shaped breads. The few misshaped loaves we make each day add the human touch to the process.

PRACTICE AND PATIENCE ARE THE KEYS TO SUCCESS

As each day passes, we refine our definition of the quintessential bread. It gets heartier, earthier, and more fragrant at each new level we reach. Mastering fermentation is the baker's biggest challenge, and a good baker continues to learn and make changes. Trying variations of time, temperature, and starter gives you different results with each new batch of dough. Like ours, your bread will get better and better at every new level of understanding. Our constant search for better bread keeps us challenged and gives us something to look forward to. We hope you will also keep experimenting. Each time you make bread, you will become more skilled and more confident. Keep notes on what you try and what you learn. You will find your bread becoming more sophisticated, with a deeper flavor, a lighter crumb, or a crunchier crust with the next new batch you make.

THE CRAFT OF BREAD BAKING

When we opened Amy's Bread in 1992, we were part of a new generation of American bread bakers who helped to change the definition of bread in our country. Over the years the term "artisan bread" has been used to describe this return to traditional bread-making methods. Unfortunately, the term has been misused by large manufacturers to label industrial bread mixes, machine-made breads, and anything else they think they can market more successfully by calling it

"artisan." At the bakery we like to say that "we specialize in handmade, traditional breads." Today's craft bakers use traditional methods learned from centuries-old European bakeries in France, Germany, and Italy, and they adapt the process to their modern bread bakeries. From New York to California, this kind of bread baking is still on the rise. Once people taste hearth-baked loaves made with longer fermentation times, thick crusts, and chewy crumbs, they have trouble going back to soft processed bread. We're pleased that the time has come for delicious artisan breads to replace the soft, squishy plastic-bagged bread so long associated with America.

Craft bakers have returned to making bread in smaller batches, using their hands to shape the dough, and reviving practices that had become a lost art. True artisan bakers use the best flour, often from organically grown wheat that is milled in smaller mills, and they leaven their bread with sourdough starters and other pre-ferments, using natural fermentation to enhance the flavor and texture of their breads. Like us, these bakers are driven by the desire to make a better "staff of life" and to reeducate the public about how good real bread tastes, and how important the daily ritual of buying bread locally can be.

Traditional craft bakeries are part of their communities, with small, abundantly stocked stores filled with fresh baked goods that people buy on a daily basis. These breads are made with wholesome ingredients, little fat or sugar, and no preservatives, and they make an important contribution to a healthful diet. The USDA's Food Guide Pyramid recommends six to eleven servings of bread and grains—especially whole grains—per day, so fresh-baked bread is the natural accompaniment to a healthy meal.

Since we wrote our first book more than thirteen years ago, we have gotten to know many wonderful bakers and bakery owners around the country. Without these friendships and the sharing of knowledge among bakers, we would not be where we are today. Bakers like Leslie Mackie of Macrina in Seattle, Craig Ponsford of Artisan Bakers (Sonoma,

California), Mary Mackay from Terra Breads (Vancouver, British Columbia), Steve Sullivan of Acme (San Francisco), Joanne Chang from Flour Bakery (Boston), Lynn and Jim Williams from Seven Stars (Providence), Didier Rosada (the Master) from Uptown Bakers (Hyattsville, Maryland), and Jim Lahey, Paula Oland, Noel Comess, and Dan Leader from our own New York, all inspire us to keep learning, keep baking, and keep raising the standards of bread and baked goods around the country.

Traditional bread baking has also become popular with home bakers. Through wonderful bread books like Dan Leader's *Local Breads*, Jeffrey Hamelman's *Bread: A Baker's Book of Techniques and Recipes*, Maggie Glezer's *Artisan Baking Across America*, and Peter Reinhart's *Crust & Crumb: Master Formulas for Serious Bread Bakers*, professional recipes based on classical techniques have been made accessible to home bread bakers. Our purpose in writing this book is to carry on this tradition of sharing, as well as to satisfy the many recipe requests we have had from our loyal customers. We're not attempting to write the "definitive" bread book, whatever that may be. Rather, we're passing along our favorite recipes and the techniques we use to make loaves that live up to our high expectations. We hope you will get as much pleasure and satisfaction from them as we do.

ESSENTIALS FOR MAKING GOOD BREAD

INGREDIENTS: BUILDING BLOCKS FOR DELICIOUS LOAVES

One of the most wonderful things about bread baking is that something so beautiful and satisfying to eat can be made with just four simple ingredients: flour, water, salt, and yeast. By combining different types of flours and adjusting the amounts of water and yeast, you can make a wide variety of delicious loaves. If you expand the ingredients list to include cracked grains, nuts, seeds, fruits, vegetables, sweeteners, dairy products, eggs, and fats, the possibilities are endless. At Amy's Bread the only ingredient taboos we have are fast-acting yeast products and additives or preservatives that artificially extend shelf life. Our preference is for organic products, although not everything we use falls into this category. Our general rule is to use natural products of the highest quality that have been minimally processed.

Flour

Flour is a subject of intense interest for artisan bakers. So many kinds are available, each with its own special characteristics that affect the volume, flavor, texture, and aroma of a finished loaf of bread. But the fact is you don't really need to know a tremendous amount about different flours to make delicious loaves in your home oven. At first, simply follow the specifications for flour types in each recipe and use whichever brand is available to you at the supermarket or the nearest natural food store. Once you've mastered the techniques and feel confident working with those flours, go for it! Experiment with the wide variety of interesting flours available from mail-order sources (see page 269) and gourmet specialty stores. Avoid self-rising flours and instant flours, which are unsuitable for bread baking, but don't be afraid to mix and match. Do taste tests using organic and nonorganic flours. We think organic flours win hands down, but don't take our word for it. Eventually you'll develop your own unique list of favorites.

Wheat flour

Wheat flour is the main ingredient in most of our recipes because this flour is the highest in gluten-forming plant proteins. It is these proteins that combine with water to form the flexible web in kneaded dough that traps carbon dioxide gas to make bread rise. Generally the more protein there is, the stronger the web of gluten, though the quality of the protein is also a factor. Protein quality requires a lengthy discussion that we won't address in this book. The amount of protein in a specific wheat flour is determined by the variety of wheat from which it is milled and the part of the wheat kernel from which it is extracted. Hard wheats are highest in protein, and red spring wheat and durum wheat are the hardest wheats grown.

Unbleached all-purpose flour is made from a combination of hard spring wheat and softer winter wheat, so it can be used for a variety of different baking jobs. It is milled from the starchy endosperm of the wheat grain. Strictly speaking, the flour is not "unbleached," as it has in fact been whitened by a natural aging process, but "bleached flours" are lightened with chlorine compounds and other chemicals. We prefer the light cream color of unbleached flour over the unnatural whiteness of chemically bleached all-purpose flour. There are many good all-purpose flours available in today's supermarkets and natural food stores.

Bread flour is a high-protein "white" flour, generally milled from the endosperm of hard red spring wheat. Good-quality bread flour can now be found in most supermarkets and natural food stores. Specialty gourmet food stores and mail-order catalogues (see page 269) are other good sources. We prefer not to use the bleached and bromated versions.

High-gluten flour is unbleached flour with a protein content of about 14 percent. It is most commonly used for making bagels and pizza dough. Don't confuse high-gluten flour with an ingredient called "vital wheat gluten." Vital wheat gluten is what's left when the starch has been removed from wheat flour through a water-washing process. It is essentially a natural gluten booster for yeast breads that are made with weaker nonwheat flours and/or significant amounts of nuts, seeds, and raisins. None of the recipes in this book call for this product, because they all use gluten-rich wheat flours as their main ingredient. Vital wheat gluten is approximately 40 percent protein.

Store grains and flours in thoroughly airtight containers in a cool location. Whole-grain flours and berries are especially susceptible to heat and humidity because the oil in the germ goes rancid quickly. If you're not going to be using them on a regular basis, the refrigerator or freezer is the best place for them. Remember to let cold flour come to room temperature before you use it, or be sure to factor in the cold flour temperature when determining the water temperature for your dough.

Patent durum flour is a fine, silky grind milled from a super-hard cold-weather wheat variety of the same name. Never bleached, this flour retains its lovely pale yellow color. Its high protein content makes it a wonderful flour for bread, but it's best combined with a softer flour. At the bakery we use it in combination with unbleached all-purpose flour to make our Italian-style semolina breads. When durum wheat is ground less fine, as coarse as cornmeal, it is called semolina flour, used primarily for pasta. Don't use semolina flour to make semolina bread—you'll get dense yellow rocks! The protein content of durum flour is about 12 percent.

Pastry flour and cake flour are both fine-milled from soft winter wheat. Whole wheat pastry flour is milled using the whole kernel; unbleached pastry flour and cake flour are milled from the endosperm. Cake flour is almost always bleached and enriched. At the bakery we use unbleached pastry flour in combination with all-purpose flour to lower the gluten content when making certain quick breads and other sweets. The protein content of pastry flour is around 9 percent. Cake flour is about 8 percent protein.

Whole wheat bread flour is milled using the whole kernel of hard red spring wheat. It contains not only the complete endosperm, but also the hull and germ, which are rich in fiber and nutrients. At the bakery we use organic stone-ground whole wheat flours, both coarse grind and fine grind. We love the coarser texture and wheaty fragrance and flavor they impart to breads. Being milled from hard wheat, they are generally high in protein, around 13 percent or more.

Wheat bran is the outer hull of the wheat, separated from the rest of the kernel during milling. We use it occasionally for additional texture in some of our whole-grain breads. Wheat germ is the nutrition-rich heart, or embryo, of the wheat kernel. It contains a high percentage of oil and must be kept refrigerated to keep it from turning rancid. It can be used raw or lightly toasted to add a slightly crunchy texture and a rich, nutty flavor to breads.

Rye Flour

Rye flour and pumpernickel flour that we use at the bakery are both milled from whole rye berries, containing the bran, germ, and endosperm. Our finely ground organic rye flour is the rye equivalent of fine whole wheat flour. Pumpernickel, sometimes called "rye meal," is the rye equivalent of coarse whole wheat flour. Although rye flour does contain some gluten, the percentage is so low that rye flour is almost always combined with some type of wheat flour when used for making bread. This fragrant, fruity-smelling grain is especially prone to fermentation and, as a result, it makes a good base for a sourdough starter (page 61). We love to use it in our "white" bread recipes to add depth and complexity to their flavor and texture. There is also a white rye flour, milled from the endosperm of the rye berry, but none of our recipes use this product.

The chart below lists the protein content of a few of the flours commonly available in most areas of the United States. In the Tips and Techniques section of our recipes, we tell you the protein content of the flours we used, if we had that information available.

FLOUR PROTEIN COMPARISON CHART

FLOUR BRAND	FLOUR TYPE	PROTEIN %
Arrowhead Mills	Unbleached Enriched "White" Flour	11.7
Arrowhead Mills	Organic Rye Flour	N/A
Ceresota/Hecker's	Unbleached All-Purpose Flour	11.8
Gold Medal	Unbleached All-Purpose Flour	11.0
Gold Medal	Harvest King	12.0
King Arthur	Organic Select Artisan All-Purpose	11.3
King Arthur	Unbleached All-Purpose Flour	11.7
King Arthur	Unbleached Bread Flour	12.8
King Arthur	All Natural White Whole Wheat	13.2
King Arthur	Organic White Whole Wheat	14.5
King Arthur	Traditional Whole Wheat	14.0
King Arthur	Organic Whole Wheat	13.0
N.D. Mills	Dakota Maid Bread Flour	12.0
Pillsbury	Softasilk Cake Flour	6.0 to 8.0
Pillsbury	Unbleached All-Purpose	10.5
Pillsbury	Unbleached Bread Flour	12.0
Swans Down	Cake Flour	6.0 to 8.0
Whole Foods 365	Organic Unbleached All-Purpose	11.5
Whole Foods 365	Organic Whole Wheat	13.0 to 14.0

Cornmeal

Cornmeal adds extra flavor and crunch to some of our breads. We like to use it in our semolina breads to enhance the yellow color and slightly sandy texture of the durum flour. We also use it to dust peels, baking pans, and stones to prevent dough from sticking before baking. We prefer the coarse-textured bright yellow stone-ground variety to the finer pale cornmeal that is found in supermarkets. It is available at natural food stores, through mail-order sources (see page 269), and sometimes in the ethnic food sections of supermarkets. Bob's Red Mill medium cornmeal works well in our recipes. You can also substitute Italian polenta for cornmeal in any of our recipes.

Oats

Rolled oats are used in several of our recipes. Full of protein, minerals, and fat, they add flavor and moisture to breads, keeping them fresh longer. We prefer the heavy old-fashioned variety to the lighter quick-cooking kind, so if you only have the quick-cooking oats available, be sure to use the weight rather than the cup measure called for in the recipe to achieve consistent results.

Liquids

Moisture is necessary in bread making to activate the yeast and promote the formation of gluten strands from the protein in the flour. Water is the liquid we use most often because it helps create a loaf with the chewy crumb and crunchy crust that we prefer. At the bakery and at home we use plain tap water except when we're making sourdough starters. Fortunately, in New York City we're blessed with excellent-tasting water right out of the faucet. If your tap water doesn't taste so great, you may want to use bottled spring water, or boil and cool your tap water before you use it. If you're in doubt, try a recipe once with tap water and once with bottled or boiled water, and let your taste buds make the decision for you. When a recipe specifies "very warm water" or "warm water," we suggest adding a little boiling water to cold tap water, or warming the water in the microwave until you get the desired temperature, to avoid water softeners and other undesirables that may come through your hot water pipes.

Milk in bread dough softens the crust and gives it a rich brown color. It also contributes to a finer-textured, more tender crumb and helps the bread stay fresh longer. We use milk in some of our yeasted sweet breads and many of our quick breads and breakfast items. If you prefer, skim or low-fat milk can be substituted when whole milk is called for.

Salt

Salt helps control the activity of yeast, tightens the gluten, and enhances the flavor of the other ingredients in bread dough. At Amy's Bread we prefer to use kosher salt because we like its mild flavor and the fact that it contains no additives. It has a coarser texture than regular salt, but the crystals are actually fine flakes. We think the flakes dissolve more easily in dough and can be sprinkled more evenly on pizza, focaccia, rolls, bread sticks, and the like. If you want to substitute kosher salt for regular salt in other bread recipes, be sure to double the measured amount (not the weight) of salt specified in the recipe; for example, if the recipe calls for a tablespoon of regular salt, substitute two tablespoons of kosher salt. The reverse is true if you want to substitute regular salt for the kosher salt in our recipes—use half the measured amount specified. Kosher salt and regular salt are actually equal if you weigh them; that is, half an ounce of kosher salt can be substituted for half an ounce of regular salt. In any case, you may want to adjust the amount of salt in a recipe to suit your personal taste.

The kosher salt marketed in some regions of the country looks like small rock-salt crystals instead of flakes. If your kosher salt is this type, you will probably want to use a slightly smaller measure of salt than specified in our recipes; e.g., if a recipe calls for two tablespoons of kosher salt, use about one tablespoon plus two-and-a-half teaspoons of these larger crystals. [Or weigh the salt instead—the two types of kosher salt should be equivalent. See page 27 of Paula Wolfert's *Cooking of Southwest France* (Wiley, 2005) for more information and measurements.]

Sweeteners

Granulated sugars (white and brown), honey, molasses, and maple syrup are the sweeteners we use to enhance the flavor of certain doughs. Sweeteners can accelerate yeast activity if used in small amounts, but will inhibit yeast activity if used in large amounts. They can also tenderize the crumb and cause the crust to brown faster during baking.

Fat

Butter, olive oil, canola oil, and walnut oil are the fats that you will see in our recipes. We use them when we want to add richness to the flavor of the bread and softness and moisture to the crumb. Breads that contain fat stay fresh longer. In addition, you will notice that doughs that contain fats are usually softer, smoother, and more pliable than those that are fat-free.

Eggs

Using eggs in a bread gives it a tender, almost cakelike texture. The yolks add color, richness, and moisture, and the whites increase the volume of the loaf. We use them in our sweet yeast breads and quick breads.

Specialty Ingredients

In artisan bread baking, specialty ingredients are anything other than the four most basic ingredients of flour, water, salt, and yeast. When we consider all the things that can add an incredible variety of flavors, textures, and colors to a simple loaf of bread, we sometimes feel like kids in a candy store. The possibilities are endless! You'll see many of our favorite ingredient combinations in the recipes in this book; we hope these will serve to inspire you to try new combinations of your own.

Grains and seeds add crunch as well as flavor. We like to use whole wheat berries and rye berries, as well as the cracked versions of these grains. Cracked grains should be covered with boiling water and soaked at room temperature overnight, and the whole berries should be cooked until they become nice and plump and tender, then drained and cooled before you use them. If you store cooked berries in the refrigerator in an airtight container, they will keep for at least a week. You will also find millet, flaxseed, poppy seeds, sunflower seeds, and sesame seeds in our recipes. We prefer the rich, earthy flavor of natural unhulled sesame seeds (available in natural food stores) to the tasteless white hulled variety found in most supermarkets.

Nuts are another of our favorite crunchies. Chopped or whole almonds, hazelnuts, pecans, and walnuts add their own unique flavors and textures to a loaf of bread. We always toast our nuts before we use them. Generally, we add nuts at the end of mixing the dough, after most of the gluten development has already taken place. If you add the nuts early in the mix, the sharp-edged pieces have a tendency to break the developing strands of gluten.

Olives are one of the most traditional and widely used ingredients for specialty breads. We stay away from the canned varieties and choose instead the more flavorful cured imports, such as Greek Kalamata, Amfissa, and Atalanti olives. Use your own favorites, and try a combination of complementary types. Rinse any brine from the olives and drain them before incorporating them into the dough at the end of the kneading time. If you add olives to a recipe, you may want to decrease the amount of salt to allow for the saltiness of the olives.

Dried fruits add sweetness to bread without using sugar. Cut into coarse chunks, they add color and texture as well. Use them as they are, or soak them briefly (fifteen to thirty minutes) in just enough warm water to cover them. Drain off the water and save it to use as part of the liquid in your dough. Our recipes use dark raisins, golden raisins, currants, apricots, and figs.

Vegetables add flavor, color, and extra nutrition to bread. Use them raw or lightly cooked and coarsely chopped, finely diced, or pureed. Even dried peas or beans can be cooked or ground into coarse flour and added to a bread dough. We've used onions, garlic, scallions, potatoes, red bell peppers, and pumpkin in the recipes in this book.

Fresh herbs are one of the most pleasing additions to bread dough. We particularly like basil, rosemary, sage, and thyme. When you experiment, practice moderation. The herbs should enhance the flavor of the bread, not overpower it. Dried herbs can be used, too, but often they're a pale substitute for their fresh counterparts. In general, you can substitute one teaspoon of dried herbs for one tablespoon of fresh herbs (a one-to-three ratio). However, dried herbs lose their pungency as they age, so the condition of your dried herbs should be considered when deciding how much to substitute. Let taste be your guide.

Spices, in small amounts, go a long way in a loaf of bread. We use them in both sweet and savory combinations with other ingredients. You'll see cinnamon, caraway, mustard seeds, and dill seeds in the recipes in this book.

Cheese has always been a favorite partner for bread. We incorporate imported Parmesan into one of our doughs and use several other varieties in our pizzas.

TOOLS: A FEW IMPLEMENTS TO MAKE YOUR JOB EASIER

Equipment

You don't need a lot of fancy, complicated tools and equipment to make the recipes in this book; our motto at the bakery in general is Keep It Simple. In fact, for most jobs, your hands are the best tools of all. In this section we're only listing equipment that may be difficult to find or that we believe has a major influence on whether you'll be able to duplicate our recipes successfully.

Baking Stone and Wooden Peel   We recommend using a baking stone for baking bread, often sold as a pizza stone, to simulate a stone hearth in your home oven. The best stones have a large surface area. We prefer a rectangular shape to a round one because we can fit more loaves of bread on it. You can bake bread on a parchment-lined sheet pan, too, but you'll get more oven spring (which contributes to a lighter crumb) and a better crust with a baking stone. If you use a baking stone, it helps to have a wooden peel to load bread onto the stone. It also helps to have a pizza stone brush to sweep the cornmeal off of the stone, or once the stone has cooled you can wipe it with a damp cloth. Baking stones and peels are available at kitchenware stores or you can purchase them easily through many online retailers (see page 269).

Bannetons and Baker's Linen/Canvas (Couche)   The willow baskets called *bannetons*, which can be cloth lined or unlined, and heavy baker's linen called *couche* (used in this book to line sheet pans) are tools professional bakers use for letting shaped loaves rise. They provide a structured place for the rising dough, help to stabilize the temperature of the proofing dough, and result in a finished loaf with a more attractive appearance than you would get by proofing on parchment lined sheet pans. We use a banneton for proofing the Organic Miche loaf on page 139. Linen-lined bannetons can be purchased online from www.amazon.com; choose the 10⅝-inch basket for up to three pounds of dough. You can also purchase a 10-inch lined basket by calling the San Francisco Baking Institute at 650-589-5724. Their prices are very reasonable. Go to www.sfbi.com/baking_supplies.html for information on both bannetons and couche. The King Arthur Flour online catalog, www.kingarthurflour.com, also has unlined baskets, called *brotform*, and the linen couche.

Cast-Iron Skillet   This is an inexpensive and invaluable tool for producing steam in your oven at the beginning of the bake. You can substitute another baking pan, but nothing produces the intense heat to turn water into steam quite the same way as cast iron.

Electric Stand Mixer   We prefer to knead bread by hand, but for some of our very wet or very heavy recipes an electric mixer can simplify and shorten the kneading process. Use a heavy-duty stationary electric mixer, such as a KitchenAid, with a dough hook.

Kitchen Scale   If you don't already own a digital kitchen scale, buy one. We firmly believe and know from experience that the best way to guarantee consistent results from a recipe is to weigh the ingredients instead of using measuring cups and spoons. Baking is a science that requires accurate measurements to achieve predictable results. Weights in grams are much more precise than weights in ounces, but ounces are fine if you feel more comfortable using them. At the bakery, all of our recipes are expressed in gram weights. In an effort to represent our bakery recipes as accurately as possible, we list the ingredient amounts for the recipes in this book in grams first. Once you get used to using grams, everything else will seem cumbersome. You will have the most success using the recipes in this book to duplicate the products we make in the bakery if you weigh the ingredients.

Good electronic digital kitchen scales are available in all kitchenware stores and can also be purchased online. We don't usually recommend specific brands, but we're so anxious to encourage you to purchase a scale if you don't have one that we decided to tell you about a very dependable budget-priced scale that we found while we were testing our recipes for this book. We both used the little Escali Primo scale that has a maximum capacity of 5 kilograms (11 pounds/175 ounces) and uses two AA batteries that last for a very long time. This scale is very accurate and very dependable and stands up to very heavy use. The cover on the battery compartment does like to fall off, but a piece of tape solved that problem immediately. It's available at many kitchenware stores and online at www.amazon .com, www.kingarthurflour.com, and www.target.com.

Lame A razor blade mounted on a 3- to 4-inch handle, known as a *lame*, is a safe and efficient way to score (slash) bread before it's loaded into the oven. You can also use a sharp single-edge razor blade. A lame can be ordered online at www.kingarthurflour.com, www.pastrychef.com, or from www.sfbi.com/ baking_supplies.html.

Parchment Paper Parchment paper is a valuable tool for the baker. Used to line a pan for sweet breakfast breads or bread sticks, it keeps them from sticking to the pan without a lot of extra oil or butter for greasing. It can also be used in place of cornmeal to keep loaves from sticking to a peel or pan before they are baked on a baking stone. We find that parchment works better than cornmeal when sliding loaves made from wet, sticky dough onto the baking stone. Parchment can be purchased at specialty cookware stores and in most supermarkets.

Sheet Pans In the recipes in this book we recommend using 17 X 12 X 1-inch sheet pans, called half sheet pans by professional bakers, to proof and sometimes bake shaped bread. They're made from aluminum-coated steel with a rolled edge surrounding bead wire, so they're heavier than ordinary baking sheets made for the home kitchen. They heat quickly and evenly for more uniform baking and they won't warp in the oven. They also last forever. The outside top dimensions of the pan are actually 18 X 13 inches. They have straight sides and are often called jelly roll pans, though that term is rarely used in professional kitchens. We recommend you add two of them to your collection of baking pans if you don't have them already. Once you bake with them, you won't want to use anything else. They're available in most good kitchenware stores and from many online retailers that specialize in kitchenware.

Thermometer   An instant-read digital thermometer is one of the most important tools you can buy. It is used to measure the temperature of both the water you mix into the dough and the final mixed dough. In some cases it may even be necessary to read the temperature of the flour and pre-ferments used in your dough (see Troubleshooting on page 259).

It is also helpful to have a portable room thermometer to find the ideal place for your dough to rise. It is helpful to know the temperature of the room where the dough is mixed and, more important, where it rises.

It's a good idea to buy an oven thermometer, too, since most home ovens fluctuate in temperature and their thermostat settings are not particularly accurate.

Timer   A timer is an important tool when mixing, shaping, and baking bread. Purchase a digital timer that can be set for several hours so you can use it when you're making our slow-rising doughs. It's helpful to have a timer with multiple settings, for timing several procedures at once or when making more than one batch of bread at a time.

TECHNIQUES: OUR SECRETS AND TIPS

At Amy's Bread, judging a great loaf of bread is all about flavor and texture. This chapter contains general information about techniques that will help you learn to make a great loaf of bread. (We've included more detailed technical information in Chapter 13.) Our technical skill, knowledge, and intuition have come from practical experience and we continue to learn with each passing year. Time and practice will also teach you about the best dough texture, dough temperature, rising and proofing, and how to achieve the optimum flavor of a ripened sourdough starter. You will learn about flour strength and gluten development, about molding and dough handling, and about the advantages of slow fermentation times at cool temperatures. As you apply these techniques to your bread making, you will find that the more you control the variables affecting the dough, the better your bread will be. When you get everything just right and make the big, beautiful, crusty loaf of your dreams, you'll feel the same sense of pride and satisfaction we feel every day at the bakery.

Measuring Ingredients

One technique that will greatly improve your results is to weigh all the ingredients on a kitchen scale instead of measuring their volume using measuring cups. The weather and the humidity level can affect the volume measurement of flour, and different types and brands of flour often have different volumes. In addition, each person measures flour differently. The same is true for liquid measurements.

We have found that liquid measuring cups frequently have inaccurate volume markings, so we weigh our liquids as well. Although we have given both weights and volume measures in our recipes, we strongly recommend that you use a scale for greater accuracy. In the bakery we weigh everything in grams because we believe it is the most accurate measurement to get the most consistent results. Almost all the digital scales available for home bakers today offer grams as a one of the weight options. On page 21 is information about the little digital scale we use when baking at home.

Controlling the Temperature of the Dough

Another very important technique is to control the temperature of the bread dough. Old recipes for bread using packets of commercial yeast had the dough proofing at temperatures of 85° to 90°F. This definitely made for speedy rising times but did very little to develop the flavor or texture of the bread. Allowing bread dough to ferment more slowly at cooler temperatures, 75° to 77°F, as we do in the bakery, creates the optimum environment for yeast activity (which contributes to the bread's texture and volume) and more time for the flavor of the ingredients to develop. Besides giving the bread better flavor and texture, a slow rise also gives the loaf a moister interior, which extends the shelf life without having to use preservatives.

If you don't already own one, purchase an instant-read digital thermometer and use it to check the temperature of the flour and the water you are going to use in the dough. After mixing it is also important to check the temperature of the dough. We like our final mixed dough to be in that 75° to 77°F range. Ideally, we also like to let the dough rise in a cool room that mirrors that same temperature range. We refer to this technique as a "slow, cool rise." The rising and proofing times in our recipes are based on these temperature ranges. Our recipes show suggested temperatures for the water to help you achieve the desired dough temperature, but those assume you'll be baking in a cool, temperately comfortable environment with flour temperatures that reflect that environment. The most accurate way to achieve a final dough temperature in the desired range is to use the detailed guidelines on page 259, in the Troubleshooting section.

Making Dough with the Right Amount of Moisture

One of the most common mistakes in bread baking is to make the dough too dry. Some people hold back part of the flour at first, then try to knead it all in to create a firm, resilient dough. Or they throw lots of flour on the table and on the dough as they knead it, making dough that feels more like stiff clay. This may make it easier to work with the dough in the beginning because it's not so sticky in the early stages of the kneading process, but the resulting bread comes out with a dense, tough texture, very small holes in the crumb, and much less flavor than you would get from a wetter dough. The moisture in the dough is what absorbs and distributes the flavor elements from the ingredients. Less moisture equals less flavor. More moisture equals more flavor.

We like to add all of the water and flour in the ingredient list in the beginning when mixing dough. Once you start kneading, you'll be able to feel the texture of the dough. If the dough seems firm, you can add more water by the tablespoon until it is supple and moist. Just flatten the dough on the table and dimple the surface with your fingertips. Sprinkle on one to two tablespoons of water, fold the dough in thirds, and knead gently until the water is absorbed. The dough will become slippery at first, perhaps shredding, but the shreds will come back together eventually, becoming a smooth dough mass. Moist dough feels supple and soft and stretches easily when it is properly kneaded.

The benefits of wetter dough are moist, chewy bread with a glossy crumb, a longer shelf life, an appealing texture with more open holes, and a satisfying, complex flavor. The secret to the dough we make in the bakery is wetter is better. Wetter dough is a little scary and more difficult to work with in the beginning, and it does take longer to knead, but with practice and persistence you'll soon become comfortable with it. Of course, dough can be made too wet, resulting in bread that spreads and flattens and has a sticky, gummy crumb. This might happen with our recipes if your flour is too low in protein so it can't absorb as much water. Dough that is too wet looks more like thick pancake batter or porridge; see page 259 for more information on how to deal with this problem.

After you have tried the same recipe two or three times, you'll learn how wet you should mix the dough to get the exact results you want. (To determine the moisture content of a dough you can calculate the hydration rate, or the ratio of water to flour in that dough; see page 260 for more information on this calculation.)

Resting the Dough (Autolyse)

Autolyse is a French baking term that refers to a rest period of at least fifteen to twenty minutes given to bread dough during the kneading process. This rest lets the gluten in the dough relax so that the protein in the flour can absorb more water than it otherwise would, resulting in dough that is smooth, strong, and supple. It also allows time to activate protease, an enzyme in flour that helps increase the extensibility (stretchiness) of bread dough so it's easier to lengthen loaves during shaping and helps them rise higher during the baking process. Using the autolyse method shortens the kneading time because much of the gluten development takes place while the dough is resting. Classically, with the French method, the only ingredients that are mixed together before the autolyse are flour and water, but we have tried adding other ingredients with good results. First, some or all of the dough ingredients are mixed together to form a shaggy mass. The dough is kneaded for a few minutes to begin the gluten development, then it rests, covered, for twenty minutes. After the rest, the dough is kneaded for a few more minutes, depending on the type of dough, until it is stretchy and smooth. We give specific instructions for timing the rest periods for our doughs with each recipe.

Kneading the Dough

In this revised edition of our book, we have increased the hydration rate of most of the doughs because we believe today's home bread bakers are more sophisticated and are ready to work with bread dough that is exactly as we make it in the bakery. In recipes where the dough is exceptionally difficult to handle, we recommend using an electric mixer, as indicated in the instructions. Otherwise we prefer hand kneading because we enjoy getting our hands and our whole body into the therapeutic rhythm of pushing, turning, and folding the dough. It's also interesting to feel the properties of the developing gluten as the dough changes from a lumpy, lifeless mass to a smooth, supple, stretchy, springy, dough. Once you get used to the feel of wetter dough and you practice working with a dough cutter to scrape up the dough from the table, you'll find it easy to improve any bread recipe yielding firm dough by adding a little more water.

To knead dough by hand, first mix the wet and dry ingredients together in a bowl with your fingers until the dough comes together and forms a wet, shaggy mass. Then move it to a very lightly floured surface to continue kneading. With wetter dough, don't give in to the temptation to use a lot of flour to keep it from sticking to your hands or the work table. Just keep your hands lightly floured and make good use of your dough scraper. You don't need to beat the dough or work so vigorously that you work up a sweat. The experienced baker uses a quick, confident hand that does not warm the dough too much yet provides enough strength to develop the gluten. Knead the dough by pushing it down and away from you with the palms or the flattened fingers of your hands, then lift the dough, turn it a quarter turn, pull it toward you, folding it in half, and repeat the process, using a push-turn-fold motion over and over again. Sometimes when the dough is quite

Kneading Dough

A shaggy mass takes form in the bowl.

Move the dough mass to the table where you will knead.

Pull the dough toward you.

Lift and stretch the dough.

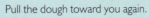

Pull the dough toward you again.

As the dough becomes more developed, scrape it up from the table.

Push and turn the dough a few more times.

The fully kneaded dough

wet, you may actually be smearing it onto the work table as you're pushing it away from you. If the dough sticks to the table during kneading, use a dough scraper to lift it off the table and scrape up the sticky dough residue, then dust lightly with more flour. If your hands get too clogged with sticky dough, you can coat them generously with flour and rub them vigorously over a trash can to "clean" them before continuing your kneading.

Using an Electric Mixer to Knead the Dough

To knead dough using a heavy-duty stationary mixer such as a five-quart Kitchen-Aid, it may work best to mix the wet and dry ingredients with a paddle first, until they gather into a moist, solid mass, then switch to a dough hook. On some older model machines, the dough hook doesn't reach the bottom of the bowl and thus is not as effective for gathering for ingredients together as the paddle. A longer hook with a more pronounced C shape has been introduced for later models of the KitchenAid mixer, making the use of the paddle unnecessary.

If you use an electric mixer for the manual recipes in this book, follow our timing instructions for hand kneading, but start by using the times at the lower end of the range specified; for example, if the range is five to seven minutes, knead for five minutes. You may also need to reduce the kneading time after the rest period by about two or three minutes if a manual kneading time longer than that is indicated.

The recipes in this book that do specify an electric stand mixer were tested with a KitchenAid stationary mixer with ten speeds, so the equivalent mixing speeds for that machine are as follows: low is #1, medium-low is #2, medium is #4, and medium-high is #6. Be sure to keep a close eye on the machine at the higher speeds because vibration can cause it to "walk" across the table and onto the floor!

Kneading Special Ingredients into the Dough

To knead special ingredients such as raisins, nuts, olives, onions, etc., into the dough, we use two equally effective methods depending on the type or texture of the dough. If you find you prefer one method over another, it's fine to use it for every recipe that calls for the inclusion of special ingredients.

1. Spread the special ingredients on top of the dough in the mixing bowl while it is resting. When the rest period is over, fold the dough over the ingredients and begin to knead it gently in the bowl until everything is evenly incorporated,

Kneading Special Ingredients into the Dough

Spread special ingredients on the dough during the rest period.

Knead the ingredient into the dough—the dough becomes shredded.

The finished dough is smooth.

two to three minutes. You may also move the dough onto a lightly floured work surface if you find kneading in the bowl is awkward for you.

2. Flatten the dough and stretch it gently with your fingers to form a rectangle about ¾ inch thick. Spread the special ingredients evenly over the rectangle. Fold the dough into an envelope as if you're folding a business letter (see page 34) and knead gently for two to three minutes, until the ingredients are well distributed. The dough should be soft, smooth, and springy. If it resists, let it rest for five minutes and then continue kneading it. Some of the ingredients may pop out of the dough, but they can easily be incorporated again after the first rise, when the dough has softened.

In both techniques, the dough may separate and look stringy before it comes together again into a smooth mass. Do not overwork the dough; if the additional ingredients keep popping out, stop kneading and wait until after the first rise, when the dough can be given a gentle turn to finish incorporating the ingredients.

Knowing When the Dough Is Fully Kneaded

The dough is fully kneaded when it is smooth, supple, and strong but stretches easily. To test dough made from mostly white flour, pull up a handful of dough and stretch it to form a thin membrane or "window pane." If you can stretch it

Window pane technique for white dough

so it's almost transparent, as thin as a balloon, it's ready. This stretch test does not always work as well with coarse-grained whole wheat or rye dough or with dough that has a lot of nuts, seeds, fruit, or chips in it. When these doughs are fully kneaded, they will feel springy and form a cohesive ball that doesn't stick to the work surface as much as it did in the early stages of the kneading process. You may still almost be able to form a membrane, but the hard bits will eventually cause it to tear.

Covering the Dough

After the dough has been kneaded, it is placed in a bowl to ferment (rise). Lightly oil the bowl to prevent the dough from sticking; we use vegetable oil. Turn the ball of dough in the bowl to coat the top with oil. Then cover the dough with plastic wrap to keep it from drying out. We spray the plastic wrap with nonstick cooking spray so it won't stick to the dough. The same piece of oiled plastic wrap can be used to cover the loaves after they have been shaped.

Letting the Dough Rise

Professional bread bakers refer to the first rising time of the dough as its fermentation period, because as the yeast in the dough is multiplying it is converting any sugars in the dough to alcohol and carbon dioxide. This chemical process is known as fermentation. In this revised edition of the book, we will generally continue to use the terms "rise" and "ferment" interchangeably, as "rise" was the word most familiar to home bakers when the book was first written.

Each rise of the dough plays an important role in the development of the bread. Some of the doughs in this book, primarily the wetter ones, will need to be deflated, or turned, partway through the first rise before they can be shaped into loaves for the final proof. If a turn is needed, it is generally done about an hour into the first rise.

During the first fermentation, the proteins in the flour continue to absorb liquid, forming a more complex network of gluten strands to strengthen the dough so it can contain the gas given off during the fermentation process, allowing the dough to rise. Organic acids are also formed that help give the dough extensibility and contribute flavor. The tangy characteristics of sourdough bread are developed at this time, and the unique flavor qualities of any special ingredients begin to permeate the dough. The gas that forms and is trapped in the gluten creates the light texture of the bread and the openness of the crumb.

If a turn is needed during the first rise, it should be done gently; punching down is not necessary nor is it desirable, as you want to preserve much of the gas that has already been trapped in the dough. After the first hour, gently deflate the dough in the middle of the bowl with your fingertips, then fold the left side over the middle, and the right side over the middle. Fold the dough in half, gently pat it down, and turn it over so the seam is underneath. Let it rise again until it has doubled in volume. When the dough is fully risen, an indentation made by poking your finger deep into the dough should not spring back. At this point your dough is ready to be shaped. When shaped loaves are set to rise, we call it proofing.

The ideal room temperature for fermenting dough is 75° to 77°F. At temperatures over 81°F, the dough will ferment too quickly and will develop a very yeasty or bitter flavor, like beer. In the bakery we have temperature-controlled environments so we can consistently produce our breads with the desired textures and flavors in a predetermined time frame. However, when baking bread at home, you may have to be creative about keeping your bread dough in the desired temperature range. If your room is very warm, you may want to mix your dough at a slightly cooler temperature, as the dough may warm quickly during the first rise. Or if your dough is already too warm and your room is warm, you may want to refrigerate it briefly to bring the dough temperature down. On the other hand, if your room temperature is too cool and the dough is too cool, putting the dough into an oven warmed by a pilot light or near a radiator for a short time (about twenty minutes) may be an option. Also try to choose a location for your dough that is free from drafts. It is wise to check the dough temperature occasionally with your digital thermometer so you can tell if it may be likely to rise faster or slower than the times given in the recipes.

Retarding the Dough (Slowing the Fermentation)

You can slow down the fermentation of the dough by retarding (refrigerating) it after the first rise has begun. Retarding intensifies the benefits of the cool rise, further enhancing the texture and flavor of your bread. Breads that have been retarded will stay fresh longer, too. After you mix the dough, let it rise for about an hour at room temperature, or until it has begun to increase in volume but has not doubled. Then chill the dough overnight or for at least eight hours and up to twenty-four. The second half of the rise takes place in the refrigerator. After the dough has been retarded, let it come to room temperature and soften before shaping and proofing it. This can take several hours depending on the temperature of your room.

Retarding dough also gives you more flexibility. You can mix it one day and finish shaping and baking it the next. Some doughs work better not chilled overnight. We indicate in each recipe whether or not the dough is enhanced by the retarding method.

Tests for Rising
Here is how to test dough to see if it has risen enough.

Small ball of unrisen dough in bowl

The dough has visibly doubled in volume.

Test the volume by poking a finger deep into dough.

The indentation does not spring back.

How to Know if the Dough Is Fully Risen
To tell if dough is fully risen, you can use three tests. The most obvious is a visual test. You can see that the dough has increased substantially in volume; most doughs will almost double in size. You can also poke the dough to see if it has risen enough. For the first rise, you should be able to push your floured finger deep into the mass of dough and leave an indentation that does not spring back. For loaves that have been shaped and are proofing, touch them lightly with your index finger. Flour your finger lightly before touching very wet dough. When they are ready for baking, the dough should feel soft and the slight indentation should not spring back. Another test for a free-form loaf when it's proofing is to gently place your fingers under the loaf and lift it up to see if the dough feels light and airy.

You will be able to tell when the network of bubbles has expanded inside the loaf because the dough will not feel as dense.

If your dough has risen too much and overproofed on the second rise so the shaped loaves are beginning to spread and deflate, gently pat the loaves to flatten them, then reshape them and let them proof again. It is almost always better to reshape them than to bake overproofed and deflating loaves. We actually prefer to leave most of our loaves very slightly underproofed in the final rise because they tend to get more "oven spring" in the early stages of baking.

Shaping the Loaves

Here we describe how to make five basic bread shapes; see page 254 for directions for other shapes. When shaping your loaves, the most important thing to remember is to be gentle with the dough. Your goal is to form an even loaf with a taut skin, while leaving some larger air holes inside.

Log   The log shape is the base for other shapes including the bâtard, baguette, and ficelle. Very lightly flour the work surface. Start by forming an envelope: Place the dough on the table. Press and flatten it gently with your fingertips to form a rectangle with a short side facing you, leaving a lot of air bubbles in the dough. Fold the top edge down over the middle of the rectangle, then fold the bottom edge up. Give the dough a quarter turn and repeat the process, folding the top edge down and the bottom edge up again and overlapping the edges slightly in the middle so the dough looks like an envelope. Pat the seam to seal it. Now you have a smaller, tighter rectangle.

Form a cylinder: Starting from the top edge of the rectangle, fold the top third of the dough over itself with one hand. With the heel of your other hand, gently press the seam to seal it. Fold the dough one third of the way down again and work from one end to the other to seal the seam. Try to keep the skin of the dough smooth and tight but not so tight that the skin tears. Repeat this process one or two more times, until the loaf is a nice round log. Seal the final seam completely with the heel of your hand. Ideally your seam should be straight and tight with no openings or flaps of dough hanging out; with practice, this will become natural. If any dough is protruding from the ends of the log, poke it back in with your finger.

The plain log shape can be placed in a loaf pan or left on a cloth for free-form proofing. From the log shape, you can make other cylindrical shapes.

Log Shaping

Flatten the dough into a rectangle.

Now we begin a business letter fold.

Business letter fold, folding the bottom up

Shaping an envelope

First fold to shape a log

Seal with the heel of the hand after the first fold.

Seal the final seam of the log.

The finished log shape

Bâtard   Begin to form the basic log shape, making an envelope. Flatten the envelope and fold the top two corners in toward the center of the rectangle to form a triangle. Using your fingers, fold the point of the triangle down into the center of the loaf, forming a half-moon shape. Then fold the dough over itself one third of the way down and, working from one edge to the other, seal the seam with the heel of your hand. Give the loaf two to three more folds, each time folding in the ends farther so they become more tapered. Seal the final seam tightly with the heel of your hand. Now roll the loaf back and forth on the table under your palms, working from the middle out to the ends of the loaf and pushing down on the ends to taper them. This technique will smooth out, elongate, and taper the loaf.

Bâtard Shaping

Flatten the dough into a rectangle, then make an envelope.

Fold in the corners of the envelope to form a half-moon shape.

Seal the first fold with the heel of your hand.

Seal the final seam.

The finished bâtard shape

The bâtard should be between eight and ten inches long, depending on the weight of the dough. Place the loaf on a floured cloth or board to proof.

Baguette   To make either a baguette or a thinner rope called a ficelle, flatten the dough into a rectangle; fold the top down and the bottom up to form a business letter. Working from one end to the other, fold the dough one third of the way down over itself and seal the seam with the heel of your hand. Repeat the process two or three times, making the log longer and thinner. Seal the final seam. Place

Baguette Shaping

Begin to shape a baguette by folding the dough over to form a business letter.

Fold the dough over once and seal with the heel of your hand.

Seal the final seam on the baguette.

Start at the center and roll the dough out to elongate the baguette.

Push your hands in two directions to elongate the baguette.

Elongate the baguette.

The final baguette shape

both palms over the middle of the loaf and roll it back and forth to elongate it, working out toward the ends. (If the loaf springs back, let it rest for two minutes, then roll it out again.) Return your hands to the center of the loaf and repeat the process, pushing down and rolling until the loaf is the length you want. Do not stretch the dough so much that the skin tears. The baguette can be placed in a mold or on a floured cloth or board to proof.

Boule   To shape the dough into a round ball-shaped loaf, or boule, place it on a very lightly floured surface and gently pat it to flatten it slightly. Then, working around the circle of dough, fold the outside edges of the dough into a point in the middle, section by section. Dust the flour off a small part of the worktable and turn the ball over onto the clean spot. Rotate the ball against the table to tighten and seal it completely: With your right hand, pull the loaf toward you and with your left hand push it away, working in a clockwise motion. You are using the stickiness of the dough to create tension against the table. Continue to shape, or round, the ball until the skin of the loaf is pulled tight, being careful not to let the skin tear. When the loaf is shaped, turn it over and rub a little bit of flour on the seam to prevent sticking, then put it seam side down in the proofing place of your choice.

Boule Shaping

Pull the sides of the dough into the center.

Rotate the dough against the table to tighten and seal the boule.

The finished boule

Roll To shape a roll, place a piece of dough on an unfloured table and cover it with your palm. Your fingers should form a cage over the roll. Rotate your curved fingers against the table in a clockwise motion and tighten the skin over the roll by pushing it against the table. The piece of dough will move under your palm in the opposite direction. Continue until the roll is firm and has a tight skin; work quickly and try not to warm up the dough too much with your hand. Place the rolls on a pan or floured cloth to proof.

Roll Shaping

Form a roll by making a cage over the dough with your fingers.

Choosing a Proofing Place for the Shaped Loaves

When you're going to bake the bread on a baking stone (see page 19), you have a choice about where to let the loaves proof. Since they must be slid onto the hot stone, it's easiest to let the shaped loaves proof on a peel or on an upside-down baking sheet covered with parchment paper. You can also let them proof somewhere else, such as the work surface, and then move them to the peel just before baking. Moving the loaves after they have proofed can work well, but there's a danger of deflating them. Wherever the loaves proof, be sure to cover them with plastic wrap so a dry skin doesn't form while they are rising.

If you are letting your bread proof on a peel, coat it generously with cornmeal before putting the loaves on it. We use coarse cornmeal because it is better than fine at keeping the loaves from sticking (and is easier to clean off the baking stone and out of the corners of the oven). With very sticky dough we put parchment paper and cornmeal on the peel to prevent the loaves from sticking and deflating. If you don't have a peel, you can use the back side of a baking sheet covered with parchment paper. Sprinkle the paper with a little cornmeal and put the loaves on the paper. When you're ready to bake, slide the loaves and the paper onto the stone. After the crust becomes firm, the paper can be removed, allowing the loaves to touch the stone for better crust development.

Bread can also proof on baker's linen/canvas (couche). At home you can use a heavy cotton dish towel with a smooth nonlooped surface or a small cotton table-cloth. Simply sprinkle a generous amount of flour over the cloth and rub it into the surface to prevent the dough from sticking. If you bake bread often, you can fold up your floured cloth to use again without washing it. Over time it will become well seasoned and dough will be released easily from it. Place the floured cloth on a counter or a pan, then place the shaped loaves on the cloth to proof.

Another option is to let the bread rise in a special proofing basket or banneton. These baskets must be well floured each time you use them. We use bannetons at the bakery to give loaves a uniform shape and to create a decorative flour pattern on the crust. Dough tends to proof more slowly in these baskets because it is insulated from the warmth of the room. They can be ordered from a baking supplier (see page 269 for mail-order sources), or you can make your own by placing a well-floured dish towel in a medium colander or in any woven basket. We have tried all sorts of different-sized deep and shallow bowls lined with a cloth. They give interesting new dimensions to boule-shaped loaves.

Standard loaf pans and baking sheets are another choice for letting bread proof. After the first rise, the loaves are shaped, then placed directly in or on the pans where they will bake. If you want to make baguettes or ficelles that are longer and straighter than those baked free-form, a baguette mold is very handy. Most molds hold two to five baguettes. Because baguettes placed in a mold are not disturbed after they are proofed, they come out fatter and more uniform after baking. The only drawback we have noticed is that the crust is not quite as crisp when baked in a mold.

If you are using a peel, cloth, pan, baking sheet, or bread mold, place the loaves seam side down to proof. Conversely, if using a cloth-lined basket or bowl, place the loaves seam side up to proof; just before baking, they will be dumped out onto the peel seam side down, revealing the tops of the loaves.

Using a Baking Stone

Any serious home baker should invest in a baking stone. A stone helps loaves bake more evenly and gives them a much better crust. If you are using a baking stone, you should preheat the stone in the oven for at least thirty minutes to ensure that it is heated through. In a gas oven, place the stone on a rack in the lower third of the oven. In an electric oven, place the stone on a rack in the center of the oven. The stone should be in the center of the rack, leaving at least one or two inches all around to let air and steam circulate if possible.

Scoring the Crust

Scoring the crust serves both functional and decorative purposes. When the yeast's activity is accelerated by the heat of the oven, the carbon dioxide gas it releases needs a place to escape, and the cuts provide the outlet. If left unscored, most loaves will crack open in undesirable places, making them less attractive. Decorative cuts on the crust are also considered the baker's signature. You can use our ideas or create your own cuts to give your loaves a beautiful appearance and make them unique.

Scoring bread properly requires a sharp blade and a quick, steady hand. At the bakery we use a lame, a double-edge razor blade mounted on a three-inch handle. To make a cut that opens to form a flared ridge on a loaf such as a baguette, hold the blade at a 30-degree angle, nearly parallel to the loaf. This allows you to cut just below the surface, or skin, of the loaf. A blade held at a 90-degree angle, or perpendicular to the loaf, will create a smooth opening with no ridge. This is nice when cutting a star, a cross, or a tic-tac-toe pattern on a round loaf. Whatever cut you choose, it is important to keep it shallow but long. Don't drag the blade too slowly, or the skin will gather or tear. And don't use a heavy hand when you score the bread, because too much pressure on the loaf will cause it to deflate. Certain heavy-grained doughs do not require much scoring because they are not high in gluten and will not burst open in the oven.

Scissors work well for scoring very wet doughs, where a blade would drag, or on decorative loaves such as crowns or epi. Additional ideas for scoring and making decorative patterns can be found on page 257.

Sliding Loaves onto the Baking Stone

When you are ready to slide proofed loaves onto a preheated baking stone, shake the peel gently to release them or loosen the loaves with your fingers. To slide the loaves onto the stone, simply hold the peel over the stone and use a smooth, quick

Scoring the Crust

Here is the technique for scoring bread using a lame to create a flared cut on the loaf. Note the angle and direction of the cuts.

Start the cut at the center of the tip of the loaf.

Angle to hold the blade for a flared ridge on the loaf

This is the correct pattern of the cut from one tip of the loaf to the other for best appearance.

Baguette Scoring

This is the correct pattern of the cut from one tip of the loaf to the other, and the correct angle of the blade to get a flared cut on your baguette.

Flat, Smooth-Opening Scoring

Angle to hold the blade for a flat, smooth opening

jerking motion to release the loaves. Draw the peel out smoothly so the loaves land where you want them to be. If you have lined the peel with parchment and sprinkled it with cornmeal, then you just slide the parchment onto the baking stone with the loaf when you load the oven. This is especially helpful with very wet, sticky dough that might stick to the wooden peel.

If your batch of dough makes more loaves than will fit on your baking stone, you can hold one or two proofed loaves in the refrigerator while you bake the other loaves. After the first batch has baked, let the stone heat again for about five minutes. Then take the waiting loaves from the refrigerator and bake them. It's usually best to refrigerate the "holding" loaves before they are completely proofed as they'll continue to rise in the refrigerator.

Steam in the Oven

Creating a good amount of steam in the oven at the beginning of the bake keeps the dough moist for the first few minutes to maximize the oven spring (see page 43) and helps make the crust browner and glossier. It also helps produce a thin, crunchy crust. The best ways to create steam in a home oven are to pour boiling water into a preheated cast-iron pan in the oven and to spray the loaves with water from a plastic water sprayer at the beginning of the baking process and again after the first minute or two of baking.

It is also helpful if you create a slightly moist oven environment prior to loading the bread to bake. Do this by placing a small baking pan, such as a mini loaf pan, on the same level as the water pan. Preheat it along with the baking stone and the water pan. Then, ten minutes prior to loading the bread, place two ice cubes (three if your cubes are small) in that pan and shut the oven door.

If you're using a water pan, place it directly on the bottom of a gas-fired oven, or on an oven rack directly under the baking stone in an electric oven. Put the pan in the oven at the same time you put the stone in to preheat. We recommend using a wide, shallow cast-iron pan, such as a skillet, that retains maximum heat and will let the water evaporate more quickly. Use an old, dispensable pan, because it will become rusted. After you slide the risen loaves onto the baking stone, mist the loaves with water, then quickly but carefully pour one cup of boiling water into the hot pan and quickly shut the oven door. You may want to wear an oven mitt while doing this to avoid being burned by the hot steam that will immediately rise from the pan. (In our home ovens, one cup of hot water will have evaporated completely after ten to twelve minutes of baking; the amount you will need depends on your oven and the size of your water pan. After the first ten to twelve minutes of baking, the oven should be allowed to dry out so the crust can develop the crunch you want.) After one or two minutes, open the oven door and quickly mist the loaves again with a plant sprayer. (If you've made a decorative flour pattern on the loaves, omit this step.) If you don't use a water pan, mist the loaves and the oven walls eight to ten times when you put the bread into the oven. Repeat the misting process two minutes later and again after two more minutes, shutting the oven door rapidly each time.

If the crust develops white streaks as it bakes and is not browning because you don't have enough steam in the oven, you can brush the loaf with a little oil during the last ten to fifteen minutes of baking. Although the crust won't be as crisp as you might like, the oil will make it browner and more attractive.

Understanding Your Oven and Rotating the Loaves

Use an oven thermometer to check the accuracy of your oven temperature. Many home ovens have some hot spots or other unevenness. Check the bread as it bakes to see that it is coloring evenly. We usually rotate the loaves from one side of the oven to the other and turn them around halfway through the baking time to get more even coloration. If you are baking on two different oven racks, it is essential that you switch the position of the loaves at least once. Quickly shut the oven door after you rotate the bread.

(Note: To test our recipes, we baked our breads in old New York City gas ovens. You may find that with newer ovens with tightly sealed doors or with electric ovens, the oven temperatures we give are too hot. If your oven temperature proves to be accurate when tested with an oven thermometer, and if your loaves seem to be browning too fast, lower the temperature by 10°F or more in all our recipes.)

Oven Spring

When raw yeast dough is placed in a hot oven, the drastic change in temperature causes the yeast to act rapidly. It gives off carbon dioxide in a last flurry of life before reaching 140°F, the temperature at which it expires. The carbon dioxide gas is trapped in the web of gluten in the dough, leaving open air bubbles in the bread. This action of bursting is known as oven spring. To get the fullest rise from your loaves, be sure the oven has had time to preheat and the dough is not overproofed when you are ready to bake it. Breads with a lighter texture, such as baguettes, are best baked slightly underproofed. The loaves will rise higher in the oven, giving them a more open-holed crumb. The cuts will also burst open farther, making the loaf more attractive.

All About the Crust

For many people the texture and the flavor of the crust are the most memorable parts of a loaf of bread. Getting a perfect crust takes practice, and, no matter what, factors beyond our control, such as humidity and the kind of oven you use, can change the results. To get the best texture in the crust, make sure to start with a moist dough and see that it has a good first rise and is properly proofed after shaping. Use a baking stone that has been preheated for at least thirty minutes at 425°F or hotter, and use plenty of steam in the oven. Bake the loaves until they have a deep brown color; a pale crust will soften and have less flavor. More information about the crust can be found starting on page 262.

To get a crunchier crust, bake the bread at a temperature over 425°F. For loaves without any sweet ingredients such as raisins or honey, the oven can be preheated to 450°F or 500°F and turned down to 400°F or 425°F after the first ten or twenty minutes of baking. Sweet breads require a cooler oven, between 375° and 400°F. Experiment with your oven to see what temperature gives the bread a good rise and a crisp, dark crust without burning the bottom of the loaf.

After the bread is baked, the best way to keep the crust dry and crisp is to let air circulate around the loaf, both during and after cooling. Don't wrap the bread in plastic wrap or chill it, or the crust will soften. If the bread has softened, you can restore a crunchy crust by reheating the bread for five to eight minutes in a preheated 400°F oven.

Testing for Doneness

Telling whether or not bread is fully baked is easy. The first test is color. A properly baked loaf will range from golden to deep brown. Pick up the loaf and tap it on the bottom. It should sound hollow and produce a nice "thunk" when tapped. If it feels heavy and does not quite sound hollow, bake it for five minutes longer and check it again.

Another test for doneness is to check the internal temperature of the loaf. Push an instant-read thermometer into the center of the bread: It should register between 200° and 210°F. After baking, the bread should be allowed to cool on a rack before cutting. It will continue to firm up and finish cooking on the inside as it cools.

Slicing Bread

We enjoy tearing right into a freshly baked loaf, but you might prefer to slice it with a serrated bread knife. Serrated knives stay sharp for a long time and the teeth cut through a thick, hard crust without compressing the loaf. A bread knife is a small but worthwhile investment for any bread lover. When you cut a loaf yourself, you can make thick, rustic slices, unlike those produced by a slicing machine.

Storing Bread

To store fresh bread, it's best to leave it at room temperature for the first two days. Leave the bread unwrapped, and place the loaf cut side down on a bread board, in a cupboard, or in a bread box. Leaving the bread unwrapped keeps the inside of the loaf soft and the outside crusty. After a couple of days, you can put the bread in a plastic bag to keep it moist.

To refresh bread, or return it to its just-baked state, cut off the amount you want to serve and mist the crust with water. Put the bread directly on an oven rack in a preheated 400°F oven. (An oven that is too cool will draw the moisture out of the bread, leaving it tough and dry.) Let it crisp for five to eight minutes, until it feels very hot and just slightly crisp and crusty. Remove it from the oven, let it rest for a few minutes, then slice and serve warm.

You can also freeze freshly baked bread as soon as it has cooled completely. Wrap the loaf tightly in foil, place it in a heavy-duty freezer bag or wrap it in two layers of plastic wrap, and freeze. Allow the bread to thaw in the wrapping at room temperature, then unwrap and refresh the loaf in the oven. We do not recommend refrigerating bread. It may keep a long time in the refrigerator, but it dries out. We absolutely never microwave bread. It becomes spongy at first, then rock-hard.

Kendall Jacques

Customer service is spelled with a capital *K* at Amy's Bread. In fact it's spelled with two exceptional capital *K*'s—Kendall Jacques and Kerrie McDevitt.

Kendall Jacques is our Customer Service Manager, the quiet powerhouse behind the customer service team that serves the bakery's 250-plus wholesale customers (including our own retail stores) 365 days of the year. Kendall and her staff of three customer service representatives are responsible for answering all the calls that come into the main phone number at the Chelsea Market location, taking wholesale orders, entering them into the computer, generating production paperwork for the bread kitchen and the pastry kitchen, fielding special requests, and troubleshooting all the problems, questions, and emergencies that arise

when serving a select population of wholesale customers who expect the best from Amy's Bread. On top of all that, she also organizes and manages nine delivery drivers and their routes to be sure our bread is delivered on time and in good condition to restaurants, hotels, and retail outlets throughout the day. And she's our "Z-Bake Wizard"—the only person in the entire bakery who knows all the ins and outs and secrets of the bakery's complex computer system.

A super-efficient perfectionist with a great sense of humor, Kendall's been part of our bakery team for nine years at this writing. Even after all that time she still loves our baguettes warm from the oven, and volunteers for Pain au Chocolat tasting at every opportunity. She's also been known to take her own hamburger buns to restaurants so she can have her burger on Amy's bread. Did we mention she's a total bread snob and one of our most loyal fans? Transplanted to New York City from North Carolina, her work experience included baking, making deliveries, and assisting with office administrative responsibilities in a small bakery, as well as waitressing in restaurants. In Kendall's own words, "I might be one of the few people in the world who enjoyed being a waitress." Sounds like a woman who loves to serve customers. She supports her staff with that same kind of dedication to service and encourages them to carry it to our customers. We feel fortunate to have her at the head of our Amy's Bread wholesale customer service team.

Kerrie McDevitt is the bakery's Retail Division Manager. She moved to New York from Boston eight years ago to be with her boyfriend, who is now her husband. At home, she's the mother of two, a daughter who's four and a son who just turned one at this writing. At the bakery, she's the mother/coach/cheerleader/role model/disciplinarian for her eight retail managers and assistant managers and the 35-plus members of their retail teams at all three Amy's Bread retail stores. She can be found most days behind the counter at our busy Hell's Kitchen location, encouraging the staff to serve our customers efficiently while still maintaining a pleasant, patient disposition—not always an easy task when faced with demanding, harried New Yorkers who always seem to be in a hurry. Kerrie and her team at all three locations have turned many of those crazed New Yorkers into happy regular customers who know they'll be greeted personally by name and their orders will be served exactly as they like them.

Behind the scenes, Kerrie and her team also constantly review sales data and place daily orders for bread and pastries (that are ultimately turned into kitchen production sheets by Kendall Jacques and her team) to ensure that each bakery location will have the products their customers want most when they come into the store. She interacts with the kitchen managers, passing along complaints as well as compliments from the customers to help maintain the standard of quality that is expected from Amy's Bread.

A native of Rhode Island, Kerrie is the youngest of eight children, so she knows what it's about when it comes to group dynamics. Training, service, and sales are the words in Kerrie's personal mantra as a manager. A tough taskmaster, she is always training her team with techniques to provide customers with better service so they can achieve higher sales revenues for the bakery, which will eventually translate to raises and bonuses. She constantly pushes the team to excel, never satisfied that they've reached their highest level. Beneath the tough exterior, there is a warm, caring, nurturing woman who is always ready to be there for staff members who need support and advice during times of personal stress. We've been blessed to have Kerrie at the head of our retail customer service team for the past eight years at this writing, and we hope she'll be with us for many more years to come.

Kerrie McDevitt

THE MAGIC OF MAKING BREAD RISE

Mix up a little flour, water, and salt, add some leavening such as yeast or sourdough, and the magic begins! *Webster's New World Dictionary* says the word leaven comes from the Latin *levare*, "to make light, lift up, raise." In France leavening is called *levure* or *levain*, in Italy *lievito* or *biga*. No matter where you are or what you call it, the leavener is the miracle ingredient that gives life to a lump of dough.

One warm summer morning when the bakery had only been open for about a month, we found out just how much life leavened dough can have. Susan, the mixer, made a large batch of our Country Sourdough and portioned it into several shallow plastic dough boxes. She stacked them inside the small walk-in refrigerator so the dough could have its first cool rise. About an hour later, while we were working up front in the retail store, we heard Susan open the door to the walk-in. Suddenly there was a shriek of surprise, and the *I Love Lucy* theme song came floating out of the refrigerator. The scene that greeted us as we peered around the open door really did look like something that only Lucy and Ethel could have cooked up. Great globs of creamy-colored dough were oozing out of the plastic boxes like rivers of lava. The boxes themselves were tipping and tilting in a crazy slow-motion rumba to the rhythm of the fast-rising dough. It was quite a mess!

The dough felt almost hot when we touched it. Susan recalled that the dough temperature had been a few degrees higher than usual at the end of the mix because of the warm weather. The extra warmth accelerated the activity of the yeast in the dough, and the madly reproducing yeast generated even more heat as the dough began to rise. The shallow plastic boxes acted like insulators, keeping the dough's heat in and the cool air of the refrigerator out. We learned a lot about leavening power that day.

At the bakery we use many different kinds of leaveners, including baker's yeast and starters. All of them help to make the bread rise using yeast in one form or another. Yeast is a minute one-celled fungus that is present in everything around us. There are at least 160 different species in the air, on our skin and on the skins of fruits and vegetables, and in the flour we use for baking. Not all of these fungi are benevolent. Some can cause food to rot, others promote a variety of unpleasant diseases. Baking yeast, however, belongs to a favorable genus called *Saccharomyces* (sugar fungi). These yeasts thrive and multiply in any warm, moist environment where they can feed on carbohydrates (sugars and starches). As they eat, the yeasts metabolize the carbohydrates through a process called anaerobic fermentation. Alcohol and carbon dioxide are the by-products. In bread dough, the carbon dioxide is trapped by a complex web of gluten strands in the moist dough, causing it to expand, or rise, and creating a spongelike network of holes throughout the dough. In the intense heat of baking, the yeast dies and the alcohol evaporates, but the network of holes remains to give leavened bread its wonderful characteristic texture.

Sugar in small amounts increases yeast activity. However, large quantities of sugar in dough will have just the opposite effect, actually slowing down the yeast. That's why most recipes for sweet breads require larger amounts of yeast.

Salt also retards yeast activity. If you forget to add salt to your bread dough, it will rise much faster and exhaust the yeast supply sooner than it would otherwise. At the bakery we always taste a tiny bit of each batch of dough after it is mixed to be sure the salt has been included, because it is one ingredient that you cannot see in the dough.

At Amy's Bread we use the minimum amount of yeast necessary to leaven our bread. We want the dough to rise slowly at a temperature of about 77°F so the flavors of the wheat and any other grains will be more prominent than the flavor of the yeast. Yeast generates heat as it metabolizes the sugars and starches in the dough. A large amount of yeast can result in too much activity, making it difficult to control the temperature of the dough and the proofing time. To help control rising time, we use less yeast in our doughs during the hot summer months (when yeast activity is intensified) than we do in the cooler months. Most of the recipes in this book contain considerably less yeast than standard bread recipes.

USING BAKER'S YEAST

There are four types of commercial baking yeast: active dry yeast, compressed cake yeast (sometimes called fresh yeast), quick-rise yeast, and instant yeast.

Active dry yeast is what we use in the recipes in this book, because it is the easiest to find. Most grocers carry the strips of three ¼-ounce foil packets. Each packet contains about 2¼ teaspoons of dried yeast granules. Look for boxed displays of Fleischmann's or Red Star brand yeast in the dairy case; sometimes it is with the flour and baking supplies. Be sure to check the expiration date that's stamped on the back of the package, and don't buy it if it's past the date. You can store the unopened packets at room temperature, but they retain their potency better in the freezer. Once a package has been opened, store any leftovers in an airtight container, or the yeast will be damaged by exposure to warmth, air, and moisture.

You can also buy active dry yeast in 4-ounce jars or in bulk from your local natural food store. Be sure to get active dry yeast, not brewer's yeast or torula yeast, which are intended for nutritional purposes only and will not cause bread to rise. Keep the yeast in an airtight container in your freezer to extend its shelf life.

You don't have to bring active dry yeast to room temperature or proof it before you use it. In the recipes in this book, we give the yeast a head start by dissolving it in a little warm water and letting it sit for about three minutes. If you're dubious about the potency of your yeast, proof it by adding a pinch of sugar to the yeast and warm water and let it sit a while longer. If the yeast is nice and bubbly after ten minutes, you can use it.

Compressed cake yeast is cultivated from a different genetic strain of the same species as dry yeast and has very different characteristics. The moisture content of cake yeast is 70 percent, compared to the 8 percent of dry yeast. We use compressed cake yeast at the bakery because it activates more easily at the cooler dough temperatures we prefer and has a milder flavor than dry yeast. If you want to use it in place of active dry yeast in our recipes, you must double the measured amount of yeast specified; for example, if the recipe calls for half a teaspoon of active dry yeast, use a full teaspoon of cake yeast to replace it. Some grocers stock small 0.6-ounce cubes or larger 2-ounce cakes of moist yeast in the dairy case. You may also be able to purchase a chunk of it from a local bakery. In either case, the yeast should have an even light tan color with no mold or discoloration. It should feel slightly moist and crumble easily, breaking with a clean edge. Don't be surprised by its pungent yeasty odor.

Cake yeast must be kept refrigerated, wrapped in plastic wrap and/or put in an airtight container. It survives freezing well and maintains its potency longer if frozen than if refrigerated. It stays potent for only a week or two if refrigerated; if frozen, it's good for up to two months. Don't buy more than you'll be able to use within that period of time and, of course, don't buy a package that has passed its expiration date. If you're in doubt, proof the yeast by dissolving it with a pinch of sugar in a quarter-cup of very warm water (105° to 115°F). If it's nice and bubbly in ten minutes, you can use it.

Quick-rise yeast is a different strain of the same low-moisture granulated yeast as active dry yeast. You can cut your rising time in half with this product because it proofs at a higher temperature, which accelerates the activity of the yeast, but the flavor and texture of the bread will generally suffer. We don't recommend it because we prefer the quality produced by a slow, cool rise. If it's the only kind of yeast you can find, follow the directions on the package but use slightly less than the amount of yeast specified in our recipes to slow down the rising time somewhat. Quick-rise yeast is packaged the same way as active dry yeast and should be stored in the same manner.

Instant yeast is yet another dry yeast product. The most commonly available brands are imported from Europe. It is a very low-moisture granulated yeast, but it is combined with a sugar and an emulsifier so it will activate immediately upon contact with warm liquid. We don't recommend it because the dough has to be very warm to activate instant yeast (at least 85°F), and some manufacturers suggest eliminating the first proofing period of the dough. Obviously, it doesn't lend itself to our "slow, cool" philosophy of bread making. If you want to try instant yeast just for the experience, you can find small bulk packages at gourmet cooking stores or through mail-order sources (see page 270 for a list of suppliers). Follow the directions on the package.

USING STARTERS

A starter is the bread baker's "magic." It is made from flour, water, and some type of leavening (either wild or commercial yeast), which are mixed, allowed to ferment for several hours, and then mixed into bread dough. Starters, also referred to as pre-ferments by professional bakers, help the bread rise, but they do many other things as well. They provide a wonderful aroma and a more complex flavor to the bread, improve the browning of the crust, create a chewier crumb and a larger hole structure, and make the bread moister so it has a longer shelf life. It takes only a few minutes to mix up a starter, and after it has been given time to ferment, it will enhance your bread more than any other technique or ingredient. Dough made with starter will have a head start on flavor development because it contains an ingredient that has already been fermenting for several hours.

For bread bakers, starters are the most interesting and challenging ingredients to learn about. It takes some skill and practice to be able to understand just when a starter is perfectly fermented and ready to use. The only way to become skilled is to try some bread recipes that call for starters and see what happens.

This chapter will provide you with the basic information needed to make all of the starters used in the recipes in this book. It is not meant to be an in-depth study on sourdough starters, but we do give you simple instructions for starting your own sourdough starter and feeding it to make the other special starters we use in our recipes. If you already have an active sourdough starter going, don't bother to start a new one. Just use some of your existing starter in the recipes.

Another way to simplify the process of creating a sourdough starter is to buy one already made. In commercial bakeries in Europe, it is a common practice to purchase dehydrated starter to use in daily bread production. We have purchased a pre-made sourdough starter from King Arthur Flour (see page 270) and had great results with it. It saves a lot of time, and the starter is very strong and active. Buying pre-made sourdough starter is a great option if you feel at all intimidated about the whole process.

Starters can be made with commercial yeast or can be started with only wild yeast. The simplest starter to make is Poolish (page 54). It's made from flour, water, and a tiny bit of yeast. It takes six to eight hours to ferment, but it's worth the effort because the resulting bread is much more interesting than bread made with straight yeasted dough. When you mix your final dough using some of the poolish, you are adding six to eight hours of flavor development to your bread, so it's already off to a good start.

At Amy's Bread, out of the twenty different kinds of bread dough we make each day, there are only three straight doughs that don't contain at least one kind of starter. We hope that you will make an effort to bake with starters. You'll be rewarded with excellent bread.

Four starters that are perfectly fermented and ready to use. Clockwise from top left: Liquid Levain, Biga Starter, Poolish, and Rye Salt Sour Starter.

Poolish

Poolish has become our favorite starter in the bakery. We enjoy using it because it gives our bread a moist, open-holed crumb, a chewy texture, and a sweet, pleasant flavor of fermentation without any sourness.

Don't be discouraged by the process of making a starter. Poolish is very easy to make and adds so much character to breads like French Baguettes (page 79) and Rustic Italian Bread (page 85). It's made from the tiniest bit of yeast we can measure, combined with equal weights of water and flour. The mixing takes about 3 minutes, and the rest of the work is done by the yeast, which slowly ferments with the flour and water. The poolish should be mixed 6 to 24 hours before you plan to make your bread. When used in your dough, the final result will be sophisticated bread that makes you look like a professional baker.

Small Batch

Makes 285 grams / 10 ounces / scant 1½ cups

INGREDIENTS	GRAMS	OUNCES	VOLUME
Very warm water (105° to 115°F)	57	2.00	¼ cup
Active dry yeast	⅛ teaspoon	⅛ teaspoon	⅛ teaspoon
Cool water (75° to 78°F)	85	3.00	¼ cup plus 2 tablespoons
Unbleached all-purpose flour	142	5.00	1 cup

Large Batch

Makes 454 grams / 16 ounces / 2¼ cups

Equipment: one 2-quart clear plastic or glass container with high sides

INGREDIENTS	GRAMS	OUNCES	VOLUME
Very warm water (105° to 115°F)	57	2.00	¼ cup
Active dry yeast	¼ teaspoon	¼ teaspoon	¼ teaspoon
Cool water (75° to 78°F)	170	6.00	¾ cup
Unbleached all-purpose flour	227	8.00	1½ cups plus 2 tablespoons

1. In the container, combine the very warm water and yeast and whisk together until the yeast has dissolved. Allow the mixture to stand for 3 minutes. Add the cool water and flour and stir vigorously with a wooden spoon or your hand for 1 minute, until a smooth, somewhat elastic batter has formed. The starter will be thick and stretchy. It gets softer and thinner after it has risen.

2. Scrape down the starter from the sides of the container and cover the container with plastic wrap. Mark the height of the starter and the time on a piece of tape on the side of the container so you can see how much it rises. Make sure it has room to triple in volume.

3. Let the starter rise at room temperature (75° to 78°F) for 6 to 8 hours. Or let it rise for 1 hour at room temperature, then chill it in the refrigerator for 8 hours or overnight. Remove it from the refrigerator and let it sit at room temperature for 3 to 4 hours to warm up and become active before use. When it is ready, it will have tripled in volume, and lots of bubbles and small folds will appear on the surface. The starter should be used in the next 2 to 4 hours, before it begins to deflate. If you use the starter while it's still cold from the refrigerator, be sure to compensate for the temperature by using warm water (85° to 90°F) in your dough instead of the cool water specified in the recipe.

TIPS AND TECHNIQUES

Take the temperature of your water with an instant-read thermometer before adding it to the yeast. If the water is too hot, it will damage the yeast, and if it is too cool, the yeast will take much longer to activate and the starter will rise very slowly, if at all.

Biga Starter

Many of our recipes use a biga starter made from flour, water, and a small amount of yeast. Biga, which is the Italian word for starter, was called Sponge Starter in the first version of *Amy's Bread*, but today the word *biga* is well known by bread bakers so we decided to use it here as well. Biga usually refers to a starter made with yeast, not sourdough, although sourdough biga (*biga naturale*) can be found in some Italian recipes. This starter, which is thicker than poolish, is allowed to ferment for at least 8 hours. It can then be used immediately or stored in the refrigerator, covered with plastic wrap, for up to 24 hours. We like breads made with biga because they have a moist, chewy texture with more flavor, a nicer crust, and a longer shelf life than straight yeasted breads. These are many of the same qualities that make sourdough breads so appealing, but you can achieve them without the extended process of making a sourdough starter.

Small Batch

Makes 400 grams / 14 ounces / 1¾ cups

INGREDIENTS	GRAMS	OUNCES	VOLUME
Very warm water (105° to 115°F)	200	7.00	¾ cup plus 2 tablespoons
Active dry yeast	⅛ teaspoon	⅛ teaspoon	⅛ teaspoon
Unbleached all-purpose flour	227	8.00	1½ cups plus 2 tablespoons

Large Batch

Makes 800 grams / 28 ounces / 3½ cups

Equipment: one 2-quart clear plastic or glass container with high sides

INGREDIENTS	GRAMS	OUNCES	VOLUME
Very warm water (105° to 115°F)	397	14.00	1¾ cups
Active dry yeast	¼ teaspoon	¼ teaspoon	¼ teaspoon
Unbleached all-purpose flour	454	16.00	3¼ cups

1. In a medium bowl, mix the warm water and yeast together and stir to dissolve the yeast. Add the flour and stir vigorously with a wooden spoon for 1 to 2 minutes, until a smooth, somewhat elastic batter has formed. The batter will be fairly thick and stretchy; it gets softer and more elastic after it has risen. Scrape the biga into the container, mark the height of the starter and the time on a piece of tape on the side of the container so you can see how much it rises, and cover the container with plastic wrap.

2. Let it rise at room temperature (75° to 78°F) for 6 to 8 hours. Or let it rise for 1 hour at room temperature, then chill it in the refrigerator for 8 hours or overnight. Remove it from the refrigerator and let it sit at room temperature for 3 to 4 hours to warm up and become active before use. Biga should more than double in volume. If you use the starter while it's still cold from the refrigerator, be sure to compensate for the cold temperature by using warm water (85°F to 90°F) in your dough, instead of the cool water specified in the recipe. Use the starter while it is still bubbling up, but before it starts to deflate.

CREATING A SOURDOUGH STARTER

Using sourdough starters is part of the fun of being a bread baker. Creating your own sourdough starter may seem mysterious and complicated, but if you take on the project with a good attitude and a willing spirit, the process of making your own starter from scratch need not be difficult at all. We have given instructions for starting a white starter with organic unbleached flour (page 59), or a rye starter (page 61) with organic rye flour. Either basic starter can be used to make the other sourdough starters in this chapter, and both kinds of flour make very nice starters. If you think you will make more white sourdough bread in the future, start with white flour. Otherwise use rye flour because it ferments faster, has a nice flavor, and comes back to life quickly after being stored in the refrigerator for extended periods of time without refreshment.

Basic Information about Sourdough Starters

As you mix up your batch of starter, you are activating the natural yeasts found in the air, in the flour, and on the skins of the grapes that you're mixing together. We prefer to use organic ingredients when starting a sourdough starter because they have no pesticides on them. The wild yeasts in your starter will thrive on the natural sugars and starches in flour and will bubble up with activity after each refreshment. Feeding or refreshing the starter means giving it more food so it can become stronger and more active in preparation for being used to make bread dough. Starter that has not been refreshed has no power to leaven the bread and usually tastes very sour, tangy, and acidic, giving an unpleasant taste to your bread. Starter that has been refreshed regularly and is ready to use tastes sweet and only mildly sour. It has lots of bubbles on the surface and around the edges, and smells fragrant like wine. If your starter has not been refreshed for days or weeks, it will take two to three refreshments to prepare it to be used in your bread dough.

TIPS AND TECHNIQUES

We recommend using glass or plastic containers and wooden utensils instead of metal bowls and spoons when working with sourdough. The metal can react with the acid in sourdough starter.

SOURDOUGH STARTER TERMINOLOGY

What shall we call our sourdough starters? Many professional bakers use the French word *levain* to describe their sourdough starters, and that's what we use at Amy's Bread. That lets us know we are talking about sourdough and not a starter derived from yeast. In this chapter and throughout the book you will see the word *levain* used to describe the sourdough starters needed for each recipe, such as Liquid Levain (page 62), Firm Levain (page 63), Miche Levain (page 64), Spelt Levain (page 68), and so on.

STARTER	CHARACTERISTICS OF THIS STARTER
Liquid Levain	Thinner white sourdough starter made without yeast
Firm Levain	Firm white sourdough starter made without yeast
Rye Salt Sour	Thick rye sourdough starter with salt, made without yeast
Miche Levain	Thick whole wheat sourdough starter made without yeast
Spelt Levain	Thick spelt sourdough starter made without yeast

NON-SOURDOUGH STARTERS

Poolish	Thinner white starter made with equal weights of flour and water, and a tiny bit of yeast
Biga	Thicker white starter made with flour, water, and a tiny bit of yeast

White Sourdough Starter

Stage 1

Equipment: one 1-quart clear plastic or glass container with high sides

INGREDIENTS	GRAMS	OUNCES	VOLUME
Organic grapes, rinsed	40	1.41	¼ cup
Cool water (75° to 78°F)	113	4.00	½ cup
Organic unbleached all-purpose flour	72	2.54	½ cup

Put the grapes in the container and press them a little with a fork or your fingers to break the skins. Add the water and flour and stir with a wooden spoon until the flour is moistened. Take the temperature of the starter. For best results it should be between 75° and 80°F. Cover with plastic wrap and a rubber band to hold the plastic in place. Mark the height of the starter on a piece of tape on the side of the container so you can see how much it rises. Also write down the time you stirred it together, and keep simple notes on the starter's activity and the time you refresh it each day. Let it sit at room temperature (75° to 78°F) until it starts to bubble. This will take 12 to 24 hours, longer if your room is cool.

First refreshment

INGREDIENTS	GRAMS	OUNCES	VOLUME
Cool water (75° to 78°F)	113	4.00	½ cup
Organic unbleached all-purpose flour	72	2.54	½ cup

If the starter is bubbly and active and smells slightly fermented, about 24 hours after you first mixed it together, add the water and flour and stir it vigorously with a wooden spoon to combine. Take note of the time and the condition of your starter. Cover it again with plastic wrap and a rubber band and let it rise at room temperature for 12 to 24 hours. If the starter does not look active, refresh it anyway, but use slightly warmer water (80°F) and let it rise for 12 to 24 hours.

Second refreshment

INGREDIENTS	GRAMS	OUNCES	VOLUME
Organic unbleached all-purpose flour	36	1.27	¼ cup

If the starter is bubbly and active within 12 to 24 hours after you refreshed it, stir it together well and scoop the grapes and a little of the starter out of your container and discard them. Add the flour and stir vigorously with a wooden spoon to combine. Take note of the time and the condition of your starter. Cover again with plastic wrap and a rubber band and let it rise at room temperature for 12 to 24 hours.

Third refreshment

INGREDIENTS	GRAMS	OUNCES	VOLUME
Cool water (75° to 78°F)	113	4.00	½ cup
Organic unbleached all-purpose flour	72	2.54	½ cup

About 24 hours after you refreshed it the second time, the starter should be bubbly and active and should smell a little sour and fermented. Stir it well. Discard about half of the starter. Add the water and flour and stir vigorously with a wooden spoon to combine. Take note of the time and the condition of your starter. Cover again with plastic wrap and a rubber band and let it rise at room temperature for 12 to 24 hours.

Making the final starter

Twelve to twenty-four hours after the third refreshment, if the starter is active and bubbly and smells sour and fruity, it is ready to be made into a specific starter to use in your dough. Follow the instructions for creating the starter that is used in the bread you will be making. From this point forward you can continue to maintain ½ cup of your original starter as a base starter to use for different recipes in this book. Just follow the instructions for maintaining your base starter, and keep a little of the starter in your refrigerator for months, if not years, giving it a feeding every one to two weeks.

Maintaining your starter for the future after it is active

After your starter is active and you're ready to make it into one of the starters for a specific recipe, you can save a little of your basic starter in a container, and continue to refresh and maintain it for future baking. *Never use up all of your sourdough starter.* When you are making a specific starter for a recipe in this book, remember to save a little bit of your base starter and refresh it so you can perpetuate it for years to come. If you don't bake often, you can store the starter in the refrigerator and refresh it once every week or two. Stir together the starter, discard all but ½ cup of it, and feed the remaining starter with 1 cup flour and ½ cup water. This refreshment with more flour than water gives the starter "food" to sustain it for extended periods of time between feedings. Stir it, cover it, and put it back in the refrigerator. Continue to maintain your starter in this manner until you are ready to refresh it and prepare it for making another sourdough bread recipe.

Rye Sourdough Starter

You can follow the exact same procedure for creating and building a white sourdough starter but substitute organic rye flour for the organic un-bleached all-purpose flour in the first feeding and each refreshment. Use ½ cup rye flour, which weighs 65 grams/2.3 ounces, in place of the unbleached flour, except when ¼ cup is called for. Then use ¼ cup of rye flour. The rising times and temperatures for both types of starter are nearly the same. You may see fermentation activity and bubbles earlier with a rye starter, but after the first two refreshments it will ferment at the same rate as the white starter. Keep the temperature of rye sourdough starter between 75° and 79°F. If the rye starter gets warmer than 80°F, it can develop a bitter taste that is unpleasant in bread. When the rye starter has been refreshed three times it will be ready to use in the other starter recipes that follow. Use the same maintenance feeding described above to keep your rye starter active between the times you use it to make bread.

When most Americans think of sourdough, they picture the crusty, assertively sour loaves that are produced in the bread mecca of America, San Francisco. But bread made from a sourdough starter doesn't have to be intensely sour. The level of acidity that produces the sour taste depends to a large extent on the consistency and maturity of the starter that is used. If you're one of those people who dislikes sourdough bread, don't stop reading here. We're going to show you how to make a starter that will produce a loaf as mild or as sour as you like.

The proportion of water to flour in a sourdough starter affects the fermentation rate. Wet starters ferment more quickly and generally have a higher level of acidity than drier starters. So if you want a mild-flavored sourdough bread, use a firm levain–style starter, as we do in our recipe for Country Sourdough (page 121). For a more San Francisco–style sourdough, use a liquid levain, as we do in our recipe for Tangy Twenty-Four-Hour Sourdough (page 129).

Liquid Levain

Makes 425 grams / 15 ounces / 2 cups

Equipment: one 2-quart clear plastic or glass container with high sides

This starter is used to make Tangy Twenty-Four-Hour Sourdough (page 129). Its consistency is thin and soupy, and it gives sourdough breads a tangier flavor than firm sourdough starters.

INGREDIENTS	GRAMS	OUNCES	VOLUME
Active White or Rye Sourdough Starter (pages 59 and 61)	57	2.00	¼ cup (full)
Warm water (85° to 90°F)	198	7.00	¾ cup plus 2 tablespoons
Unbleached all-purpose flour	170	6.00	1¼ cups

1. Place the active starter, water, and flour in a medium mixing bowl and stir vigorously with a wooden spoon for 1 to 2 minutes, until a smooth, somewhat elastic batter has formed. The batter will be fairly thick and stretchy; it gets softer and more elastic after it has risen. Scrape the liquid levain into the container, mark the height of the starter and the time on a piece of tape on the side of the container, and cover the container with plastic wrap.

2. Let the levain rise at room temperature (75° F to 77°F) until it has doubled in volume, 6 to 8 hours. Or if you plan to make your dough the next day, let it rise at room temperature for 1 hour, then refrigerate overnight. Remove it from the refrigerator and let it sit at room temperature for 2 to 3 hours to warm up and become active before using it. If you use the starter while it's still cold from the refrigerator, be sure to compensate for the cold temperature by using warm water (85°F to 90°F) in your dough instead of the cool water specified in the recipe.

Firm Levain

Makes 255 grams / 9 ounces / 1¼ cups

Equipment: one 2-quart clear plastic or glass container with high sides

This starter is used to make Country Sourdough (page 121), Toasty Seeded Bread Twists (page 127), and Amy's Rye with Caraway and Mustard Seeds (page 149).

INGREDIENTS	GRAMS	OUNCES	VOLUME
Active White or Rye Sourdough Starter (pages 59 and 61)	57	2.00	¼ cup
Cool water (75° to 78°)	57	2.00	¼ cup
Unbleached all-purpose flour	142	5.00	1 cup

1. In a medium mixing bowl, mix the active starter, water, and flour with your hand until it gathers into a mass. Knead it for 1 to 2 minutes until a firm, heavy dough has formed.

2. Press the levain into the bottom of the container. Mark the height and the time on a piece of tape on the side of the container, cover with plastic wrap, and let it sit at room temperature (75° to 78°F) until it has doubled in volume. (If the levain hasn't doubled within 8 hours, discard all but 57 grams/2 ounces of it and feed it again in the same manner. If it is very stiff and dry, you may have to add another tablespoon of water. Sometimes it takes more than one feeding if you haven't been refreshing the starter often enough.)

3. When the levain has doubled, it is ready to use in a recipe. Measure the amount needed and discard any that remains. If you're not going to use it right away, store it for up to 24 hours in the refrigerator.

Miche Levain

Makes 273 grams / 9.53 ounces / about 1⅛ cups

Equipment: one 2-quart clear plastic or glass container with high sides

This starter is thick, brown, and sticky. It has a funny texture but a lovely, tangy, wheaty smell. It should take two refreshments to make your active starter into miche levain.

INGREDIENTS	GRAMS	OUNCES	VOLUME
Cool water (75° to 78°F)	90	3.17	⅓ cup plus 1 tablespoon
Active White or Rye Sourdough Starter (pages 59 and 61)	60	2.12	¼ cup (full)
Organic rye flour	64	2.26	½ cup
Organic whole wheat flour	64	2.26	⅓ cup plus 1 tablespoon

1. In the container, combine the water and active starter, stirring vigorously with a wooden spoon to break up the starter. Add the rye and whole wheat flours and stir vigorously until they are well combined. The consistency of this levain will be more like dough than batter, so you may have to knead it by hand two or three times to be sure the flour is completely moistened.

2. Press the levain down into the bottom of the container. Mark the height and the time on a piece of tape on the side of the container and cover the container with plastic wrap. Let the levain rise at room temperature (75° to 78°F) for 5 to 7 hours, until it has at least doubled and a network of bubbles shows throughout, then do the first refreshment. If you don't have time to do the refreshment right away, refrigerate the levain until you're ready to feed it again. The refreshment should be done within 12 hours.

3. First refreshment: From this point forward, use 60 grams/2.12 ounces/¼ cup of the newly fermented miche levain in place of the active sourdough starter, and the same quantities of the other ingredients listed in the chart for each successive refreshment. In a 1-quart clear glass or plastic container, combine the water and miche levain, stirring vigorously with a wooden spoon or your fingers to break up the levain a little. Add the rye and whole wheat flours and stir vigorously again until everything is well combined. Cover with plastic wrap. Let the levain rise at room temperature (75° to 78°F) for 5 to 7 hours, until it has at least doubled and a network of bubbles shows throughout.

4. Second refreshment: Follow exactly the same procedure as outlined in step 3. When the levain has at least doubled, refrigerate it until you are ready to mix your dough. The active levain should be used within 12 hours, or it will need to be refreshed again.

TIPS AND TECHNIQUES

If you plan to make Organic Miche (page 139) on a regular basis, once you remove the amount of levain needed to make your bread, use a piece of the remaining levain to do a refreshment as described above and store it in the refrigerator. The levain can be maintained by refreshing it at least once a week. Two days before you want to bake with it again, go through the refreshment process twice, to bring the levain back up to a very active state.

Rye Salt Sour Starter

Makes 283 grams / 10 ounces / 1¼ cups
Equipment: one 1-quart clear plastic or glass container with high sides

We use this starter to make the French Rye (page 153) as well as Toy's Teddy Bread (page 135), Chewy Pumpernickel (page 157), and our Tangy Twenty-Four-Hour Sourdough (page 129). The starter contains only rye flour, and gets its name from the generous measure of salt that is added. The salt acts to slow down the fermentation slightly, and breads made with this starter have a more complex, almost "meaty" smell and flavor. It's amazing that the simple addition of salt to a rye sourdough starter can impact the flavor of the bread so dramatically. It will take one initial feeding and one refreshment to make your active sourdough starter into the rye salt sour, so be sure to start this process two days before you want to bake the bread.

INGREDIENTS	GRAMS	OUNCES	VOLUME
Cool water (75° to 78°F)	130	4.58	½ cup plus 1 tablespoon
Active White or Rye Sourdough Starter (pages 59 and 61)	30	1.00	1 tablespoon plus 1 teaspoon
Kosher salt	¾ teaspoon	¾ teaspoon	¾ teaspoon
Organic rye flour	130	4.58	1 cup

1. In the container, combine the water, active starter, and salt, and stir with a wooden spoon. Add the flour and stir again until the flour is moistened. It should have a fairly thick pastelike consistency. Take the temperature of the starter. For best results it should be between 75° to 79°F. Using a rubber spatula, scrape down the sides and level the top of the starter. Cover it with plastic wrap. Mark the height of the starter and the time on a piece of tape on the side of the container. Let the starter rise at room temperature (75° to 78°F) for 5 to 7 hours, until it has at least doubled and a network of bubbles shows throughout, then do the first re-freshment. If you don't have time to do the refreshment right away, refrigerate the starter until you're ready to feed it again. The refreshment should be done within 12 hours.

2. The refreshment: From this point forward, use 30 grams/1 ounce/1 tablespoon plus 1 teaspoon of fermented salt sour in place of the active sourdough starter, and the same quantities of the other ingredients listed in the chart for each refreshment. In a 1-quart clear glass or plastic container, combine the water, salt sour, and salt and stir with a wooden spoon. Add the flour and stir again until the flour is moistened. Take the temperature of the starter. For best results it should be between 75° and 79°F. Using a rubber spatula, scrape down the sides and level the top of the starter. Cover it with plastic wrap. Mark the height of the starter and the time on a new piece of tape. Let the starter rise at room temperature (75° to 78°F) for 5 to 7 hours, until it has at least doubled and a network of bubbles shows throughout, then refrigerate it until you are ready to make your dough within 24 hours.

TIPS AND TECHNIQUES

Once your salt sour is established, you can keep some in a small container in the refrigerator to refresh for future use. If the starter has not been refreshed for several days, give it two refreshments to reactivate it before using it to make dough.

PEACE, BREAD, AND A DOUBLE ESPRESSO

David Chaffin is our production manager. He was born in Texas but is a true New Yorker, embracing all the city has to offer, especially enjoying art and music. He arrives at work every day on one of his many bicycles or his skateboard, with a long gray ponytail flying in the wind behind him. David joined the bakery in 1998, two years after we expanded to the Chelsea Market, and has helped to build a great team of bread bakers over the years. He loves to bake bread and couldn't be happier standing in front of a deck oven loading and unloading golden brown loaves with a wooden peel. But his special skill is peacemaking. He has taken a corps of forty-five workers from at least ten different countries and merged them into a harmonious team. He hires each baker, makes all of their schedules, counsels them, gives reviews, and keeps all of them working together—despite their many different personalities, customs, and work habits. Between filling vacation requests and sick calls, David has to work around equipment problems, too. When one of our four bread ovens needs repair, his team has to change their schedule to bake bread early or late in order to get the oven back on track. On a good day, when all the mixers, shapers, and bakers are at work, in good health and on time, and with all the equipment up and running, David can calmly enjoy his favorite moment: an aromatic double espresso, a fresh chocolate chip cookie—and a little bit of peace.

Spelt Levain

Makes 270 grams / 9.53 ounces / about 1¼ cups

Equipment: one 1-quart clear plastic or glass container with high sides

O rganic Whole Grain Spelt with Flax and Sesame (page 143) requires a starter also made from spelt flour. This starter is similar to the wheat and rye sourdough starters, though not quite as dry, and it also includes a little salt like the rye salt sour. As you can see, we tailor our starters to help us achieve a particular vision of flavor and texture as we develop the recipe for a new bread. It takes one initial feeding and two refreshments to make your active sourdough starter into a spelt levain, so be sure to start this process three days before you want to bake the bread.

INGREDIENTS	GRAMS	OUNCES	VOLUME
Cool water (75° to 78°F)	100	3.53	⅓ cup plus 2 tablespoons
Active White or Rye Sourdough Starter (pages 59 and 61)	20	0.70	1 tablespoon plus 1 teaspoon
Kosher salt	½ teaspoon	½ teaspoon	½ teaspoon
Organic whole grain spelt flour	150	5.29	1 cup

1. In the container, combine the water, active starter, and salt, stirring vigorously with a wooden spoon or your fingers to dissolve the salt and break up the starter. Add the flour and stir vigorously again. The consistency of this levain will be more like soft dough than batter, so you may have to knead it two or three times by hand to be sure the flour is completely moistened.

2. Press the levain down into the bottom of the container and cover it with plastic wrap. Mark the height of the levain and the time on a piece of tape on the side of the. Let the levain rise at room temperature (75° to 78°F) for 5 to 7 hours, until it has at least doubled and a network of bubbles shows throughout, then do the first refreshment. If you don't have time to do the refreshment right away, refrigerate the levain until you're ready to feed it again. The refreshment (feeding) should be done within 12 hours.

3. First refreshment: From this point forward, use 20 grams/0.70 ounce/1 tablespoon of the newly fermented spelt levain in place of the active sourdough starter, and the same quantities of the other ingredients listed in the chart in each successive refreshment. In a 1-quart clear glass or plastic container, combine the water, spelt levain, and salt, stirring vigorously with a wooden spoon or your fingers to dissolve the salt and break up the levain a little. Add the flour and stir vigorously again until everything is well combined. Cover the container with plastic wrap. Mark the height of the levain and the time on a new piece of tape. Let the levain rise at room temperature (75° to 78°F) for 5 to 7 hours, until it has at least doubled and a network of bubbles shows throughout, then do the second refreshment or put it in the refrigerator until you are ready to refresh it again.

4. Second refreshment: Follow exactly the same procedure as outlined in step 3. When the levain has at least doubled, refrigerate it until you are ready to mix your dough. The active levain should be used within 12 hours to make dough or it will need to be refreshed again.

TIPS AND TECHNIQUES

If you plan to make the Organic Whole Grain Spelt with Flax and Sesame (page 143) on a regular basis, you can perpetuate the spelt levain for future use. Once you remove the amount of levain needed to make your bread, use a piece of the remaining spelt levain to do a refreshment as described above and store the levain in the refrigerator. It can be maintained by refreshing it at least once a week. Two days before you want to bake with it again, go through the refreshment process twice to bring the levain back up to a very active state.

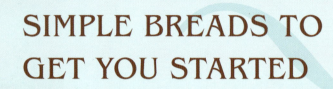

SIMPLE BREADS TO GET YOU STARTED

Here are six basic breads that taste delicious and are easy to make. Some of them are made without any type of starter. These recipes will give you a chance to try your hand at kneading, shaping, proofing, and baking, and the overall time from mixing through baking is shorter than some of the recipes found later in the book. As you try to make each kind of bread, take notes about the timing, temperature, and other observations about the dough. You will find that after you make a recipe a few times, your bread will become even better. After you have tried and perfected these recipes, you'll be ready to tackle more complex breads in the following chapters. Relax, experiment, and enjoy the process.

Golden Whole Wheat Bread

MADE WITHOUT A STARTER

Makes two 15-ounce round boules

Equipment: wooden peel and baking stone, or one 17 × 12-inch sheet pan

This is a fragrant and versatile bread that is simply made with flour, water, yeast, and salt, with the addition of wheat bran for extra fiber and flavor. Make an effort to find top-quality whole wheat flour for these loaves. We like to use organic flour or whole wheat flour from smaller mills such as Hodgson Mill or King Arthur. By using the best-quality whole grain flours, your bread will have a wheaty aroma and the flavor of real whole grains will shine through. We make this dough very wet and use two turns while it is rising to help develop better texture and enhance the flavor characteristics of the grain. This is an excellent recipe to try to learn about working with wet dough.

INGREDIENTS	GRAMS	OUNCES	VOLUME
Very warm water (105° to 115°F)	57	2.00	¼ cup
Active dry yeast	1 teaspoon	1 teaspoon	1 teaspoon
Organic whole wheat flour	312	11.00	2½ cups
Unbleached bread flour	220	7.76	1½ cups
Wheat bran	22	0.75	½ cup
Kosher salt	10	0.35	1 tablespoon plus ¼ teaspoon
Cool water (75° to 78°F)	454	16.00	2 cups
Cornmeal, for sprinkling	as needed	as needed	as needed

1. Combine the warm water and yeast in a small measuring cup and stir with a fork to dissolve the yeast.

2. Combine the whole wheat flour, bread flour, bran, and salt in a medium bowl. With your fingers, mix in the yeast mixture and the cool water until the dough is a granular mass. Fold the dough over onto itself and knead briefly in the bowl for about 2 minutes. If the dough seems too firm, add 1 to 2 tablespoons of water. It should be very loose and sticky.

3. Move the dough to a lightly floured work surface and continue to knead until it becomes somewhat cohesive, 3 to 4 more minutes. You should use very little flour to knead this dough. It will stick to the surface, but use a scraper to lift it and clean

the surface rather than using too much flour. After kneading, the dough will still be granular and will not become springy yet.

4. Put the dough back into the mixing bowl, cover with oiled plastic wrap, and let rest for 20 minutes to smooth out and develop elasticity.

5. Return the dough to the lightly floured surface and knead it for 6 to 7 minutes. The dough will already feel stretchy, and will become smooth and develop strength with kneading. Do not knead extra flour into the dough. It should be soft and loose.

6. Place the dough in a lightly oiled bowl. Cover the dough with oiled plastic wrap and allow it to rise at room temperature (75° to 78°F) for 1 hour.

7. After 1 hour, turn the dough while it is still in the mixing bowl. Gently deflate the dough in the middle of the bowl with your fingertips, then fold the left side over the middle, and the right side over the middle. Fold the dough in half, gently pat it down, and then turn it over so the seam is underneath.

8. Let it rise again for 1 hour and repeat the turning process. This dough gets stronger and springier each time it is turned.

9. Let it rise again for 1 to 1½ hours, until it doubles in volume. When the dough is fully risen, an indentation made by poking your finger deep into the dough should not spring back.

10. Sprinkle a peel or the back of a sheet pan generously with cornmeal or line it with parchment paper. Place the dough on a very lightly floured surface. Divide the dough into two equal pieces, about 515 grams/18.1 ounces each. Shape each piece tightly into a boule (see page 37). Place the loaves seam side down on the peel or pan, leaving 3 to 4 inches between them for rising. Cover with oiled plastic wrap and allow the loaves to rise for about 1½ hours, until they have nearly doubled in size. Watch the loaves carefully; if they begin to grow together, bake them a little early, even if they are slightly underrisen.

11. Thirty minutes before baking, preheat the oven to 450°F. Prepare the oven by placing a cast-iron skillet and a smaller pan (a mini loaf pan) on the floor of the oven or on the lowest possible rack in an electric oven. Place an oven rack two rungs above the cast-iron pan, and if you have one, put a baking stone on the rack. Fill a plastic spray bottle with water. Fill a teakettle with water to be boiled later, and have a metal 1-cup measure with a straight handle available near the kettle.

12. Five to 10 minutes before the loaf is ready to bake, turn the water on to boil, and carefully place two or three ice cubes in the small loaf pan in the bottom of the oven. This helps to create moisture in the oven prior to baking.

13. Snip a shallow circle or crown pattern into the top of each loaf with scissors (see page 255), or use a lame to score a tic-tac-toe cut on top of each loaf. Open the oven door and gently slide the bread onto the stone. (If you're baking without a stone simply slide the sheet pan with the scored loaves onto the empty oven rack.) Quickly mist the loaves with water 6 to 8 times, pour 1 cup of boiling water into the skillet, and immediately shut the oven door. After 1 minute, quickly mist the loaves with water again, then shut the oven door.

14. Bake for 15 minutes, then reduce the oven temperature to 375°F and bake for 13 to 18 minutes longer, until the loaves are deep golden brown and sound hollow when tapped on the bottom.

15. Place the loaves on a rack to cool. Serve warm or cool—and enjoy the wheaty fragrance.

TIPS AND TECHNIQUES

We used unbleached bread flour with a protein content of 12.7% for this dough. Organic or conventional whole wheat flour can be used.

MY GRANDPARENTS' FARM

Memories of bread smells wafting from the oven and filling the big kitchen transport me to Pleasant View Farm, the family farm where my mother, her father, and his father were raised. Built in 1892, the house has been warm and welcoming to family, friends, and neighbors for more than a century. Today my cousin lives there and carries on the family tradition with a beautiful farm stand, filled with homegrown produce from the lush rolling fields of the farm.

When I was growing up, we would drive to the farm on Sunday afternoons to visit my grandparents and to take in the sights and smells of the country. As soon as we entered the house, our senses were awakened. From my grandmother's kitchen came the fragrant aromas of roasting chicken or roast beef with caramelized onions and carrots. Pots simmered on the stove and steam clouded the windows. The table was set for lots of people and anticipation was in the air. Above all of the wonderful smells was the lingering aroma of those big, beautiful white pan loaves perched on their racks to cool. They were golden brown, plump, and still slightly warm. To me they were the highlight of the meal, with a soft, tender texture that would almost melt in your mouth. We always had strawberry or raspberry jam with dinner. That was to show off my grandmother's preserves, made with fresh berries from her extraordinary garden. I remember holding a soft slice of fresh bread, its edges gently drooping over the sides of my small hand, and spooning on the wonderful homemade jam! Who needed the roast beef?

A.S.

French Baguette

Makes two 14-inch-long baguettes

Equipment: electric stand mixer with dough hook; baking stone and wooden peel, one 17 x 12-inch sheet pan; baker's linen or heavy smooth cotton towel

We included a recipe for baguettes in our first edition of this book, which was written two years after the bakery was opened. Over the years we've learned a lot about making traditional French-style baguettes, using various techniques to produce superior flavor and texture. Making a consistently excellent baguette is not an easy task. Professional bread bakers can learn many things about the level of a colleague's skill and craftsmanship by looking at one of their baguettes.

We now have fresh baguettes coming out of our ovens in the Chelsea Market location three times a day, and we think our team of baguette bakers does an outstanding job making what many of our customers say is the best baguette in the city. We have French expatriates who come to Amy's Bread to get their daily baguettes, and many French tourists have told us our baguettes are better than the ones that are made in France these days. From our own experiences on trips to France, we know there may be some truth to that, but we know that in Paris better baguettes are on the rise (no pun intended). We also know that there are a handful of master bakers there who make their baguettes with great skill and pride, and some of them have generously shared their techniques with us. We will always be grateful to them for their willingness to share that knowledge.

When baking baguettes in a regular home oven, it's very difficult to get the kind of thin, crackly crust that comes from using a steam-injected deck oven like the ones we have in the bakery. But don't let that discourage you from using this recipe. You may not be able to duplicate the crust, but with a little practice you'll be able to make baguettes that have a sweet, milky flavor and aroma and an openholed texture that will make you proud. Have one for breakfast, spread with sweet butter, your favorite jam, and a steaming cup of café au lait on the side. You could almost be in Paris—or at Amy's Bread.

These baguettes are shorter than the ones we make at the bakery to accommodate the limitations of baking in a home oven.

INGREDIENTS	GRAMS	OUNCES	VOLUME
Very warm water (105° to 115° F)	57	2.00	¼ cup
Active dry yeast	⅜ teaspoon	⅜ teaspoon	⅜ teaspoon
Unbleached bread flour	250	8.82	1⅔ cups
Poolish (page 54)	140	4.94	½ cup
Very cool water (65° to 70° F)	95	3.35	⅓ cup plus 1 tablespoon
Kosher salt	2¼ teaspoons	2¼ teaspoons	2¼ teaspoons
Ascorbic acid solution (see Tips and Techniques)	¼ teaspoon	¼ teaspoon	¼ teaspoon
Barley malt syrup	¼ teaspoon	¼ teaspoon	¼ teaspoon
Coarse cornmeal or polenta, for sprinkling	as needed	as needed	as needed

1. Combine the very warm water and yeast in a measuring cup and stir to dissolve the yeast. Let stand for 3 minutes.

2. In the bowl of an electric stand mixer fitted with a dough hook, combine all of the ingredients including the yeast and mix on medium low speed for 3 minutes, or until all the flour is moistened and gathers into a ball of dough. Slide the dough down from the top of the hook (to be sure all of the dough will be evenly kneaded), increase the speed to medium and knead the dough for 3 more minutes. Slide the dough down from the hook again, increase the speed to medium-high and continue kneading for another 3 minutes, or until the dough begins to slap the sides of the bowl and is beginning to pull up from the bottom of the bowl but does not clean the bottom of the bowl. The dough should be about 80 percent developed at this point. It should have some strength and elasticity but it will be soft and a little sticky and you will not be able to pull a transparent sheet without having it tear. The dough temperature should be around 77°F.

3. Put the dough in a large oiled bowl, cover it with oiled plastic wrap, and allow it to rise for 1 hour. It should look and feel puffy but it will not have doubled.

4. Give the dough a turn while it is still in the mixing bowl. Gently deflate the dough in the middle of the bowl with your fingertips, then fold the left side over the middle, and the right side over the middle. Fold the dough in half, gently pat it down, and then turn it over so the seam is underneath.

5. Let it rise again for 45 to 50 minutes. The dough will almost double during this time and it should feel strong and supple by the end of the rising period. You will be able to pull a transparent sheet—the final development of the dough occurs while it is rising.

6. Pour the dough out onto a lightly floured work surface and divide it into two equal pieces, about 260 grams/9 ounces each. Pre-shape each piece by patting it into a small rectangle about 8 X 4 inches, positioned so the short sides are at the top and the bottom of the rectangle. If the dough sticks to the work surface, lift it gently with a dough scraper and lightly reflour the surface. Starting with the upper edge of the dough, gently fold the top third down and the bottom third up, like a business letter, so you have three equal layers. Seal the seam along the top edge to form a log and roll it over so the seam is on the bottom. The pre-shaping prepares for the final lengthening of the baguette. Cover these shapes with the oiled plastic wrap and let them rest on the work surface until they feel puffy and have almost doubled. This could take anywhere from 30 minutes to an hour or more depending on the temperature of the dough and whether the pre-shaping was tight or loose.

7. While the dough rests, prepare a proofing pan for the baguettes by lining a 17 X 12-inch sheet pan with baker's linen so that the cloth hangs over the side of the pan, and sprinkling it with a moderate amount of flour; or a heavy smooth cotton towel sprinkled generously with flour; or just line the pan with parchment paper and sprinkle the parchment with a moderate amount of flour.

8. Use a dough scraper to lift one of the almost-doubled pieces of dough and gently flip it over onto the lightly floured work surface. With lightly floured hands, pat the dough gently into an oval about 10 X 4 inches with the long edge facing you. (Don't be too heavy-handed with the patting; you want to preserve some of the gas bubbles in the dough so you'll have a nice airy crumb in your finished baguette.) Shape each piece into a baguette (see page 36). The baguettes should be 13 to 14 inches long and about 1¾ inches in diameter. Don't go beyond 14 inches or they won't fit on a baking stone. This length is good even if you're baking on a sheet pan without a stone because it will give you a good crust-to-crumb ratio for a piece of dough this size. The longer you make it, the less crumb you have on the inside of the loaf. Place one loaf lengthwise on the prepared pan touching against the edge of the pan (be sure the edge of the pan is covered by the floured cloth). Pull up a 3-inch pleat of cloth to separate the two loaves and place the second loaf on the pan next to the first loaf. Pull up another pleat of cloth on the outside of the second loaf to support it while it rises. If you're using a parchment-lined pan, place the loaves about 2 inches in from the sides and leave about 3 or 4 inches between the two loaves. Cover the loaves with oiled plastic wrap and let them rise until they have almost doubled. They should look plump and hold a slight indentation when pressed lightly your finger. This could take 1 or 2 hours depending on the temperature of the dough and how tightly the baguette is shaped. Baking them when they're slightly underproofed guarantees more oven spring, which contributes to a more open, airy crumb in the finished loaf.

9. At least 30 minutes before the loaves are ready to bake, preheat the oven to 480°F. Prepare the oven by placing a cast-iron skillet and a smaller pan (a mini loaf pan) on the floor of the oven or on the lowest possible rack in an electric oven.

Place an oven rack two rungs above the cast-iron pan, and if you have one, put a baking stone on the rack. Fill a plastic spray bottle with water. Fill a teakettle with water to be boiled later, and have a metal 1-cup measure with a straight handle available near the kettle.

10. Five to 10 minutes before the bread is ready to bake, turn the water on to boil, and carefully place two or three ice cubes in the small loaf pan in the bottom of the oven. This helps to create moisture in the oven prior to baking.

11. At the same time, 5 to 10 minutes before the baguettes are ready to go into the oven, lightly sprinkle the wooden peel with coarse cornmeal or polenta and gently lift each loaf from the proofing pan onto the peel. The easiest way to do this is to put one hand under each end of the baguette and gently scoot them in toward the center of the loaf so the middle will be supported instead of stretching out during the move. Try not to stretch the loaves beyond 14 inches, and leave enough space between them to allow for spreading in the oven. Leave them uncovered so a light skin forms on the surface, which makes the loaves easier to score. (If you're baking without a stone, just leave the risen loaves on the parchment-lined baking pan and remove the plastic for the last few minutes of proof time.)

12. When the loaves are ready, use a lame or a sharp razor blade to make three or four slashes down the length of each baguette. The cuts should run from one end of the loaf to the other, rather than across it, and the blade should be held at a 30-degree angle to the loaf to create cuts that will pop open in the oven. Use the plastic spray bottle to mist the loaves evenly with water. Slide the loaves onto the baking stone, being mindful not to stretch them or they'll fall off the end of the stone. (If you're baking without a stone simply slide the sheet pan with the scored and misted loaves onto the empty oven rack.) Pour 1 cup of boiling water into the water pan and immediately shut the oven door. After about 1 minute, quickly mist the loaves 6 to 8 times, then shut the oven door.

13. Check the loaves after 12 minutes and rotate them if necessary to ensure even browning. Bake the baguettes for a total of 23 to 28 minutes, until they are uniformly golden brown in color, have a crisp crust, and sound hollow when tapped on the bottom.

14. Cool them on a wire rack and enjoy them slightly warm or at room temperature. Baguettes are best eaten the same day they are baked.

TIPS AND TECHNIQUES

We used unbleached bread flour with a protein content of 12.7% for this dough. The poolish was made with unbleached all-purpose flour with a protein content of 11.7%.

Ascorbic acid is a natural crystalline form of vitamin C. It's an essential nutrient found in most fruits and vegetables. Your body requires it but it can't be made or stored in the body so it must be acquired through eating food. There is no reason to be concerned about adding a tiny bit of ascorbic acid to your bread. Ascorbic acid crystals can be purchased at any health food store. Be sure they are pure, without additives. This is added to improve the elasticity of the dough.

To make ascorbic acid solution, stir ½ teaspoon of pure ascorbic acid crystals into 300 grams/10.6 ounces/1⅓ cups of cold water until completely dissolved. Store the solution in an airtight container in the refrigerator. Do not use more than the specified amount. A little ascorbic acid goes a long way, and it can be counterproductive if too much is used. We're not sure what the actual shelf life of this solution is (though it's probably at least several weeks) so if you don't use it frequently, simply discard it and make a new batch the next time you bake.

In the bakery we proof our baguettes on wooden boards lined with baker's linen that has been lightly floured (see page 270 for sources). If you don't have baker's linen, heavy smooth cotton towels (preferably unbleached) work just as well if you rub them with lots of flour. You can also use a sheet pan lined with parchment that has been sprinkled with flour, but your final baguette will have a flatter profile.

You can also proof your baguettes directly on the wooden peel you use to load them into the oven, but if the dough is very sticky, line the peel with parchment, then sprinkle with cornmeal, or they may stick to the peel.

If the loaves collapse when you move them from the cloths to the peel, you'll know they've been proofed too long. You can still bake the collapsed loaves but they probably won't rise much in the oven and their flavor and texture will be less than ideal. If the loaves collapse when you score them you'll know they've been proofed too long. What to do about this? There is nothing to do at this point. It's too late to fix them. Just bake them anyway.

Rustic Italian Bread (page 85), Rustic Italian Bread Sticks (page 88), and Prosciutto and Black Pepper Bread (page 89)

Rustic Italian Bread

Makes 2 large 1½-pound bâtard-shaped loaves

Equipment: electric stand mixer with dough hook; baking stone and wooden peel, one 17 × 12-inch sheet pan; baker's linen or heavy smooth cotton dish towel

This white bread with an airy open crumb is our version of ciabatta bread. At Amy's Bread we use this dough to make our crusty rectangles of Rustic Italian Bread in two sizes, as well as Country White Boules and Country White Bâtards. We love it because it has so much versatility. It can be cut into flat rectangle-shaped loaves of varying sizes that are more crust than crumb, or into long, chewy bread sticks covered in sesame seeds and salt. With the addition of ground prosciutto and a sprinkling of black pepper, you can turn it into a slightly lighter but just as delicious version of the Amy's Prosciutto and Black Pepper bread. Spread it on a sheet pan and top it with a few slices of fresh tomato, a sprinkling of olives, and a little olive oil for a dairy-free pizza treat. The possibilities are limited only by your imagination. This recipe explains how to make the big torpedo-shaped bâtards because we use slices of these loaves in the Turkey and Avocado on Country White Bread sandwiches on page 218, but we also give you instructions for shaping the Rustic Italian loaf, and for making other variations.

This is a very wet dough that develops much of its strength and elasticity while it proofs in the bowl after being mixed. It takes practice to get used to handling and shaping a dough this wet, but with a little persistence you'll soon be an expert and will want to use this recipe again and again.

INGREDIENTS	GRAMS	OUNCES	VOLUME
Very warm water (105° to 115° F)	57	2.00	¼ cup
Active dry yeast	1 teaspoon	1 teaspoon	1 teaspoon
Poolish (page 54)	454	16.00	1⅞ cups
Very cool water (65° F)	365	12.87	1⅔ cups
Unbleached bread flour	605	21.34	4 cups
Kosher salt	13	0.46	1 tablespoon plus 1¼ teaspoons
Coarse cornmeal or polenta, for sprinkling	as needed	as needed	as needed

1. Combine the very warm water and yeast in a measuring cup and stir to dissolve the yeast. Let stand for 3 minutes.

2. In the bowl of an electric stand mixer fitted with a dough hook, combine all of the ingredients including the yeast mixture and mix on low speed for 30 seconds to gather the ingredients together. Increase the speed to medium-low and continue mixing for 3 minutes, or until all the flour is moistened and looks like a thick batter. Slide the dough down from the top of the hook if necessary (to be sure all of the dough will be evenly kneaded), increase the speed to medium-high, and knead the dough for 6 more minutes. Slide the dough down from the hook and let it rest in the bowl for 20 minutes before continuing the mix.

3. After the rest period, with the mixer on medium-high speed, resume mixing the dough for 16 to 18 more minutes, until the dough just begins to slap the sides of the bowl and is beginning to pull away from the sides and bottom of the bowl but does not clean the bottom of the bowl. The dough should be about 75 percent developed at this point. It should have some strength and elasticity but it will still be soft and sticky, and you will not be able to pull a transparent sheet without having it tear. The dough temperature should be around 77°F.

4. Put the dough in an oiled bowl that is large enough to allow it to almost double, cover it with oiled plastic wrap, and allow it to rise for 1 hour. It should look and feel puffy but it will not have doubled. Give the dough a turn while it is still in the mixing bowl. Gently deflate the dough in the middle of the bowl with your fingertips, then fold the left side over the middle, and the right side over the middle. Fold the dough in half, gently pat it down, and then turn it over so the seam is underneath.

5. Let it rise again for 45 to 50 minutes. The dough will almost double during this time and it should feel strong and supple by the end of the rising period. You will be able to pull a transparent sheet—the final development of the dough occurs while it is rising.

6. While the dough rises, prepare a proofing pan for the loaves by lining a 17 X 12-inch sheet pan with baker's linen so it overlaps the sides and sprinkle it with a moderate amount of flour, or a heavy smooth cotton towel sprinkled generously with flour, or just line the pan with parchment paper and sprinkle the parchment with a moderate amount of flour.

7. Pour the dough gently out onto a well-floured work surface. By pulling and patting gently with your hands, shape the dough into a big rectangular pillow, about 16 X 10 inches, with the long sides at the top and bottom. Try not to deflate the dough too much. Using a dough scraper, cut the rectangle in half from top to bottom so you have two 10 X 8-inch pieces, with the short sides at the top and bottom. To shape the bâtards, follow the instructions on page 35. The bâtards should be about 14 inches long after shaping. Place the first loaf lengthwise on the prepared pan, right against one edge (be sure the edge of the pan is covered by part of the floured cloth). Pull up a 3-inch pleat of cloth to separate the loaves, then place the second bâtard next to the first loaf. Pull up another pleat of cloth on the outside of the second loaf to support it while it rises. If you're using a parchment-lined pan, place the loaves about 2 inches in from the sides and leave 3 or 4 inches between the two loaves. Cover the loaves with oiled plastic wrap and let them rise until they have almost doubled. They should look large and plump and hold a slight indentation when pressed lightly with your finger. This could take 1 hour or more, depending on the temperature of the dough and how tightly the bâtard is shaped. (Baking the loaves when they're slightly underproofed guarantees more oven spring, which contributes to a more open, airy crumb in the finished loaf.)

8. At least 30 minutes before the loaves are ready to bake, preheat the oven to 480°F.

9. Prepare the oven by placing a cast-iron skillet and a smaller pan (a mini loaf pan) on the floor of the oven or on the lowest possible rack in an electric oven. Place an oven rack two rungs above the cast-iron pan, and if you have one, put a baking stone on the rack. Fill a plastic spray bottle with water. Fill a teakettle with water to be boiled later, and have a metal 1-cup measure with a straight handle available near the kettle.

10. Five to 10 minutes before the bread is ready to bake, turn the water on to boil, and carefully place two ice cubes in the small loaf pan in the bottom of the oven. This helps to create moisture in the oven prior to baking.

11. At the same time, 5 to 10 minutes before the loaves are ready to go into the oven, sprinkle the wooden peel with coarse cornmeal or polenta and gently lift each loaf from the proofing pan onto the peel. The easiest way to do this is to put one hand under each end of the loaf and gently scoot them in toward the center of the loaf so that it will be supported during the move. Try not to stretch the loaves, and leave enough space between them to allow for spreading in the oven. Cover them again with the oiled plastic wrap to rest for a few minutes.

12. When the loaves are ready, use a lame or a sharp razor blade to score the loaves by making one long cut down the center of each bâtard. The cut should run from one end of the loaf to the other leaving 1 to 2 inches unscored at each end. Use the plastic spray bottle to mist the loaves lightly with water. Quickly but carefully fill the metal 1-cup measure with boiling water, open the oven and slide the bâtards onto the baking stone, being mindful not to stretch them too much, then quickly but carefully pour the boiling water into the cast-iron pan and immediately close the oven door. (If you're baking without a stone simply slide the sheet pan with the scored and misted loaves onto the empty oven rack.) After 3 minutes, pour in another ½ cup of boiling water.

13. Check the loaves after 20 minutes and rotate them if necessary to ensure even browning. Bake them for a total of 45 to 50 minutes, until they are uniformly dark golden brown in color and sound hollow when tapped on the bottom.

14. Cool them completely on a wire rack before cutting them.

Other variations using the same dough:

RUSTIC ITALIAN (CIABATTA) SHAPE Follow the procedures for making the dough through step 5, except that you must generously flour the proofing cloth with a half-inch thickness of flour. Pour the dough gently onto a well-floured work surface. Pat it gently with your hands into a big rectangular pillow, about 14 X 10 inches, with the long sides at the top and bottom. Be careful not to deflate the dough or lose any air bubbles. Using a dough scraper, cut the rectangle in half across the dough so that the long side of the rectangle is the long side of each loaf. Lift each rectangle of dough carefully and place it on the well-floured cloth to rise. This loaf requires no shaping, but you must place the loaf neatly on the cloth with the edges square for the best results. Pull up a 3-inch pleat of cloth between the two loaves and carefully place the second loaf. Cover the loaves with well-oiled plastic wrap and let them rise for 35 to 45 minutes. They should be slightly underproofed before baking so they spring up in the oven.

Prepare the oven in the same manner as for the bâtard shape. To load the loaves into the oven, sprinkle a peel generously with cornmeal, then very gently place one hand under each end of a loaf and carefully lift and flip it over, then place it on the peel so that the floured side is up. Slide the loaf onto the baking stone leaving room for the second loaf, then load the second loaf in the same manner. Now add the boiling water to the cast-iron skillet to create steam and quickly close the oven door. Follow the baking instructions for the bâtard shape.

RUSTIC ITALIAN BREAD STICKS Place 1½ cups of unhulled sesame seeds and 1 tablespoon of coarse sea salt in a 17 X 12-inch sheet pan with 1-inch sides. Shake the pan to distribute the seeds and salt evenly. Use one of the 10 X 8-inch pieces of dough to make the bread sticks. Mist one side of the dough with water and quickly flip it, wet side down, onto the pan of sesame seeds. Press it gently to coat the dough with seeds. Lift the dough off onto the unfloured work surface, seeded side down, and shake the sheet pan to evenly redistribute the seeds. Mist the top of the dough and flip it on to the pan of seeds, once again pressing down to coat it with seeds. Move the seeded dough back onto the unfloured work surface. Pat the dough into a roughly 12 X 8-inch rectangle and use a dough cutter to cut 18 strips that are each about 8 inches long. Line two 17 X 12-inch sheet pans with parchment paper and place 9 bread sticks crosswise on each pan, allowing them to stretch and lengthen to 12 inches as you move them onto the pan. Let them rise for 10 minutes and bake them with steam in a 480°F oven for 20 to 25 minutes, until they're lightly browned and crusty.

PROSCIUTTO AND BLACK PEPPER BREAD Use one batch of dough to make three small loaves. Divide the dough equally into three pieces, each weighing about 500 grams/17.64 ounces. Pat each piece into a rectangle and sprinkle it evenly with freshly ground black pepper. Spread ½ cup of finely chopped imported prosciutto onto the dough, covering the entire surface evenly. Press the ham into the dough so it sticks. Fold the rectangle into thirds like a business letter, then with the short sides at the top and bottom roll the rectangle into a log and seal the length of the seam with the heel of your hand. Tuck in the ends and seal those too. Let the loaves rise on a lightly floured, cloth-covered pan for about an hour, until almost doubled in volume. Move the loaves onto a peel that has been sprinkled with cornmeal, score the loaves by making three short cuts across the top of each loaf, mist them with water, and bake them in a 480°F oven with steam. Bake for 10 minutes, reduce oven temperature to 450°F, and bake 25 minutes longer, or until the loaves are dark golden brown and sound hollow when tapped on the bottom.

TIPS AND TECHNIQUES

We used unbleached bread flour with a protein content of 12% for this dough. The poolish was made with unbleached all-purpose flour with a protein content of 11.5%.

If the dough is still weak and not fully developed at the end of step 4 in the recipe, fold and turn it again. Let it rise for 30 minutes or more, until it has almost doubled. Check it again to see if you can pull a transparent sheet. It should be ready to divide at the end of that third turn.

Cinnamon Raisin Bread

Makes two 9 x 5-inch loaves

Equipment: two 9 x 5-inch loaf pans, oiled or buttered

This easy recipe for cinnamon raisin bread makes a nice breakfast loaf that can be sliced and toasted to accompany a morning meal of eggs, bacon, and fresh fruit. Save the extra slices, if there are any, and use them for French toast the next day. First you prepare a simple bread dough, and then sprinkle on cinnamon and sugar to taste, followed by lots and lots of raisins. The dough is carefully and tightly rolled so that the raisins form a swirl through each slice. If you prefer a more modest amount of raisins, hold some back to make a lighter loaf.

INGREDIENTS	GRAMS	OUNCES	VOLUME
Very warm water (105° to 115°F)	57	2.00	¼ cup
Active dry yeast	1¼ teaspoons	1¼ teaspoons	1¼ teaspoons
Biga Starter (page 56)	397	14.00	1¾ cups
Cool water (75° to 78 °F)	368	13.00	1½ cups plus 2 tablespoons
Unbleached all-purpose flour	574	20.25	4½ cups
Kosher salt	12	0.42	1 tablespoon plus 1 teaspoon
Dark raisins	425	15.00	3 cups
Sugar	65	2.29	¼ cup plus 1 tablespoon
Ground cinnamon	1 tablespoon	1 tablespoon	1 tablespoon

1. Combine the very warm water and yeast in a medium bowl and stir with a fork to dissolve the yeast. Let stand for 3 minutes.

2. Add the biga and cool water to the yeast mixture and mix with your fingers for 2 minutes, breaking up the starter. The mixture should look milky, chunky, and slightly foamy. Add the flour and the salt and mix with your fingers until the dough forms a shaggy mass. Fold the dough over onto itself and knead briefly in the bowl.

3. Move the dough to a lightly floured work surface and knead until it is smooth and supple, about 4 minutes. If it feels stiff or dry, add cool water, 1 tablespoon at a time.

4. Put the dough back into the mixing bowl, cover with oiled plastic wrap, and let rest for 20 minutes to smooth out and develop elasticity.

5. Return the dough to the lightly floured surface and knead it for 5 to 7 minutes. The dough will already feel stretchy, and will become silky and elastic with kneading. Do not knead extra flour into the dough. It should be soft and loose.

6. Place the dough in a lightly oiled bowl. Cover the dough with oiled plastic wrap and allow it to rise at room temperature (75° to 77°F) for 1 hour.

7. After 1 hour, turn the dough while it is still in the mixing bowl. Gently deflate the dough in the middle of the bowl with your fingertips, then fold the left side over the middle, and the right side over the middle. Fold the dough in half, gently pat it down, and then turn it over so the seam is underneath.

8. Let it rise again for 1 to 1½ hours. When the dough is fully risen, an indentation made by poking your finger deep into the dough should not spring back.

9. While the dough is rising, place the raisins in a bowl or a plastic container and add warm water to come just below the top of the raisins. (If you use too much water, you will rinse away the natural sweetness of the raisins.) Combine the sugar and cinnamon in a small bowl and set aside.

10. Place the dough on a very lightly floured surface. Gently deflate the dough and pat it into a rectangle about 14 X 12 inches with the long sides at the top and bottom edges. Cut the dough into two equal rectangles, about 680 grams/24 ounces each, by cutting the dough in half lengthwise. Sprinkle each piece of dough with cinnamon sugar to taste. Drain the raisins well and divide them evenly between the two pieces of dough. Spread them evenly over the entire surface of the dough and press them in. Starting at the short side of one loaf, roll the dough tightly into a log, keeping the skin of the dough slightly taut and tucking in any raisins that fall out, but don't stretch the dough so tight that the skin tears. Seal the seam of the log gently but tightly against the surface of the table using the heel of your hand, or pinch it shut with your fingers.

11. Place each loaf seam side down in a prepared pan. Gently press down on the loaves to spread them to fill the corners of the pan, and cover with oiled plastic wrap. Let the bread rise for 1 to 1½ hours, until it has doubled and risen about 1 inch above the sides of the pan.

12. Thirty minutes before baking preheat the oven to 450°F, and prepare the oven by placing a cast-iron skillet and a smaller pan (a mini loaf pan) on the floor of the oven or on the lowest possible rack in an electric oven. Place an oven rack two rungs above the cast-iron pan, and make sure there is enough height between the rack and the top of the oven for a pan of bread to fit. Fill a plastic spray bottle with water. Fill a teakettle with water to be boiled later, and have a metal 1-cup measure with a straight handle available near the kettle.

13. Five to 10 minutes before the loaf is ready to bake, turn the water on to boil, and carefully place two or three ice cubes in the small loaf pan in the bottom of the oven. This helps to create moisture in the oven prior to baking.

14. When the loaves are ready, quickly but carefully fill the metal 1-cup measure with boiling water, open the oven, and place the loaf pans on the oven rack, then using a plastic spray bottle, quickly mist them 6 to 8 times. Quickly but carefully pour the boiling water into the skillet and immediately close the oven door.

15. Bake for 15 minutes, then reduce the oven temperature to 375°F and bake for 18 to 25 minutes longer, until the crust is brown and the loaves sound hollow when tapped on the bottom. The crust may color quickly because of the cinnamon and raisins in the dough; watch carefully and cover the tops of the loaves loosely with foil if they are browning too fast.

16. Let them cool in the pans for 5 minutes, then remove the bread from the pans and place the loaves on a rack to cool. Let cool completely before slicing, or the bread will fall apart. This bread keeps well for at least 2 days.

TIPS AND TECHNIQUES

We used unbleached all-purpose flour with a protein content of 11.7% for this dough.

Crispy Bread Sticks with Anise, Coriander, and Mustard Seeds

MADE WITHOUT A STARTER

Makes 40 long bread sticks

Equipment: three 17 x 12-inch sheet pans

Everyone loves these bread sticks. They are loaded with aromatic spices and are delicious on their own or served with dips, soups, or salads. Try them, for example, dipped in hummus or baba ganoush. Lay them across the top of a bowl of soup or on a composed salad as an attractive garnish. Almost eighteen inches long, they make an eye-catching centerpiece displayed in a tall crock or a basket. They are fun to serve at a party, and if you have any leftovers, they still taste great the next day. The dough goes together quickly and only requires a short rise after they are cut, so you can have bread sticks in the oven just two hours after kneading them. Make sure to use fresh spices to get bread sticks with the fullest flavor.

INGREDIENTS	GRAMS	OUNCES	VOLUME
Very warm water (105° to 115°F)	57	2.00	¼ cup
Active dry yeast	1¾ teaspoons	1¾ teaspoons	1¾ teaspoons
Mustard seeds	19	0.65	1 tablespoon plus 2 teaspoons
Anise seeds	11	0.40	1 tablespoon plus 2 teaspoons
Warm water (85° to 90°F)	454	16.00	2 cups
Extra virgin olive oil	85	3.00	⅓ cup plus 1 tablespoon
Molasses	1 tablespoon	1 tablespoon	1 tablespoon
Unbleached all-purpose flour	737	26.00	5¾ cups
Sesame seeds	31	1.10	3 tablespoons
Kosher salt	16	0.56	1 tablespoon plus 2 teaspoons, plus extra for sprinkling
Ground coriander	8	0.30	1 tablespoon plus 2 teaspoons
Olive oil for brushing			
Fine cornmeal, for sprinkling	42	1.50	3 tablespoons

1. Combine the very warm water and yeast in a medium mixing bowl and stir with a fork to dissolve the yeast. Let stand for 3 minutes.

2. If you have a spice grinder, briefly pulse the mustard seeds and anise seeds, 10 to 20 seconds, to chop them slightly; do not grind them to a fine powder. You can also crush the spices using a mortar and pestle. Or spread them on a work surface, cover with a thin towel, and crush them with the bottom of a heavy pot.

3. Add the lukewarm water, olive oil, and molasses to the yeast mixture and mix with a wire whisk until well combined.

4. Combine the flour, mustard, anise, sesame seeds, salt, and coriander in a large bowl and mix with your fingers to blend. Pour the yeast mixture over the dry ingredients and mix with your fingers, scraping the sides of the bowl and folding the dough over onto itself until it gathers into a mass. The dough will be moist. If it feels too firm, add more warm water 1 tablespoon at a time.

5. Move the dough to a lightly floured surface and knead for 5 to 8 minutes, until the dough becomes smooth and elastic, using as little additional flour as possible. The dough should be slightly firm, bouncy, and supple.

6. Pat the dough into a rectangle. Brush it on both sides with olive oil and place it on an oiled space on your work surface. Cover it with plastic wrap and let it rise at room temperature (75° to 77°F) for about 1 hour, until not quite doubled in volume.

7. Lightly flour a 22 × 7-inch area on the work surface and sprinkle it with fine cornmeal, keeping in mind that you will be cutting the bread sticks on this surface. Keeping the dough flat, gently move it to the cornmeal-sprinkled area and stretch and pat it to form a narrow rectangle about 20 inches long and 6 inches wide.

8. Line three 17 × 12-inch sheet pans with parchment paper and sprinkle them lightly with cornmeal. Brush the dough with a little olive oil and sprinkle it lightly with kosher salt. Using a dough cutter, cut the rectangle into four equal pieces, cutting across the 6-inch width. Be careful to cut gently against your countertop so you don't scratch it. Cut each piece into 10 strips about ½ inch wide. Lift each strip and carefully stretch it as evenly as possible until it is 14 to 18 inches long (the length of your pans), and place it on the prepared sheet pan, leaving ¼ inch between each strip for rising. Cover the pans loosely with oiled plastic wrap. Let the sticks rise for about 30 minutes, just until they are slightly puffy but not fully risen.

9. While the sticks are rising, preheat the oven to 425°F. Position the oven racks in the middle and lower parts of the oven.

10. Place two of the baking sheets in the oven. (Leave the third pan of sticks at room temperature to bake when the oven is empty.) Using a plastic spray bottle, mist the sticks 6 to 8 times, then quickly shut the oven door. Spray the bread sticks again 2 minutes later.

11. Bake for 10 minutes, then rotate the pans and reduce the oven temperature to 400°F. Bake for 10 to 15 minutes longer, until the sticks are light brown and the thinner parts are crisp. Watch them carefully, because the thin parts brown quickly near the end of the baking time. (It's okay if the fatter parts are still slightly soft.) Place the sticks on racks to cool.

12. Reheat the oven to 425°F, then bake the remaining pan of bread sticks.

13. These sticks can be served as soon as they cool slightly, but they will get crunchier over time and are very good served the next day.

TIPS AND TECHNIQUES
....
We used unbleached all-purpose flour with a protein content of 11.7% for this dough.

Use very fresh spices to get the fullest flavor in your bread sticks.

HENRI LOVERA AND THE MOST BEAUTIFUL LOAVES

At one bakery where I trained in France, I worked with a baker named Henri Lovera. Half French and half Italian, he was a dedicated bread baker who worked alone all night from 10:00 P.M. to 6:00 A.M., six days a week, to make perfect baguettes for the bakery's customers. For him the most satisfying accomplishment each morning was to glance over the hundreds of finished loaves to see that each one had the proper dimensions, a gorgeous brown crust, and even cuts. He knew that inside each toasty, golden loaf was a light, delicious crumb. He was proud of the fact that he did not use additives in his dough to make the baguettes puff up, a common practice in many boulangeries at that time. Although his baguettes might have looked a little smaller than those of his neighbors, they weighed the same—the size of a baguette is governed by French law!

At the end of the night, Henri would sweep the bakery, change his clothes, and then survey the loaves again to choose the ones he would take home to his family. I was accustomed to working in restaurants where the employees chose the less-attractive products to taste, leaving the most beautiful creations for the paying customer. Not Henri! Every day he picked the two most perfect, impeccably beautiful loaves to serve at his table. He believed that after all his hard work, his family should be treated to only the best. Besides, who else would have an eye exacting enough to appreciate that perfection?

A.S.

It's a custom at Amy's Bread for everyone on the staff to say "Hi" to each of their co-workers when they come in to the bakery every day, and to make the rounds when they leave to tell everyone goodbye. When Lau (whose given name is Wen Hong Liu) first started working as the bakery's porter he was so quiet and shy and his English vocabulary was so limited that even returning these simple greetings seemed to make him uncomfortable. It was Lau's job to pit olives, pick herbs and handle any bakery cleaning and maintenance jobs that needed doing. He would stand quietly at the sink, with his back to the bread shaping table, doing his work while the radio on the shelf above the sink blared out whatever the music choice was for that hour—there were only a handful of us working there then but everyone had different tastes in music, so once every hour or so we'd let someone choose what they wanted to hear. Whenever the classical music was playing, John Stork, a former ballet dancer and one of the bread shapers at the time, would go leaping across the long, narrow kitchen doing tour jetés to liven things up a bit

and make us all laugh. That always got a laugh out of Lau, too. And when some familiar song, perhaps a rock 'n' roll oldie, a Tony Bennett ballad, or a Broadway show tune, would come on John would burst into song and then turn to Mr. Quiet Lau at the sink and shout "Sing it, Lau!" and everyone would laugh, including Lau. So we knew Lau had a sense of humor but he was still very timid about expressing himself verbally in English and of course none of us spoke Chinese. One day after Lau had been working in all this craziness for a few months, one of those old familiar songs came on and without turning around from the sink, Lau shouted, "Sing it, John!" That's when we knew that lurking under that quiet exterior was a very bright young guy who was full of surprises. Over the past seventeen years, Lau has confirmed that long-ago impression for us over and over again. As he became more comfortable communicating in English, he began making subtle jokes that showed a remarkable understanding and enjoyment of offbeat American humor. Scott Klein, a former Amy's bread baker, once played a joke on Lau by taping a note addressed to "Lau Z" on his locker. Everybody who saw it got a good laugh out of that one, including Lau, and for years the nickname stuck, with Lau understanding that it was really a term of affection and all done in good fun. Gradually, Lau made it known that he wanted to learn to bake bread. With his quick mind, his willingness to work hard, and his desire to do well at whatever he took on, Lau soon became one of our best bread bakers. Currently one of the supervisors on the bakery's elite team of baguette mixers, he works on the midnight to 7:00 A.M. shift and then goes home to take his three young children off to school. Lau's sense of humor and his quiet confidence in his own abilities make him a favorite among his co-workers. Whenever he's part of any baking crew the mood of the group always seems a little lighter and things always seem to run a little smoother. There's no question in our minds that good fortune was smiling on Amy's Bread the day Lau—Wen Hong Liu—first walked through our bakery door.

BREADS MADE WITH WHOLE WHEAT FLOUR

We love the textures and flavors of whole grains so much it's almost guaranteed we'll find a way to use them whenever we're developing new recipes. We've come a long way from the dull packaged "brown bread" our mothers made us eat when we were kids. "It's good for you," they always said. Well, Mom, here are a few basic good-for-you breads, full of the fiber and nutrients found in whole wheat flour, that you can put on your table or in the lunch box without hearing any complaints. From simple, lighter selections like the Organic Wheat Baguette and Whole Wheat Challah to more complex, denser loaves like the Coarse-Grained Whole Wheat with Toasted Walnuts, Whole Wheat Sandwich Bread with Oats and Pecans, or the Fragrant Whole Wheat Dinner Rolls, you're sure to find a "brown" bread that will have your friends and family begging for more.

Organic Wheat Baguette

Makes two 14-inch baguettes

Equipment: electric stand mixer with dough hook; baking stone and wooden peel, one 17 x 12-inch sheet pan;, baker's linen or heavy smooth cotton towel

When we started developing the breads for our organic line of products, baguettes were right on the top of our list. We definitely wanted our organic baguettes to be made with whole grain flour. The question was: Could we develop a baguette that wasn't dense and dry with a leathery crust using whole grain flour? For our customers who love our Organic Wheat Baguette, the answer is an unqualified "yes." The inside of the loaf has a nice open crumb full of uneven holes. The crust is crunchy and chewy without being leathery and the flavor is infused with the earthy sweetness of whole-grain wheat.

The recipe that we offer here is not identical to the one we use at the bakery because the unique whole grain flour we use can only be purchased in 50-pound bags from a wholesale flour distributor. However, we have put together a combination of organic flours available in health food and natural food stores that will help you make a baguette that is close in flavor and texture to the ones we sell in the bakery. The flour is, after all, only half of the equation for an outstanding baguette. The other half is technique, which you are able to duplicate in a home kitchen. It's not a whole grain baguette, but it is organic and it is delicious.

INGREDIENTS	GRAMS	OUNCES	VOLUME
Very warm water (105° to 115°F)	57	2.00	¼ cup
Active dry yeast	⅛ teaspoon	⅛ teaspoon	⅛ teaspoon
Poolish (page 54), made with organic flour	148	5.22	½ cup
Very cool water (65° to 70°F)	98	3.46	⅓ cup plus 2 tablespoons
Ascorbic acid solution (see page 83)	¼ teaspoon	¼ teaspoon	¼ teaspoon
Barley malt syrup	¼ teaspoon	¼ teaspoon	¼ teaspoon
Organic unbleached bread flour	208	9.80	1⅞ cups
Organic rye flour	18	0.88	3 tablespoons
Organic coarse whole wheat flour	18	0.88	3 tablespoons
Kosher salt	2¼ teaspoons	2¼ teaspoons	2¼ teaspoons
Coarse cornmeal or polenta, for sprinkling	as needed	as needed	as needed

1. Combine the very warm water and yeast in a measuring cup and stir to dissolve the yeast. Let stand for 3 minutes.

2. In the bowl of an electric stand mixer fitted with a dough hook, combine all of the ingredients including the yeast mixture and mix on medium-low speed for 3 minutes until all the flour is moistened and gathers into a ball of dough. Slide the dough down from the top of the hook (to be sure all of the dough will be evenly kneaded), increase the speed to medium and knead the dough for 3 more minutes. Slide the dough down from the hook again, increase the speed to medium-high and continue kneading for another 3 to 4 minutes or until the dough begins to slap the sides of the bowl and is beginning to pull up from the bottom of the bowl but does not clean the bottom of the bowl. The dough should be about 80 percent developed at this point. It should have some strength and elasticity but it will be very soft and a little sticky and you will not be able to pull a transparent sheet without having it tear. The dough temperature should be around 77°F.

3. Put the dough in an oiled bowl that is large enough to allow it to almost double, cover it with oiled plastic wrap, and allow it to rise for 1 hour. It should feel puffy but it will not have doubled.

4. Gently fold the dough in from the sides to the middle to deflate it, turn it over so the smoother bottom side is up, and cover it, and let it rise again for 45 to 50 minutes. The dough will almost double during this second rest and it should feel strong and supple by the end of the time period. You will be able to pull a transparent sheet—the final development of the dough occurs while it is resting.

5. Pour the dough out onto a lightly floured work surface and divide it into two equal pieces weighing approximately 260 grams/9 ounces each. With lightly floured hands, pre-shape each piece by patting it into a small rectangle about 8 X 4½ inches, positioned so the short sides are at the top and the bottom of the rectangle. If the dough sticks to the work surface, lift it gently with a dough scraper and lightly reflour the surface. Also keep your hands lightly floured so the dough doesn't stick to them and tear. Starting with the upper edge of the dough, gently fold the top third down and the bottom third up, like a business letter, so you have three equal layers. Seal the seam at the top edge and turn it so the seam is on the bottom. The pre-shaping prepares for the final lengthening of the baguette. Cover these shapes with the oiled plastic wrap and let them rest on the work surface until they feel puffy and have almost doubled. This could take anywhere from 30 minutes to an hour or more depending on the temperature of the dough and whether the pre-shaping was tight or loose.

6. While the dough rests, prepare a proofing pan for the baguettes by lining a 17 X 12-inch sheet pan with baker's linen so it overlaps the sides, and sprinkle it with a moderate amount of flour; or a heavy smooth cotton towel sprinkled generously with flour; or just line the pan with parchment paper and sprinkle the parchment with a moderate amount of flour.

7. Use a dough scraper to lift one of the almost-doubled pieces of dough and gently flip it over onto the lightly floured work surface. With lightly floured hands, pat the dough gently into an oval shape about 10 X 4 inches with the long edge facing you. (Don't be too heavy-handed with the patting; you want to preserve some of the gas bubbles in the dough so you'll have a nice airy crumb in your finished baguette.) Shape each piece into a baguette (see page 36). The baguettes should be 13 to 14 inches long and about 1¾ inches in diameter. Don't go beyond 14 inches or they won't fit on a baking stone. This length is good even if you're baking on a sheet pan without a stone because it will give you a good crust-to-crumb ratio for a piece of dough this size. The longer you make it, the less crumb you have on the inside of the loaf. Place one loaf lengthwise on the prepared pan touching against the edge of the pan (be sure the edge of the pan is covered by part of the floured cloth.) Pull up a 3-inch pleat of cloth to separate the two loaves and place the second loaf on the pan next to the first loaf. Pull up another pleat of cloth on the outside of the second loaf to support it while it rises. If you're using a parchment-lined pan, place the loaves about 2 inches in from the sides and leave 3 to 4 inches between the two loaves. Cover the loaves with oiled plastic wrap and let them rise until they have almost doubled. They should look plump and hold a slight indentation when pressed lightly your finger. This could take 1 or 2 hours depending on the temperature of the dough and how tightly the baguette is shaped. Baking them when they're slightly underproofed guarantees more oven spring, which contributes to a more open, airy crumb in the finished loaf.

8. Thirty minutes before baking, preheat the oven to 480°F. Prepare the oven by placing a cast-iron skillet and a smaller pan (a mini loaf pan) on the floor of the oven or on the lowest possible rack in an electric oven. Place an oven rack two rungs above the cast-iron pan, and if you have one, put a baking stone on the rack. Fill a plastic spray bottle with water. Fill a teakettle with water to be boiled later, and have a metal 1-cup measure with a straight handle available near the kettle.

9. Five to 10 minutes before the loaves are ready to bake, turn the water on to boil, and carefully place two or three ice cubes in the small loaf pan in the bottom of the oven. This helps to create moisture in the oven prior to baking.

10. At the same time, 5 to 10 minutes before the loaves are ready to bake, sprinkle the wooden peel with coarse cornmeal or polenta and gently lift each loaf from the proofing pan onto the peel. The easiest way to do this is to put one hand under each end of the loaf and gently scoot them in toward the center so the middle will be supported during the move. Try not to stretch the loaves beyond 14 inches, and leave enough space between to allow for spreading in the oven. Leave them uncovered so a light skin forms on the surface, which makes the loaves easier to score—scoring is

TIPS AND TECHNIQUES

We used unbleached bread flour with a protein content of 12.7% for this dough. The flour in the poolish had a protein content of 11.5%.

If you can't find coarse whole wheat flour, using regular organic whole wheat flour will be fine.

Refer to the Tips and Techniques for the French Baguette on page 83 for more tips on making baguettes and for instructions on making the ascorbic acid solution.

the term bread bakers use for cutting the loaves before baking. (If you're baking without a stone, just leave the risen loaves on the parchment-lined baking pan and remove the plastic wrap for the last few minutes of proof time.)

11. When the loaves are ready, use a lame or a sharp razor blade to make three or four slashes down the length of each baguette. The cuts should run from one end of the loaf to the other, rather than across it, and the blade should be held at a 30-degree angle to the loaf to create cuts that will pop open in the oven. Use the plastic spray bottle to mist the loaves evenly with water. Slide the loaves onto the baking stone, being mindful not to stretch them or they'll fall off the end of the stone. Pour 1 cup of boiling water into the skillet and immediately shut the oven door. After about 1 minute, quickly mist the loaves 6 to 8 times, then shut the oven door. (If you're baking without a stone simply slide the sheet pan with the scored and misted loaves onto the empty oven rack.)

12. Check the loaves after 12 minutes and rotate them if necessary to ensure even browning. Bake the baguettes for a total of 23 to 25 minutes, until they are uniformly golden brown in color and sound hollow when tapped on the bottom.

13. Cool them on a wire rack and enjoy them slightly warm or at room temperature. Baguettes are best eaten the same day they are baked.

THE AROMA OF GRAIN

Every summer I spent a week at my grandparents' farm, much of the time playing and exploring in the big barn. My uncle raised dairy cows and he had a huge hayloft above the cow barn where hay and straw were stored. We played on the thick rope swing that hung from the rafters, pushing off from great piles of hay bales and flying through the air from one side of the barn to the other. We stacked the bales in special configurations to make our own private forts, where we hid from each other. In hot weather the hay was pungent, nearly fermenting, and the sweet tangy smell was intoxicating. Although we weren't supposed to play in the feed storeroom on the side of the barn, sliding on the big pile of slippery oats was great fun and would kick up even more earthy, tangy, grainy smells.

Those hot days, with the grain dust sticking to my sweaty arms and legs, etched a powerful image in my memory of how real whole grains should smell. When we developed our whole wheat recipes we wanted the bread to be fragrant, like the sweet, pungent grains from my childhood. The key to achieving that goal is to use good-quality whole wheat flour with the germ and bran intact. For the best results, we recommend using organic flour or whole wheat flour produced by smaller mills.   A.S.

Whole Wheat Challah

MADE WITHOUT A STARTER

Makes one 1-pound challah round and 6 sandwich buns
Equipment: electric stand mixer with dough hook; two 17 x 12-inch sheet pans

Alice B. Chernich has been an Amy's Bread customer since the very first day we opened. Over the years she has often influenced our new product development with timely suggestions that pique our interest. This Whole Wheat Challah was one of her requests. Many of our other customers had also expressed a desire for more whole grain products, so Amy decided to tackle this challenge. Her first recipe attempts included unbleached white flour in an effort to create at least a hint of the light-textured crumb one expects in a traditional challah loaf. But the white flour took it out of the "whole grain" category, and we really wanted this to be a whole grain bread. To that end, Amy finally turned to the King Arthur Flour Company's white whole wheat flour, which solved the problem nicely. This is an exclusive product made only by King Arthur Flour but it can be obtained easily through mail order (see page 270) or at Whole Foods Markets and other natural food stores. We especially love to make this dough into sandwich rolls to be used as a light-textured, healthy whole grain alternative to fluffy white hamburger buns. This is a very wet dough that requires use of a stand mixer for best results. Alice Chernich loves this bread. We hope you will, too!

INGREDIENTS	GRAMS	OUNCES	VOLUME
Very warm water (105° to 115°F)	57	2.00	¼ cup
Active dry yeast	1½ teaspoons	1½ teaspoons	1½ teaspoons
Whole wheat flour	202	7.12	1⅓ cups
Organic white whole wheat flour	195	6.88	1⅓ cups
Coarse whole wheat flour	90	3.17	½ cup
Sugar	50	1.76	¼ cup
Kosher salt	12	0.42	1 tablespoon plus 1 teaspoon
Very cool water (65° to 70°F)	300	10.58	1⅓ cups
Eggs	100	3.50	2 large
Canola or vegetable oil	44	1.55	scant ¼ cup
Coarse cornmeal or polenta, for sprinkling	as needed	as needed	as needed

1. Combine the very warm water and yeast in a measuring cup and stir to dissolve the yeast. Let stand for 3 minutes.

2. Whisk the three whole wheat flours, sugar, and salt together in a medium bowl. Set aside.

3. In the bowl of an electric stand mixer fitted with a dough hook, combine the yeast mixture, very cool water, eggs, and canola oil and mix on medium speed for 1 minute. Add the flour and mix on medium-low speed for 2 minutes until all the flour is moistened. Increase the speed to medium and continue mixing for 6 minutes. If necessary, scrape the bowl and slide the dough down from the top of the hook (to be sure all of the dough will be evenly kneaded). Increase the speed to medium-high and knead for 2 more minutes. At this point the dough is beginning to pull away from the sides of the bowl but does not clean the bottom of the bowl. The dough should be about 60 percent developed. It should have some strength and elasticity but it will be very soft and sticky and you will not be able to pull a transparent sheet. The dough temperature should be around 75°F. Let the dough rest in the bowl for 15 to 20 minutes.

4. After the rest period, begin mixing on medium-low speed for 1 minute, to gather the dough together, then increase the speed to medium-high and finish mixing for 3 more minutes. The dough should be about 80 percent developed. You can stretch it into a sheet but it will begin to tear.

5. Put the dough in an oiled bowl that is large enough to allow it to almost double, cover it with oiled plastic wrap, and allow it to rise for 1 hour. It should feel puffy but it will not have doubled. After 1 hour, turn the dough while it is still in the mixing bowl. Gently deflate the dough in the middle of the bowl with your fingertips, then fold the left side over the middle, and the right side over the middle. Fold the dough in half, gently pat it down, and then turn it over so the seam is underneath.

6. Let it rise again for another hour. The dough will almost double during this second rest and it should feel strong and supple by the end of the time period. You will be able to pull a transparent sheet—the final development of the dough occurs while it is rising.

7. Pour the dough out onto a lightly floured work surface and divide it into six small pieces weighing approximately 84 grams/3 ounces each. (There will be slightly more than half the dough remaining.) With lightly floured hands, shape these pieces into rolls (see page 38), placing them on a parchment-lined sheet pan in two rows of three, leaving as much space as possible around the sides and between the rolls so they won't touch the pan or grow together as they proof. Cover them with oiled plastic wrap to proof.

8. With the remaining piece of dough, on a lightly floured surface with floured hands, gently flatten the dough into a rectangle, then shape it into a cylinder by rolling it up tightly from left to right, as if you were shaping a baguette (see page

36). Seal the seam well. Place both hands over the center of the cylinder and roll it back and forth from the center out to the ends to elongate it until you have a rope about 27 inches long. If the dough is tight and difficult to lengthen, let it rest to relax for 5 or 10 minutes before elongating it further. Roll the rope lightly in flour and shape it into a coil, following the instructions on page 254.

9. Place the loaf seam side down on a peel or the back of a sheet pan that has been covered with parchment and sprinkled with cornmeal. Cover it with oiled plastic wrap. Allow the shaped pieces to rise for 1½ to 2 hours, until almost doubled in bulk but still slightly underproofed. The loaf and rolls will look light and airy and will not hold an indentation when pressed lightly with your finger.

10. Thirty minutes before baking, preheat the oven to 400°F. Prepare the oven by placing a cast-iron skillet and a smaller pan (a mini loaf pan) on the floor of the oven or on the lowest possible rack in an electric oven. Place an oven rack two rungs above the cast-iron pan, and if you have one, put a baking stone on the rack. Position another oven rack two rungs above the stone. Fill a plastic spray bottle with water. Fill a teakettle with water to be boiled later, and have a metal 1-cup measure with a straight handle available near the kettle.

11. Five to 10 minutes before the loaves are ready to bake, turn the water on to boil, and carefully place two or three ice cubes in the small loaf pan in the bottom of the oven. This helps to create moisture in the oven prior to baking.

12. Mist the loaf and the rolls with water, then open the oven and gently slide the loaf onto the baking stone with the parchment paper underneath. (If you're baking without a stone, just leave the risen loaf on the parchment-lined baking pan.) Place the pan of rolls on the rack above the baking stone. Pour 1 cup of boiling water into the skillet and immediately shut the oven door. After 1 minute, quickly mist the loaf and the rolls again, then shut the oven door.

13. Bake for 10 minutes, then rotate the pan of rolls and reduce the oven temperature to 375°F. Bake the rolls for 5 to 7 minutes longer, or until they are lightly and evenly browned on the top. Slide them off the pan onto a rack to cool. The loaf should be rotated when the rolls are removed from the oven, and continue baking for 7 to 10 more minutes for a total bake time of 24 to 28 minutes. It should be lightly browned and an instant-read digital thermometer should read 190° to 200°F. Transfer the bread to a rack to cool completely before slicing.

TIPS AND TECHNIQUES

If you can't find coarse whole wheat flour, using additional regular whole wheat flour will be fine, though the dough may be slightly wetter because the fine whole wheat flour won't absorb as much water as the coarse flour. The crust on this bread should be thin and somewhat soft, not crunchy or leathery. You may want to try brushing the loaf and the rolls very lightly with canola oil before you bake them.

Coarse-Grained Whole Wheat with Toasted Walnuts

Makes two 1-pound round boules

Equipment: baking stone and wooden peel, or 17 x 12-inch sheet pan

Amy developed this recipe when she was working at a restaurant called Mondrian in New York City. The chef, Tom Colicchio, wanted a bread that was crunchy and earthy, with a deep walnut taste, to complement a new prosciutto and fig dish. The bread was served lightly toasted to enhance its nuttiness. When the fig dish was dropped from the menu, the bread remained—to be served with nothing less than foie gras! If you don't have any foie gras around, it tastes perfectly good by itself, or with richly flavored cheeses such as aged, soft Camembert or St. André. In the bakery we use it for a sandwich filled with Brie, crisp apple slices, and watercress.

INGREDIENTS	GRAMS	OUNCES	VOLUME
Very warm water (105° to 115°F)	57	2.00	¼ cup
Active dry yeast	¾ teaspoon	¾ teaspoon	¾ teaspoon
Whole wheat flour	255	9.00	1¾ cups
Unbleached bread flour	128	4.50	⅞ cup
Medium yellow cornmeal or polenta, plus additional for sprinkling	28	1.00	3 tablespoons
Kosher salt	9	0.30	1 tablespoon
Cool water and/or reserved wheat berry cooking liquid (75° to 78°F)	227	8.00	1 cup
Biga Starter (page 56)	227	8.00	1 cup
Honey	16	0.56	1 tablespoon
Walnut or vegetable oil	12	0.42	1 tablespoon
Walnut pieces, toasted (see "Toasting Nuts," page 111)	170	6.00	1½ cups
Cooked wheat berries (see "Cooking Wheat and Rye Berries," page 110)	85	3.00	½ cup

1. Combine the very warm water and yeast in a large bowl and stir with a fork to dissolve the yeast. Let stand for 3 minutes.

2. Whisk the whole wheat flour, bread flour, cornmeal, and salt together in a medium bowl. Set aside.

COOKING WHEAT AND RYE BERRIES

To save time, you can cook the wheat berries a day ahead. Place the berries in a saucepan with water to cover them by at least 1 inch, cover, and bring to a boil. Reduce the heat to low and cook until they're plump, 30 to 40 minutes. Let the berries cool, then drain, saving the cooking liquid to use as part of the water called for in the recipe. Refrigerate in an airtight container if you don't plan to use them immediately. Whole rye berries can be cooked the same way, but you should increase the cooking time by 10 minutes.

Wheat berries and rye berries triple in volume when they are cooked. To determine the quantity of dry berries you need to cook, simply divide the measured amount in the recipe by three (for example, if the recipe calls for ¾ cup of cooked berries, you need to cook at least ¼ cup of dry ones). Or cook a bit more to sprinkle on your morning cereal or toss with a salad.

3. Add the cool water, biga, honey, and oil to the yeast mixture and mix with your fingers for 2 minutes, breaking up the biga. The mixture should look milky and slightly foamy. Add the flour mixture and stir with your fingers to incorporate the flour, scraping the sides of the bowl and folding the dough over itself until it gathers into a shaggy mass.

4. Move the dough to a very lightly floured surface and knead for 7 to 8 minutes, until it becomes supple and elastic, using as little additional flour as possible. This dough should be very soft, not stiff. If it feels too stiff, knead in cool water, 1 tablespoon at a time, until it becomes more pliable. Put the dough back into the mixing bowl, cover with oiled plastic wrap, and let rest for 20 minutes to relax and develop elasticity. You should be able to stretch it easily, though it will eventually tear because of the cornmeal.

5. Spread out the dough in the mixing bowl and evenly sprinkle on the walnuts and wheat berries. Press them into the dough, then pull the dough from the edges of the bowl and fold it in toward the middle. Knead the dough in the bowl until the nuts and wheat berries are evenly incorporated, 2 to 3 minutes.

6. Gather the dough into a loose ball, lift it up and oil the bowl, then place it back in the bowl, along with any loose nuts and berries. Turn the dough to coat with oil, cover the bowl with oiled plastic wrap, and let it rise at room temperature (75° to 77°F) for 1½ to 2 hours, until it doubles in volume. When the dough is fully risen, an indentation made by poking your finger deep into the dough should not spring back.

7. Gently remove the dough from the bowl and place it on a lightly floured work surface, pressing in any loose nuts and wheat berries. Divide it into two equal pieces and shape each piece into a boule (see page 37). Line a peel or a baking sheet with parchment paper and sprinkle with cornmeal. Place the loaves on the peel or sheet, seam side down, leaving several inches between them so they won't grow into each other as they rise. Cover with oiled plastic wrap and allow to proof for 1 to 2 hours, or until they have doubled in size (a finger pressed lightly into the dough will leave an indentation).

8. Thirty minutes before baking, preheat the oven to 450°F. Prepare the oven by placing a cast-iron skillet and a smaller pan (a mini loaf pan) on the floor of the

oven or on the lowest possible rack in an electric oven. Place an oven rack two rungs above the cast-iron pan, and if you have one, put a baking stone on the rack. Fill a plastic spray bottle with water. Fill a teakettle with water to be boiled later, and have a metal 1-cup measure with a straight handle available near the kettle.

9. Five to 10 minutes before the loaves are ready to bake, turn the water on to boil, and carefully place two or three ice cubes in the small loaf pan in the bottom of the oven. This helps to create moisture in the oven prior to baking.

10. When the loaves are ready, spray them with water and cut a shallow *X* on top of each one with a lame or a very sharp knife. Slide them onto the baking stone. (If you're baking without a stone simply slide the sheet pan with the scored and misted loaves onto the empty oven rack.) Pour 1 cup of boiling water into the skillet and immediately shut the oven door. After about 1 minute, quickly mist the loaves again, then shut the oven door.

> ### TOASTING NUTS
>
> To toast walnuts or other nuts, spread them on a cookie sheet and toast in a preheated 350°F oven, stirring once or twice, for about 8 minutes, until they begin to smell fragrant. Let cool.

11. After 20 minutes, reduce the oven temperature to 400°F and rotate the loaves if necessary to ensure even browning. Bake them for another 20 minutes or until they are dark brown in color and sound hollow when tapped on the bottom (an instant-read digital thermometer should register around 210°F).

12. Cool them completely on a wire rack. This bread freezes well, wrapped tightly in aluminum foil and a heavy-duty plastic freezer bag.

TIPS AND TECHNIQUES

We used unbleached bread flour with a protein content of 12.7% and regular whole wheat flour with a protein content of 14.5% for this dough. The biga was made with all-purpose unbleached flour with a protein content of 11.7%.

Use the same container for weighing/measuring both the honey and the oil. Pour the oil into the container first, then pour the specified amount of honey on top of the oil. When you add them to the ingredients in your mixing bowl, the honey will be released easily from the cup without sticking, giving a more accurate measure and an easier clean-up. (When using volume, measure the oil first, then use the same tablespoon to measure the honey.)

This dough can be refrigerated overnight to intensify its walnut flavor and to allow the walnut skins to impart a slightly purple color to the dough. After the dough is kneaded, let it rise at room temperature (75° to 77°F) for 1 hour or until it looks slightly puffy but has not doubled. Refrigerate the dough overnight, covered securely with oiled plastic wrap. Remove the dough from the refrigerator and allow it to rise at room temperature for 2 hours to warm and soften before you divide it and shape it into loaves.

Whole Wheat Sandwich Bread with Oats and Pecans

Makes two 9 x 5-inch loaves

Equipment: two 9 x 5-inch loaf pans, oiled

Mildly sweet and slightly crunchy, our version of whole wheat–oatmeal bread is great for tuna sandwiches. Cut in thick slices, it's perfect for French toast. Shape it into rolls for a dinner party or a family picnic. For variety, add two cups (ten ounces) of golden raisins to the dough and shape half of it into twists (see page 128); crusty and delicious, they're good for breakfast-on-the-go and afternoon snacks. This versatile bread is sure to become one of your favorites.

INGREDIENTS	GRAMS	OUNCES	VOLUME
Very warm water (105° to 115°F)	57	2.00	¼ cup
Active dry yeast	1 teaspoon	1 teaspoon	1 teaspoon
Whole wheat flour	524	18.48	3½ cups
Unbleached bread flour	354	12.50	2⅓ cups
Old-fashioned rolled oats	170	6.00	2 cups
Kosher salt	20	0.70	2 tablespoons
Cool water (75° to 78°F)	622	22.00	2¾ cups
Biga Starter (page 56)	340	12.00	1½ cups
Honey	42	1.50	2 tablespoons plus 2 teaspoons
Molasses	35	1.23	2 tablespoons
Canola or vegetable oil	20	0.70	2 tablespoons
Pecan pieces, toasted (see "Toasting Nuts," page 111)	227	8.00	2 cups
Extra oats, for topping the shaped loaves			

1. Combine the very warm water and yeast in a large bowl and stir with a fork to dissolve the yeast. Let stand for 3 minutes.

2. Whisk the whole wheat flour, bread flour, oats, and salt together in a medium bowl. Set aside.

3. Add the cool water, biga, honey, molasses, and oil to the yeast mixture and mix with your fingers for 2 minutes, breaking up the biga. The mixture should look milky and slightly foamy. Add the flour mixture and stir with your fingers to incorporate the flour, scraping the sides of the bowl and folding the dough over itself until it gathers into a shaggy mass.

4. Move the dough to a very lightly floured surface and knead for 7 to 8 minutes, until it becomes supple and elastic, using as little additional flour as possible. This dough should be very soft and moist but not mushy. If it feels too wet, add another tablespoon or so of bread flour as you knead. If it feels too stiff, add cool water 1 tablespoon at a time until you have a pliable dough. It will feel sticky in the beginning but become compact and elastic as you knead it. Put the dough back into the mixing bowl, cover with oiled plastic, and let rest for 20 minutes to relax and develop elasticity. You should be able to stretch it easily but you won't get a transparent sheet with this dough, because of the chunky oatmeal.

5. Spread out the dough in the mixing bowl and evenly sprinkle on the pecans. Press them into the dough, then pull the dough from the edges of the bowl and fold it in toward the middle. Knead the dough in the bowl until the nuts are evenly incorporated, 3 to 4 minutes.

6. Gather the dough into a loose ball, lift it up and oil the bowl, then place it back in the bowl, along with any loose nuts. Turn the dough to coat with oil, cover the bowl with oiled plastic wrap, and let it rise at room temperature (75° to 77°F) for about 2 to 2½ hours, until it doubles in volume. When the dough is fully risen, an indentation made by poking your lightly floured finger deep into the dough should not spring back.

7. Gently remove the dough from the bowl and place it on a lightly floured work surface, pressing in any loose nuts. Divide it into two equal pieces and shape each piece into a log (see page 34).

8. Spread a thin layer of the extra oats for topping on a flat plate or baking sheet. Use a pastry brush or plastic spray bottle to lightly moisten the top of each log with water, then roll the tops of the loaves in the oats. Place each loaf seam side down in one of the oiled 9 x 5-inch loaf pans. Cover with oiled plastic wrap and allow to proof for about 2 hours or until they have doubled in size (a finger pressed lightly into the dough will leave an indentation).

9. Thirty minutes before baking, preheat the oven to 450°F. Prepare the oven by placing a cast-iron skillet and a smaller pan (a mini loaf pan) on the floor of the oven or on the lowest possible rack in an electric oven. Place an oven rack two rungs above the cast-iron pan, and if you have one, put a baking stone on the rack.

Fill a plastic spray bottle with water. Fill a teakettle with water to be boiled later, and have a metal 1-cup measure with a straight handle available near the kettle.

10. Five to 10 minutes before the loaves are ready to bake, turn the water on to boil, and carefully place two ice cubes in the small loaf pan in the bottom of the oven. This helps to create moisture in the oven prior to baking.

11. When the loaves are ready, place the pans on the baking stone. (If you're baking without a stone simply slide the bread pans onto the empty oven rack.) Pour 1 cup of boiling water into the skillet and immediately shut the oven door. After about 1 minute, quickly spray the loaves with water, then shut the oven door.

12. After 20 minutes, reduce the oven temperature to 400°F and rotate the loaves if necessary to ensure even browning. Bake them for another 25 to 30 minutes, until the loaves sound slightly hollow when tipped out of the pan and tapped on the bottom (an instant-read digital thermometer should register around 210°F). The sides and bottom of the loaves should feel firm and slightly crusty. If the tops are browned but the sides are still somewhat soft, place the loaves directly on the stone or the oven rack to bake for 5 to 10 more minutes.

13. Cool the loaves completely on a wire rack before slicing. This bread freezes well, wrapped tightly in aluminum foil and a heavy-duty plastic freezer bag.

TIPS AND TECHNIQUES

We used unbleached bread flour with a protein content of 12.7% and regular whole wheat flour with a protein content of 14.5% for this dough. The biga was made with all-purpose unbleached flour with a protein content of 11.7%.

Use the same container for weighing/measuring the honey and molasses and the oil. Pour the oil into the container first, then pour the specified amounts of honey and molasses on top of the oil. When you add them to the ingredients in your mixing bowl, the sticky sweeteners will be released easily from the cup without sticking, giving a more accurate measure and an easier clean-up. (When using volume, measure the oil first, then use the same tablespoon to measure the honey and the molasses.)

If you want to duplicate the Whole Wheat Oat Pecan bread we sell in the bakery, add 290 grams/10.25 ounces/2 cups of golden raisins to the dough when you add the pecans; divide the dough into four equal pieces and shape them into bâtards (see page 35) before proofing and baking. You may have to bake two of the loaves on a sheet pan if they won't all fit on your baking stone.

You can also refrigerate this dough overnight and shape and bake it the next day. After mixing, let it rise for 1 hour at room temperature or until it looks slightly puffy but has not doubled, before refrigerating. The next day, let it rise for 2 hours at room temperature to warm and soften before shaping it.

Fragrant Whole Wheat Dinner Rolls

MADE WITH POOLISH

Makes 12 rolls

Equipment: one 9-inch square baking pan, oiled

Flavored with earthy sesame seeds and sweet, toasty wheat germ, these fragrant whole wheat rolls will complement any menu. For large dinner parties, you can double the recipe and bake the rolls in a 13 X 9-inch pan. You may want to do that anyway and freeze the extras for another meal. Wrap them in aluminum foil first, then in a heavy-duty freezer bag. Let them thaw at room temperature for an hour and reheat them in the oven just before serving. For a deliciously satisfying snack, split one in half, toast it lightly, then make a mini sandwich with a schmear of hummus topped with another schmear of basil pesto. One won't be enough!

INGREDIENTS	GRAMS	OUNCES	VOLUME
Very warm water (105° to 115°F)	57	2.00	¼ cup
Active dry yeast	1¼ teaspoons	1¼ teaspoons	1¼ teaspoons
Whole wheat flour	190	6.70	1¼ cups
Unbleached bread flour	128	4.51	⅞ cup
Cooked wheat berries (see "Cooking Wheat and Rye Berries, page 110)	85	3.00	½ cup
Natural unhulled sesame seeds	42	1.48	¼ cup
Toasted wheat germ	35	1.23	⅓ cup
Kosher salt	12	0.42	1 tablespoon plus 1 teaspoon
Poolish (page 54)	275	9.70	1⅓ cups
Cool water (75° to 78°F)	220	7.76	1 cup
Honey	28	1.00	1½ tablespoons
Canola or vegetable oil	10	0.35	1 tablespoon
Additional sesame seeds, for topping	40	1.41	¼ cup

1. Place the very warm water and yeast in a large bowl. Stir with a fork to dissolve the yeast and allow to stand for about 3 minutes.

2. Whisk the whole wheat flour, bread flour, wheat berries, sesame seeds, wheat germ, and salt together in a medium bowl. Set aside.

3. Add the poolish, cool water, honey, and oil to the yeast mixture and mix with your fingers for 2 minutes, breaking up the poolish. The mixture should look milky and slightly foamy. Add the flour mixture and stir with your fingers to incorporate the flour, scraping the sides of the bowl and folding the dough over itself until it gathers into a shaggy mass.

4. Move the dough to a very lightly floured surface and knead for 8 to 9 minutes, until it becomes supple and elastic, using as little additional flour as possible. This dough should be very moist, almost mushy. It feels very sticky in the beginning but becomes more manageable as you knead it. Keep your hands lightly floured but expect the dough to stick to them anyway. When it sticks to the table use a dough scraper to lift it up, lightly flour the table and continue kneading until it becomes a cohesive mass and is starting to feel slightly firm and stretchy. Cover it with oiled plastic wrap and let it rest on the work surface for 20 minutes to relax and develop more elasticity. At the end of the rest period, you should be able to stretch the dough easily but it will still tear slightly.

5. Knead the dough again for 1 to 2 minutes, until it is smooth and springy. You will be able to pull a transparent sheet at this point. Place the dough in an oiled bowl. Turn it to coat the top with oil, cover the bowl with oiled plastic wrap, and let it rise at room temperature (75° to 77°F) for 1 hour until it looks puffy but has not doubled.

6. After 1 hour, turn the dough while it is still in the mixing bowl. Gently deflate the dough in the middle of the bowl with your fingertips, then fold the left side over the middle, and the right side over the middle. Fold the dough in half, gently pat it down, and then turn it over so the seam is underneath. Let it rise again for 1 to 1½ hours, or until it doubles in volume. When the dough is fully proofed, an indentation made by poking your lightly floured finger deep into the dough should not spring back.

7. Pour the extra sesame seeds into a small bowl and set it off to one side. Gently remove the dough from the bowl and place it on a lightly floured work surface. Divide it into 12 equal pieces, weighing about 86 grams/3 ounces each, and shape them into rolls (see page 38). The dough will be sticky but try to use a minimum of flour on your hands and the table. As the rolls are shaped, dip the tops in the sesame seeds and place them seam side down in an oiled 9-inch square pan, arranging them in three rows of four rolls each. Cover with oiled plastic wrap and allow to proof for about 1 hour, until they have almost doubled in size (a finger pressed lightly into the dough will barely leave an indentation).

8. Thirty minutes before baking preheat the oven to 450°F. Prepare the oven by placing a cast-iron skillet and a smaller pan (a mini loaf pan) on the floor of the oven or on the lowest possible rack in an electric oven. Place an oven rack two rungs above the cast-iron pan, and put a baking stone on it if you have one. Fill a plastic spray bottle with water. Fill a teakettle with water to be boiled later, and have a metal 1-cup measure with a straight handle available near the kettle.

9. Five to 10 minutes before the rolls are ready to bake, turn the water on to boil, and carefully place two or three ice cubes in the small loaf pan in the bottom of the oven. This helps to create moisture in the oven prior to baking.

10. When the rolls are ready, spray them lightly but thoroughly with water and place the pan on the baking stone. (If you're baking without a stone simply put the pan onto the empty oven rack.) Pour 1 cup of boiling water into the skillet and immediately shut the oven door. After about 1 minute, quickly spray them again, then shut the oven door.

11. After 15 minutes, rotate the pan if necessary to insure even browning. Bake them for another 10 to 15 minutes, until the rolls are nicely browned and sound slightly hollow when tipped out of the pan and tapped on the bottom (an instant-read digital thermometer should register around 210°F). Tip the rolls out of the pan and transfer them to a wire rack. They can be served warm or at room temperature. To ensure that they stay moist, don't separate the rolls until just before serving.

TIPS AND TECHNIQUES

We used unbleached bread flour with a protein content of 12.7% and regular whole wheat flour with a protein content of 14.5% for this dough. The poolish was made with all-purpose unbleached flour with a protein content of 11.7%.

Use the same container for weighing/measuring both the honey and the oil. Pour the oil into the container first, then pour the specified amount of honey on top of the oil. When you add them to the ingredients in your mixing bowl, the honey will be released easily from the cup without sticking, giving a more accurate measure and an easier clean-up. (When using volume, measure the oil first, then use the same tablespoon to measure the honey.)

Oven temperatures and baking characteristics vary widely, so keep a careful eye on these rolls as they are baking. If they're browning too fast, reduce the oven temperature to 400°F for the last 10 to 15 minutes of baking. If they're browning too slowly, put a second rack in the middle of the oven, above the baking stone, and move the pan of rolls up onto that rack for the last 10 to 15 minutes of baking.

SOURDOUGH BREADS

Before Amy opened the bakery, she worked as a baker at Mondrian restaurant for two and a half years. Every day she made a batch of Country Sourdough that she shaped into loaves and dinner rolls for lunch and dinner service. Over the years she kept hundreds of pages of notes on little variations in the formula and the process of making the dough. Finally, when the bakery opened, Amy's Country Sourdough was ready for the big time. She knew that New Yorkers were ready for sophisticated sourdough that was chewy and flavorful with a wheaty aroma—but without the knockout punch of a really tangy sourdough.

For the first several years after we opened, Country Sourdough was by far our most popular bread, and this dough was the base for more than a third of our products. It was so essential to our production that the name typed on top of the formula was "Basic Dough." Country Sourdough was made into baguettes, ficelles, boules, ovals, prosciutto and black pepper bread, walnut strips, apple-walnut-raisin rolls, five kinds of bread twists, olive fougasse, French loaves, dinner rolls, and pan loaves. On many occasions we had to educate our customers about how mild and delicious our sourdough bread was. And when they tried it, they loved it. Within a year of opening we added our tangy, San Francisco–style sourdough and several other breads made with sourdough starter. Today they are still popular for their moist, chewy crumb and their hearty crust. Here we share the recipes for some of our most popular sourdough products.

Country Sourdough Boule

Makes two 1½-pound boules

Equipment: two round baskets 7½ to 8½ inches in diameter; baker's linen or heavy smooth cotton towels for lining baskets; wooden peel and baking stone, or 17 × 12-inch baking sheet

This is a scaled-down version of the Country Sourdough recipe we use at the bakery. The big beautiful loaves that burst open when we bake them in our steam-injected deck oven are so crusty and flavorful that we were sure we'd never be able to duplicate the same results in a home oven. But when we tested this recipe in our apartment kitchens, the loaves of bread were so satisfying and delicious we couldn't stop eating them. You may be amazed to find you can produce a sourdough bread this good in your own oven. At the bakery, Country Sourdough is one of our largest batches of dough, and we still feel exhilarated when we mix up a perfect batch of this wet, creamy, stretchy dough. There is nothing like watching the giant fork mixer turning a 250-pound batch as it snaps and slaps in its gentle rotation around the bowl. After sixteen years, it's still a best seller, because it goes so well with everything, and it is great for sandwiches such as our Grilled New York State Cheddar Cheese Sandwich (page 225). We love it plain, but for variety you can knead in toasted walnuts, chopped fruit and raisins, or imported olives, and you can shape it into baguettes, ovals, or triangles to keep your creative spirit engaged.

INGREDIENTS	GRAMS	OUNCES	VOLUME
Very warm water (105° to 115°F)	57	2.00	¼ cup
Active dry yeast	¾ teaspoon	¾ teaspoon	¾ teaspoon
Unbleached all-purpose flour	680	24.00	4¾ cups plus 2 tablespoons
Pumpernickel flour	130	4.60	1 cup
Kosher salt	18	0.64	2 tablespoons
Firm Levain (page 63)	212	7.50	1 cup
Cool water (75° to 78°F)	567	20.00	2½ cups
Medium cornmeal, for sprinkling	as needed	as needed	as needed

1. Place the very warm water and yeast in a medium bowl and stir with a fork to dissolve the yeast. Allow to stand for about 3 minutes.

2. Whisk the all-purpose flour, pumpernickel flour, and salt together in a bowl. Set aside.

3. Add the levain starter and cool water to the yeast mixture and mix with your fingers for 2 to 3 minutes, just long enough to soften the levain and break it up into small pieces. Add the flour mixture and stir with your fingers to incorporate the flour, scraping the sides of the bowl and folding the dough over itself until it gathers into a shaggy mass.

This bread is easy to make, but you need to start planning for it several days in advance. Make the levain starter a day or two before you make the dough because you have to feed the levain more than once to boost its leavening power. If your levain starter doesn't quite double within 8 hours, you can still use it, but your bread may take longer to rise and it may not achieve as much volume; although the recipe includes a small amount of commercial yeast, the levain is its primary leavener.

4. Move the dough to a lightly floured surface and knead for 6 to 8 minutes, until it becomes supple and somewhat elastic. The dough will be very sticky at first; keep your hands and the work surface lightly floured, using a dough scraper if necessary to prevent the dough from sticking and building up on the work surface. As you continue kneading, the dough will become more elastic and easier to handle. Shape the dough into a loose ball, return it to the bowl, cover with oiled plastic, and let rest for 20 minutes to smooth out and develop elasticity.

5. Knead the dough again on the lightly floured surface for 2 to 3 minutes, until it becomes very smooth and springy. Shape the dough into a loose ball and place it in a lightly oiled bowl. Cover the bowl tightly with oiled plastic wrap and let rise at room temperature (75° to 77°F) for 1 hour.

6. After 1 hour, turn the dough while it is still in the mixing bowl. Gently deflate the dough in the middle of the bowl with your fingertips, then fold the left side over the middle, and the right side over the middle. Fold the dough in half, gently pat it down, and then turn it over so the seam is underneath. Let it rise again for 1 to 1½ hours, until it doubles in volume. When the dough is fully risen, an indentation made by poking your finger deep into the dough should not spring back.

7. Line 2 round baskets with well-floured cloths; if you don't have baskets, use 2 round-bottomed (not flat-bottomed) bowls or colanders. Gently remove the dough from the bowl and place it on a lightly floured work surface. Divide it into two equal pieces, about 780 grams/27.5 ounces each. Shape each piece into a boule (see page 37), being careful not to tear the outer surface of the loaf by exerting too much pressure during shaping. Lift each loaf, put a handful of flour on the seam of the boule, and place the loaves seam side down in the prepared baskets. Cover them with oiled plastic wrap and let rise for about 1 to 1¾ hours, until they have not quite doubled in volume. These loaves burst open and look nicer if they are slightly underproofed when you bake them.

8. Thirty minutes before baking, preheat the oven to 450°F. Prepare the oven by placing a cast-iron skillet and a smaller pan (a mini loaf pan) on the floor of the

oven or on the lowest possible rack in an electric oven. Place an oven rack two rungs above the cast-iron pan, and if you have one, put a baking stone on the rack. Fill a plastic water sprayer with water. Fill a teakettle with water to be boiled later, and have a metal 1-cup measure with a straight handle available near the kettle.

9. Five to 10 minutes before the loaves are ready to bake, turn the water on to boil, and carefully place two or three ice cubes in the small loaf pan in the bottom of the oven. This helps to create moisture in the oven prior to baking.

10. Cut parchment paper to fit the top of the peel or back of a sheet pan, then sprinkle with medium cornmeal. Carefully tip each loaf out of the basket onto the prepared peel or baking sheet, leaving the loaf seam side up. (If the floured cloths have stuck to the loaves, gently peel them away.) Open the oven and quickly slide each loaf onto the baking stone, leaving at least 2 inches between them to allow for oven spring. (If your stone isn't large enough to accommodate both loaves, cover one loaf with plastic wrap and refrigerate it until the first loaf has finished baking, then bake the second loaf.) If you're baking without a stone simply slide the sheet pan with the scored loaves onto the empty oven rack. Quickly pour 1 cup of boiling water into the water pan and immediately shut the door. After 1 minute, using a plastic water sprayer, quickly mist the top and sides of the oven 6 to 8 times, then immediately shut the oven door. (Avoid spraying the bread when misting, or the flour on the top will look blotchy and unappetizing.) Repeat the misting procedure 1 minute later.

11. Bake for 20 minutes, then reduce the oven temperature to 400°F and bake for 20 to 25 minutes longer, until the loaves are a deep golden brown and sound hollow when tapped on the bottom. Transfer them to a rack and allow to cool before serving.

TIPS AND TECHNIQUES

We used unbleached all-purpose flour with a protein content of 11.7% for this dough. The firm levain starter was made with unbleached all-purpose flour with a protein content of 11.7% as well.

We use pumpernickel flour in this recipe, but it is difficult to find in stores. (King Arthur Flour makes a pumpernickel flour; see page 270.) As a substitute, you can use whole wheat flour mixed with added bran to duplicate the pumpernickel flour; mix 120 grams/4.2 ounces/1 cup minus 2 tablespoons whole wheat flour with 28 grams/ 1 ounce/¼ cup wheat bran.

This dough is used to make Toasty Seeded Bread Twists (page 127.) If you enjoy variety, you can split the dough in two equal pieces and make half into a boule and the rest into bread twists.

We also make this dough into a traditional pan-shaped loaf and slice it to make our Grilled New York State Cheddar Cheese Sandwich (see page 225). To make pan loaves, after dividing the dough into two equal pieces, shape each piece into a log following the instructions on page 34. Place each loaf seam side down in a lightly oiled 9 x 5-inch loaf pan. Gently press down on the top of the loaf to spread it to fill the corners of the pan, and cover it with oiled plastic wrap. Let the loaves rise for 1½ to 2 hours, until they have doubled and risen about ¾ inch above the sides of the pan. To bake the loaves, follow steps 8 and 9 above. For step 10, place the pans directly onto the baking stone or an empty oven rack that has been positioned in the center of the oven, spray the tops lightly with water, and use the boiling water as described in step 10 to create steam in the oven. Continue with the baking instructions in step 11 above.

DAINER AGUIRRE

Dainer Aguirre keeps the oven in his head. That's only one of the reasons he's one of the best bread bakers we know. When Dainer joined the Amy's Bread baking team a year after the bakery opened, he was handsome, young, and single, with a strong work ethic and a cheerful disposition. A Colombian immigrant living with his close-knit family in one of New York's outer boroughs, he had been working with our friend and colleague Paula Oland at Ecce Panis in Manhattan. Paula was the one who gave Dainer his first lessons in bread baking. Though his grasp of English was a little tenuous at times, he and Paula learned to communicate with each other using the language of baking bread. She was the one who told Dainer that once he put something in the oven he had to carry that oven with him in his head until whatever he was baking had been taken out of the oven. He shared that story with Toy one day when they were baking baguettes together.

As this is written, Dainer has been with us for fifteen years. He's now a married man with a son and is an American citizen. A natural bread baker who instinctively understands the ins and outs of making bread, he has the magic touch when shaping bread dough. He can take an ugly baguette shaped by a newbie and with one or two effortless strokes of his hands turn it into perfection. He treats the loaves like they're his children, with sensitivity and pride. When mixing dough, without thinking he automatically adjusts the hydration to accommodate changes in the weather or the condition of the flour. Given new responsibilities with a different routine, within a couple of weeks he'll have developed techniques and systems to do the job more efficiently than it was done before. He's currently one of the full-time bakers at our Chelsea Market location who is in charge of the organic bread production. This means he comes in at 5:30 A.M. five days a week and mixes the dough, shapes the loaves, and bakes them for our complete organic bread line. And because he's Dainer, he has enough time left over to help the other bakers with their tasks too. Dainer bakes beautiful bread. We're proud to have him as part of our team and we're happy to know that the oven in Dainer Aguirre's head has Amy's Bread in it.

Toasty Seeded Bread Twists

Makes sixteen 6-inch twists

Equipment: one 17 × 12-inch baking sheet

Seeded bread twists are one of our most popular snack items at the bakery. Some of our wholesale restaurant customers cut them in half and use them in their bread baskets. We like the flavor combination of our mild, chewy sourdough coated with delicious toasty seeds, rich olive oil, and a sprinkling of kosher salt. These twists are quite substantial and make a nice addition to a light meal of a salad or pasta. They are great for parties or picnics to spread with dips or cheeses, and they are also nice eaten alone. Some people even cut them in half lengthwise to make funny, narrow sandwich rolls. One batch of Country Sourdough makes a large batch of twists, but you can always split the dough in two pieces, and make one large boule and eight beautiful twists.

INGREDIENTS	GRAMS	OUNCES	VOLUME
Country Sourdough Boule (page 121), prepared through Step 5	1560	55.00	1 recipe
Natural unhulled sesame seeds	50	1.85	⅓ cup
Poppy seeds	34	1.20	¼ cup
Extra virgin olive oil	57	2.00	4 tablespoons
Kosher salt, for sprinkling	to taste	to taste	to taste
Additional olive oil, for brushing (optional)	as needed	as needed	as needed

1. After the Country Sourdough dough has risen for 1 hour (in Step 5 above), dust your work surface lightly with flour and dump the dough onto it. Pat it into a 12-inch square.

2. Combine the sesame and poppy seeds in a small bowl. Sprinkle the dough lightly with about one third of the seed mixture. Fold the dough in thirds like a business letter, folding the top third of the square down and the bottom third up over the middle, to make a 12 × 4-inch rectangle. Gently pinch the open ends of the rectangle to seal. Using a plastic water sprayer, generously mist the dough with water. Coat both sides of the dough completely with the remaining seed mixture; make sure there are no bare spots. Gently brush the dough on both sides with the extra virgin olive oil and sprinkle it with salt.

3. Line a 17 X 12-inch sheet pan with parchment paper, and oil the edges of the pan. Place the seeded dough rectangle on the pan and cover it with oiled plastic wrap. Let it rise at room temperature for 30 to 45 minutes. The dough should be soft but will not have doubled.

4. Lightly oil a 16 X 4-inch area on the work surface. Place the dough on the oiled area, brush the top with a little olive oil, and sprinkle it lightly with kosher salt. Using a dough cutter, gently mark sixteen 1-inch strips, then cut all the way through the dough, being careful not to damage the surface below. Lift each stick, stretch it slightly so it's 6 inches long, and twist it once, then lay it back on the baking sheet starting at the edge of the pan. Place the twists side by side with no space between them. You want them to touch each other as they rise and to bake together. Let rise for 20 to 35 minutes, until slightly puffy but not quite fully risen.

5. Right after shaping, while the twists are rising, preheat the oven to 450°F. Prepare the oven by placing a cast-iron skillet and a smaller pan (a mini loaf pan) on the floor of the oven or on the lowest possible rack in an electric oven. Place an oven rack two rungs above the cast-iron pan, and if you have one, put a baking stone on the rack. Fill a plastic water sprayer with water. Fill a teakettle with water to be boiled later, and have a metal 1-cup measure with a straight handle available near the kettle.

6. Five to 10 minutes before the twists are ready to bake, turn the water on to boil, and carefully place two or three ice cubes in the small loaf pan in the bottom of the oven. This helps to create moisture in the oven prior to baking.

7. When they are ready to bake, mist the twists with water, then open the oven and place the pan of bread on the baking stone. (If you're baking without a stone simply put the pan onto the empty oven rack.) Quickly pour 1 cup of boiling water into the water pan and immediately shut the oven door. After 1 minute, mist the twists with water 6 to 8 times, then quickly shut the oven door.

8. Bake for 15 minutes, then reduce the oven temperature to 375°F and bake for 10 to 15 minutes longer, until the twists look golden brown and sound slightly hollow when tapped on the bottom but are still soft inside. Brush the hot bread twists with a little olive oil if desired, transfer them to a rack, and let cool for at least 15 minutes before serving. Leave the twists connected until ready to serve, then pull them apart.

Tangy Twenty-Four-Hour Sourdough

MADE WITH LIQUID LEVAIN AND RYE SALT SOUR STARTER

Makes three 13-ounce round boules

Equipment: 1 deep 2-quart clear plastic container; baking stone and wooden peel, or 17 × 12-inch sheet pan; baker's linen or heavy smooth cotton towel

This tangy bread is similar to a San Francisco sourdough. The sharp, sour flavor is achieved by making a sourdough sponge that is allowed to develop for several hours, and then by giving the bread a long, slow fermentation. We have also made this bread without the long fermentation, resulting in a milder sourdough flavor. We developed this formula when our customers asked for a sharp-tasting bread made without commercial yeast. It is very challenging to bake using only starter, and we wanted to try to make our own version, to show that we too could be "sourdough purists"! Today our Tangy Sourdough is still very popular for two reasons. First, it tastes great to those who love that sharp, tangy flavor. Second, we have always been committed to keeping a few of our products extremely affordable for those who don't want to spend a lot on bread. For the first fifteen years we were open, this 12-ounce loaf sold for only $1.00. Just in the past couple of years have we raised it above this mark because our ingredient costs have increased so dramatically. It's still extremely popular, and it is still a terrific bargain.

INGREDIENTS	GRAMS	OUNCES	VOLUME
Sponge			
Liquid Levain (page 62)	411	14.50	2 cups (full)
Rye Salt Sour Starter (page 66)	64	2.25	¼ cup
Very warm water (105° to 115°F)	283	10.00	1¼ cups
Unbleached bread flour	262	9.25	1¾ cups
Dough			
Unbleached all-purpose flour	280	9.80	2 cups
Organic whole wheat flour	100	3.50	½ cup plus 2 tablespoons
Kosher salt	16	0.56	1 tablespoon plus 2 teaspoons

1. For the sponge: Place the liquid levain and rye salt sour in a medium bowl. Add the very warm water and mix with your fingers, breaking up the starter and letting it dissolve in the water until it is fully blended, about 2 minutes.

2. Add the bread flour and stir rapidly about 2 minutes to make a thick, batterlike mixture. Scrape it into a deep 2-quart clear plastic container. Mark the level of the sponge and the time on the side of the container with a marker or tape. Cover with plastic wrap and let sit at warm room temperature (77° to 78°F) for 2½ to 4 hours to mature. When the sponge is bubbly and has almost doubled its original height, it is ready to be used in the dough.

This bread contains no commercial yeast. Its only leavening is the sourdough starters, so be sure the liquid levain and the rye salt sour starter are fresh and active before you make this recipe. If your starters have not been fed on a daily basis, you should refresh them for two or three days in a row so they are strong enough to leaven this bread. We use liquid levain, rather than firm levain starter, because wetter sourdough starters are usually more acidic and sharper in flavor. Instructions for building and maintaining the starters can be found on pages 57 to 58.

3. Taste the sponge: It should be slightly sweet with a tangy aftertaste. This is the moment to use it, even if you want a very tangy bread. If the sponge tastes very sour and sharp with no hint of sweetness, either your starters were too mature or your sponge has aged too long. You can still use the sponge, but it may take longer to get the bread to rise and the loaves will be denser than usual.

4. For the dough: Scrape the sponge into a large mixing bowl. Add the all-purpose flour, whole wheat flour, and salt and mix to form a rough, shaggy mass. Knead the dough for about 2 minutes, until the wet and dry ingredients are well combined.

5. Move the dough to a lightly floured surface and knead for about 4 minutes, until an elastic dough has formed. If the dough feels too firm, knead in additional cool water (75° to 78°F) 1 tablespoon at a time.

6. Put the dough back into the mixing bowl, cover with oiled plastic wrap, and let rest for 20 minutes to smooth out and develop elasticity.

7. Knead the dough again for 3 to 4 minutes, until it is very smooth and supple. Place the dough in an oiled bowl, cover it with oiled plastic wrap, and let it rise at room temperature (75° to 77°F) for about 1 to 1½ hours, until the dough looks slightly puffy but has not doubled.

8. Turn the dough while it is still in the mixing bowl. Gently deflate the dough in the middle of the bowl with your fingertips, then fold the left side over the middle, and the right side over the middle. Fold the dough in half, gently pat it down, and then turn it over so the seam is underneath. Cover the bowl of dough tightly with plastic wrap or a large plastic bag. Put the dough in the refrigerator to chill for at least 12 hours, or preferably overnight. From the beginning of the sponge stage through the final rise, this dough should age for at least 18 to 24 hours before baking.

9. Remove the dough from the refrigerator and let it sit at room temperature for 2 to 3 hours, until it warms up, feels soft, and is beginning to rise again.

10. Place the dough on a lightly floured surface and divide it evenly into 3 pieces, about 440 grams/15.5 ounces each. Shape each piece into a boule (see page 37), and place on well-floured baker's linen or a heavy smooth cotton towel on a baking sheet, leaving 3 inches between the loaves for rising. Cover the loaves with oiled plastic wrap and let rise for 2 to 4 hours, until they have almost doubled in volume and feel fairly light and airy when gently lifted. This bread rises best at about 78°F in a draft-free place; it is important to check the room temperature and the dough temperature to make sure you are in the optimum range. If your room and dough are too cool, move the bread to a warm place in the sun or near a radiator to get it moving.

11. Thirty minutes before baking, preheat the oven to 475°F. Prepare the oven by placing a cast-iron skillet and a smaller pan (a mini loaf pan) on the floor of the oven or on the lowest possible rack in an electric oven. Place an oven rack two rungs above the cast-iron pan, and if you have one, put a baking stone on the rack. If you can fit only 2 loaves on your baking stone, you will have to bake the third on a pan placed on an oven rack above the stone, so make sure there is enough space between the racks. Fill a plastic spray bottle with water. Fill a teakettle with water to be boiled later, and have a metal 1-cup measure with a straight handle available near the kettle.

12. Five to 10 minutes before the loaves are ready to bake, turn the water on to boil, and carefully place two or three ice cubes in the small loaf pan in the bottom of the oven. This helps to create moisture in the oven prior to baking.

13. When the loaves are ready to bake, sprinkle a peel and/or baking sheet generously with cornmeal or line with parchment paper. Gently lift the loaves from the towel and place them seam side down on the peel and/or sheet pan(s), allowing 2 to 3 inches between them for spreading. Mist the loaves with water, then score each loaf with a lame or a sharp razor blade, making five cuts across the loaf that gather into a point. Slide the bread gently onto the stone. If necessary, place the baking sheet with the third loaf on the rack above. (If you're baking without a stone simply slide the first sheet pan with the scored loaves onto the empty oven rack.) Quickly pour 1 cup of boiling water into the skillet and immediately shut the oven door. After 1 minute, mist the loaves again 6 to 8 times, then quickly shut the oven door. Mist again after 1 more minute.

14. Bake for 15 minutes, then reduce the oven temperature to 400°F and bake for 17 to 22 minutes longer, until the loaves are a deep golden brown with a glossy, bubbly crust. They should sound hollow when tapped on the bottom. Place the loaves on a wire rack to cool completely before serving.

NOTE: To make this bread less sour, shorten the fermentation time of the sponge to 2 hours or less. Don't refrigerate the dough; after mixing the dough, let it take a full first rise until doubled, 2 to 4 hours. Divide and shape the loaves, let them rise again for 2 to 3 hours, and bake according to the directions above.

TIPS AND TECHNIQUES

We used unbleached bread flour with a protein content of 12.7% and unbleached all-purpose flour with a protein content of 11.7% for this dough. Organic or conventional whole wheat flour can be used.

This bread tends to look streaky when it is baked in a home oven. It is nearly impossible to duplicate the powerful steam found in commercial ovens. Without that steam and an airtight seal around your oven, a bread made with 100 percent sourdough will always look a little dull, and not as brown as one baked in a bakery.

SAMPLE TIMING SCHEDULE FOR TANGY TWENTY-FOUR-HOUR SOURDOUGH

Mix the sponge	15 minutes	4:15 P.M.
Rise	2½ to 4 hours	8:15 P.M.
Knead dough	6 minutes	8:21 P.M.
Dough rest period	20 minutes	8:41 P.M.
Knead dough	4 minutes	8:45 P.M.
Rise	1½ hours	10:15 P.M.
Chill overnight, remove from refrigerator	12 hours	10:15 A.M.
Warm up and rise	2 hours	12:15 P.M.
Divide and shape loaves	5 minutes	12:20 P.M.
Proof	2 to 4 hours	4:20 P.M.
Bake	35 minutes	4:55 P.M.
Cool	45 minutes	5:40 P.M.
Slice and eat!		5:45 P.M.

Note: This timetable shows the longest rising times for your dough. On a warm day, the full fermentation time will be two or three hours shorter.

Whole Grain Spelt with Flax and Sesame and Tangy Twenty-Four-Hour Sourdough

Toy's Teddy Bread

MADE WITH RYE SALT SOUR STARTER

Makes two 1½-pound boules

Equipment: electric stand mixer with dough hook; baking stone and wooden peel, or 17 × 12 inch sheet pan

Toy originally developed this recipe so she could make teddy bears out of bread dough without having them lose their shape during baking. At the bakery we called the bears "huggable edibles." They were used as table centerpieces for birthday parties and baby showers and sent as get-well gifts to hospitals. A couple of them were even permanently encased in fiberglass resin to become part of private teddy bear collections! However, this dense, chewy bread was made to be eaten. The wonderful mildly tangy flavor and grainy texture are perfect for cheese platters or sandwiches that are complemented by a fine, assertive mustard. You can also team it up with a steaming bowl of your favorite soup and a crisp green salad for a satisfying and delicious meal.

We no longer make Teddy Bread at the bakery because we can't fit it into our busy production schedule, but we still think it's a bread with exceptional flavor that should be part of any serious baker's bread repertoire.

This updated recipe uses a little yeast so it no longer takes all day to complete this bread, but it's also no longer appropriate for shaping teddy bears because it rises too much in the oven.

Be sure to feed your rye salt sour starter twice the day before you plan to make your dough (see "Preparing the Rye Salt Sour for Teddy Bread" for special feeding instructions). Also remember to soak your cracked wheat, flax, and sesame seeds overnight so they'll be ready when you start to mix the dough.

PREPARING THE RYE SALT SOUR FOR TEDDY BREAD

Start with an active Rye Salt Sour Starter (page 66). On the morning of the day before you plan to bake, do a refreshment using 130 grams/4.58 ounces of water, 130 grams/4.58 ounces of organic rye flour, 45 grams/1.58 ounces of active Rye Salt Sour, and ¾ teaspoon kosher salt. Leave at room temperature to ferment. Before you go to bed that night, refresh the rye salt sour again in this same way, and leave it at room temperature to ferment overnight. Use it to make the Teddy Bread in the morning. The sour should at least double in volume each time it is refreshed. It can remain at room temperature for up to 12 hours until you're ready to feed it again. After 12 hours it should be refrigerated.

INGREDIENTS	GRAMS	OUNCES	VOLUME
Cracked wheat	113	4.00	¾ cup
Sesame seeds	42	1.48	scant ⅓ cup
Flax seeds	42	1.48	generous ¼ cup
Boiling water	300	10.58	1⅓ cups
Very warm water (105°F to 115°F)	57	2.00	¼ cup
Active dry yeast	1 teaspoon	1 teaspoon	1 teaspoon
Unbleached bread flour	354	12.48	2⅓ cups
Coarse whole wheat flour	246	8.68	1⅓ cups
Kosher salt	17	0.60	1 tablespoon plus 2½ teaspoons
Rye Salt Sour Starter (page 66)	255	9.00	1 cup
Very cool water (65° to 70°F)	235	8.28	1 cup
Additional flax and sesame seeds, for topping (optional)	1 tablespoon of each	1 tablespoon of each	1 tablespoon of each
Coarse cornmeal or polenta, for sprinkling	as needed	as needed	as needed

1. The day before you plan to bake, feed the rye salt sour twice.

2. The night before you plan to bake, in a 1-quart heatproof container, combine the cracked wheat, sesame seeds, and flax seeds with the boiling water. Stir briefly and cover tightly with plastic wrap. Set aside at room temperature to soak overnight. (See Tips and Techniques.)

3. Combine the very warm water and yeast in a measuring cup and stir to dissolve the yeast. Let stand for 3 minutes.

4. In a medium bowl, whisk together the bread flour, whole wheat flour, and salt. Set aside.

5. In the bowl of an electric stand mixer fitted with a dough hook, combine the yeast mixture, rye salt sour, and cool water and mix on medium-low speed for 1 minute to break up the salt sour. Add the soaked wheat and seeds (along with any liquid) and the flour mixture, mixing on medium-low speed for 2 minutes or until everything is well combined. Increase the speed to medium and continue mixing for another 2 minutes. Increase the speed to medium-high and mix for another 5 minutes. Turn off the mixer, and with water-moistened hands slide the dough down off of the hook. Check the dough temperature. If it is over 80°F, cover the bowl with plastic wrap and refrigerate it during the rest period. If it is cooler, cover it and leave it on the countertop to rest.

6. Mix again for 2 minutes at medium speed. This is very sticky, heavy dough with a coarse texture because of all the seeds. It will only be partially developed at

this point, but it should form a cohesive dough mass that pulls away from the sides and bottom of the bowl and begins to gather up around the dough hook. You will not be able to stretch a transparent sheet without having it tear. The rest of the dough development will take place as it rises in the bowl. The temperature of the dough should be 77° to 80°F.

7. Moisten your hands with water and shape the dough into a loose ball. Place it in an oiled bowl that is large enough to allow it to double. Cover it with oiled plastic wrap, and allow it to rise for 1 hour. The dough will not have doubled in volume, but it will be slightly puffy and feel bouncy and stronger, though still very sticky.

8. Moisten your hands with cool water and gently deflate the dough in the middle of the bowl with your fingertips, then fold the left side over the middle, and the right side over the middle. Fold the dough in half, gently pat it down, and then turn it over so the seam is underneath. Cover it and let it rise again for 1½ to 2 hours, until it has almost doubled in bulk.

9. Combine the flax and sesame seeds for topping, if using, and spread on a flat plate. Turn the dough out onto a lightly floured work surface and divide it into two equal pieces weighing about 820 grams/28.92 ounces each. Shape each piece into a compact boule (see page 37). If desired, roll the tops of the boules in the seed mixture. Sprinkle a peel generously with coarse cornmeal or polenta or cover the back of a baking sheet with parchment and dust it generously with cornmeal. Place the loaves seam side down on the peel or sheet, leaving several inches between them so they won't grow into each other as they rise. Cover them with oiled plastic wrap and let rise at room temperature until they have almost doubled in volume (a finger pressed lightly into the dough will leave a slight indentation). This should take about 1½ hours, but it could take longer if your starter is weak and/or the room is chilly.

10. Thirty minutes before baking, preheat the oven to 480°F. Prepare the oven by placing a cast-iron skillet and a smaller pan (a mini loaf pan) on the floor of the oven or on the lowest possible rack in an electric oven. Place an oven rack two rungs above the cast-iron pan, and if you have one, put a baking stone on the rack. Fill a plastic water sprayer with water. Fill a teakettle with water to be boiled later, and have a metal 1-cup measure with a straight handle available near the kettle.

11. Five to 10 minutes before the bread is ready to bake, turn the water on to boil, and carefully place two or three ice cubes in the small loaf pan in the bottom of the oven. This helps to create moisture in the oven prior to baking.

12. When the loaves are ready, cut an X on top of each one with a lame or a very sharp knife. Spray them with water and slide them onto the baking stone, repositioning them if necessary to leave space between the loaves. (If you're baking without a stone simply slide the sheet pan with the scored and misted loaves onto the empty oven rack.) Pour 1 cup of boiling water into the skillet and immediately shut the oven door. After 1 minute, quickly mist the loaves again, then shut the oven door.

13. After 20 minutes, reduce the oven temperature to 450°F and rotate the loaves if necessary to ensure even browning. Bake them for another 20 to 25 minutes, until they are dark brown in color and sound hollow when tapped on the bottom (an instant-read digital thermometer should register around 210°F).

14. Cool them completely on a wire rack. This bread freezes well, wrapped tightly in aluminum foil and then in plastic wrap or a heavy-duty freezer bag.

TIPS AND TECHNIQUES

We used unbleached bread flour with a protein content of 12.7% for this dough.

This recipe depends on coarse whole wheat flour for the best results. It's difficult to find this outside of commercial bakery suppliers, but we did uncover one source that sells their products online to home bakers. See Mail-Order Sources (page 270) for Paul's Grains wheat graham flour.

Combining the cracked wheat and seeds in boiling water to soak overnight hydrates and softens them so they won't absorb moisture from the dough. It also makes them more digestible.

When baking in the summer, or if the room temperature is very warm, use only half the measure of kosher salt from the recipe with the soaker to keep the enzymes in the grain from becoming too active. This can produce an unpleasant sour flavor when the soaker is left in a warm, moist environment for too long.

Organic bulgur wheat is an excellent substitute for cracked wheat and is often easier to find. When using bulgur, which is cracked wheat that has been parboiled and dehydrated, you don't have to boil the water for the soaker; using room temperature water for the soak is fine. The soaking time can be reduced to 1 hour or until the bulgur has softened but is not mushy and most of the soaking water is absorbed.

Be very careful about not letting your dough temperature exceed 80°F as this dough can develop an unpleasantly bitter aftertaste if it gets too warm.

Organic Miche

Makes 1 large 3-pound boule or two 1½-pound boules

Equipment: electric stand mixer with dough hook; baking stone and wooden peel, or 17 × 12-inch sheet pan; one 10⅝-inch banneton or a large colander and heavy smooth cotton towel

Huge round loaves baked so dark the crust looks almost black, with a dense, chewy crumb, a mild but complex sourdough flavor, and an aroma that smells like fresh wheat steeped in warm honey—this is the style of bread that was made popular by the late famous French bread baker Lionel Poilâne. At Amy's Bread we make miche in two sizes, a 1-pound boule to please our customers who are used to buying their own whole individual loaves, and the big 4-pound loaf that can be purchased whole or in halves or quarters. Wise bread lovers know that the big loaf is the one with the most amazing flavor and are happy to take home just a portion of the loaf. We scaled down the recipe to make one 3-pound boule so it would fit in the average home oven, but it's still an impressive loaf. Don't be afraid of the dark brown crust; those caramelized sugars are part of what gives this bread its outstanding flavor.

This is a wet, heavy dough and is best proofed in a linen-lined willow basket, called a banneton, for support. They are available in several different sizes (see page 20). Instead of the banneton, Toy used a colander lined with an unbleached heavy smooth cotton towel that served the purpose perfectly.

INGREDIENTS	GRAMS	OUNCES	VOLUME
Very warm water (105° to 115°F)	57	2.00	¼ cup
Active dry yeast	½ teaspoon	½ teaspoon	½ teaspoon
Cool water (75° to 78°F)	600	21.87	2¾ cups
Miche Levain (page 64), made with organic flour	165	5.82	⅔ cup
Organic unbleached bread flour	635	22.40	4¼ cups
Organic rye flour	200	7.00	1½ cups
Kosher salt	23	0.81	3 tablespoons
Medium cornmeal or polenta, for sprinkling	as needed	as needed	as needed

1. Combine the very warm water and yeast in a measuring cup and stir to dissolve the yeast. Let stand for 3 minutes.

2. In the bowl of an electric stand mixer fitted with a dough hook, combine the yeast mixture, the cool water, and the miche levain and mix on medium-low speed for 1½ minutes to break up the levain. Add the bread flour, rye flour, and salt and mix on medium-low speed for 2 minutes, then scrape down the sides of the bowl. Increase the speed to medium and continue mixing for another 5 minutes. Turn off the mixer, slide the dough down off the hook, then cover the bowl with plastic wrap and let the dough rest for 10 minutes.

3. Mix again for 2 minutes at medium-low speed. This wet dough will only be partially developed at this point. The rest of the dough development will take place as it proofs in the bowl. The temperature of the dough should be 77°F to 80°F.

4. Put the dough in an oiled bowl that is large enough to allow it to almost double, cover it with oiled plastic wrap, and allow it to rise for 30 minutes. The dough will not have doubled in volume, but it will be slightly puffy though still very sticky.

5. Moisten your hands with cool water or a little oil and give the dough a turn by gently folding it in from the sides to the middle to de-gas it, then turn it over so the smoother bottom side is up, cover it, and let it rise again for 30 minutes.

6. Turn it again and let it rise a third time for 30 minutes. The consistency of the dough will still be soft but it should now be stronger and feel slightly springy.

7. While the dough is rising the third time, generously flour the banneton or line the colander with the towel so the towel extends out over the edge of the colander, and then rub it generously with flour, all the way up the sides and into any folds in the cloth. The dough will stick to any unfloured areas, so be sure every inch is heavily coated with flour.

8. Pour the dough out onto a lightly floured work surface and gently shape it into a round ball. To do this, flour your hands or wet them with cool water, and, working quickly, draw the edges of the dough into the center, making a circular shape. Then turn the dough over and rotate the ball against the table in a circular motion, pushing it away from you with one hand and pulling it back toward you with the other, to tuck the edges under and tighten it. This is a little tricky because this is a big piece of fairly wet, heavy, loose dough. Keep your hands floured or moistened so they don't stick to the dough and try not to tear the skin of the dough. Place the ball seam side up in the prepared banneton or colander, cover it with the oiled plastic wrap, and let it rise until it has almost doubled. This will take about an hour or more depending on the temperature of the dough.

9. Thirty minutes before baking, preheat the oven to 480°F. Prepare the oven by placing a cast-iron skillet and a smaller pan (a mini loaf pan) on the floor of the

oven or on the lowest possible rack in an electric oven. Place an oven rack two rungs above the cast-iron pan, and if you have one, put a baking stone on the rack. Fill a plastic water sprayer with water. Fill a teakettle with water to be boiled later, and have a metal 1-cup measure with a straight handle available near the kettle.

10. Five to 10 minutes before the bread is ready to bake, turn the water on to boil, and carefully place two or three ice cubes in the small loaf pan in the bottom of the oven. This helps to create moisture in the oven prior to baking.

11. Sprinkle the wooden peel generously with medium cornmeal or polenta, or line a sheet pan with parchment. When the miche is ready, remove the plastic wrap and carefully turn it upside down onto the peel or the parchment-lined pan. If there is too much flour caked on the top of the loaf, use a clean dry pastry brush to gently brush most of it off. Holding a lame or a sharp razor blade at a 90-degree angle to the loaf, make four deep slashes as if drawing a large square on the top of the loaf. The cut lines should overlap at the corners. Open the oven and slide the miche onto the baking stone. (If you're baking without a stone simply slide the sheet pan with the scored loaves onto the empty oven rack.) Quickly pour 1 cup of boiling water into skillet and immediately close the oven door. After 3 minutes pour another ½ cup of boiling water into the skillet.

12. Check the loaf after 20 minutes and use a small metal baking cup or a metal spoon to prop the oven door open for 2 or 3 minutes to vent any residual moisture from the oven. Don't forget to use a pot holder when you remove the spoon or cup!

13. Reduce the oven temperature to 450°F. Bake for a total of 50 to 55 minutes, until the loaf is very, very dark brown in color and sounds hollow when tapped on the bottom.

14. Place it on a wire rack and cool the loaf completely before cutting into it.

TIPS AND TECHNIQUES:

We used unbleached bread flour with 12.7% protein for this dough.

If you're using a parchment-lined sheet pan instead of a baking stone, the profile of the finished loaf will be much flatter than the loaf proofed in a basket, and it will take longer to bake than a loaf baked directly on a stone.

Organic Whole Grain Spelt with Flax and Sesame

MADE WITH SPELT LEVAIN STARTER

Makes two 8½ x 4½-inch pan loaves

Equipment: electric stand mixer with dough hook; two 8½ x 4½-inch bread pans; baking stone

We probably should have named this bread "Whole Grain Ugly Bread" because there is nothing even remotely pretty about these loaves. They look like something you could build a house with and the interior crumb resembles a speckled brownish gray sponge. But once you get past the appearance and take a bite of this dense, moist, chewy bread, the flavors that envelop your taste buds make you want to sit down and eat the whole loaf. Spread with a little softened goat cheese or unsalted butter there's no other bread in the city that tastes quite like our ugly spelt bread. When our agent, Sharon Bowers, took a test loaf home to share with her family, which includes two small children, they all loved it so much they kept making the slices thinner and thinner in an effort to make it last longer.

This is truly a 100 percent whole grain bread. There is no white or unbleached flour in it at all. Even the sourdough starter is made from whole grain spelt. Spelt is considered by some to be more digestible and easier to tolerate than regular wheat, and it's higher in protein, fiber, and B complex vitamins. We also soak the flax and sesame seeds overnight to make them more digestible and make their nutrients more available. The dough is very wet, almost more like a batter, so it's a little tricky to shape into loaves, but the loaves are baked in traditional bread pans so even if you don't shape them perfectly they're likely to come out fine. There are some benefits to making "ugly" loaves!

INGREDIENTS	GRAMS	OUNCES	VOLUME
Cool water (75° to 78°F)	245	8.64	1⅛ cups
Organic flax seeds	90	3.17	½ cup
Organic unhulled sesame seeds	90	3.17	½ cup plus 2 tablespoons
Very warm water (105° to 115°F)	57	2.00	¼ cup
Active dry yeast	1⅜ teaspoons	1⅜ teaspoons	1⅜ teaspoons
Cold water (60°F)	450	15.87	2 cups
Spelt Levain (page 68)	160	5.64	1 cup
Organic whole spelt flour	696	24.60	5⅔ cups
Kosher salt	16	0.56	2 tablespoons plus ¼ teaspoon
Nonstick cooking oil spray, such as Pam or Crisco	as needed	as needed	as needed

1. The day before you plan to bake, feed the spelt levain twice (see "Preparing the Spelt Levain for Baking").

2. The night before mixing the dough, in a 1-quart plastic container, combine the flax and sesame seeds with the cool water, stir briefly, cover with plastic wrap, and set them aside to soak at room temperature overnight.

PREPARING THE SPELT LEVAIN FOR BAKING

Start with an active Spelt Levain (page 68). On the morning of the day before you plan to bake, do a refreshment using 100 grams/ 3.52 ounces of water, 150 grams/ 5.29 ounces of organic whole spelt flour, 60 grams/2.12 ounces of active spelt levain, and ½ teaspoon kosher salt. Leave at room temperature to ferment. Before you go to bed that night, refresh the spelt levain again in this same way, and leave it at room temperature to ferment overnight. Use it to make the spelt bread in the morning. The sour should at least double in volume each time it is refreshed. It can remain at room temperature for up to 10 hours until you're ready to feed it again. After 10 hours it should be refrigerated.

3. The following day, combine the very warm water and yeast in a measuring cup and stir to dissolve the yeast. Let stand for 3 minutes.

4. In the bowl of an electric stand mixer fitted with a dough hook, combine the yeast mixture, the cold water, and the spelt levain and mix on medium-low speed for 1 minute to break up the levain. Add the flour and salt, mix again on medium-low speed for 2 minutes, scraping down the sides of the bowl after the first minute. Increase the speed to medium and continue mixing for another 4½ to 5 minutes. This dough will be heavy and sticky, but it should be pulling away from the side of bowl, forming a dough mass up around the dough hook, but still sticking to the bottom of the bowl. Turn off the mixer and allow the dough to relax in the bowl for 15 minutes.

5. Add the seed mixture and mix on low speed for 1 minute to begin incorporating the seeds into the dough. The dough will start to look shredded. Slide the dough down from the neck of the hook if needed, increase the speed to medium and continue mixing for another 2 minutes. Increase the speed to medium-high and mix again for 2 minutes until the seeds are evenly distributed and the dough is beginning to gather into a mass. It will still stick to the sides and bottom of the bowl, but it should feel fairly strong and bouncy. The dough will be sticky but you should be able to stretch it to form a thin membrane that tears. The temperature of the dough should be 75°F to 77°F.

6. Leave the dough in the bowl, cover it with oiled plastic wrap, and allow it to rise for 30 to 40 minutes. The dough will not have doubled in volume, but it should be slightly puffy and feel bouncy and stronger though still very sticky.

7. Moisten your hands with cool water and gently deflate the dough in the middle of the bowl with your fingertips, then fold the left side over the middle, and the right side over the middle. Fold the dough in half, gently pat it down, and then turn it over so the seam is underneath. If the dough tears and stick to your hands, moisten them again with water and work quickly to tuck the edges under to create

enough tension to form a loose dough ball. Cover it and let it rise again for 30 minutes before you begin the shaping process.

8. Spray the two loaf pans with nonstick cooking oil. Pour the dough out onto a work surface that has been very lightly moistened with water and divide it into two equal pieces, about 885 grams/31.22 ounces each. The dough should be loose but strong and springy. With water-moistened hands, shape each piece by gently patting it into a rectangle—the exact dimensions are not important. Position the rectangle so the short sides are at the top and the bottom of the rectangle. If the dough sticks to the work surface, lift it gently with a dough scraper and lightly re-moisten the surface. Also keep your hands moist so the dough doesn't stick to them and tear. You'll need to work quickly because this dough is loose and wants to spread out if you let it sit for even a few seconds. Starting with the upper edge of the dough, gently fold the top third down and the bottom third up, like a business letter, so you have 3 equal layers. Use the dough scraper to help you do this if it makes it easier for you. Give the dough a quarter turn so the short side is at the top again and repeat the folding process. Seal the seam if necessary, though this dough is so wet it generally seals itself. Keeping your hands moist, roll the dough over so the seam is on the bottom, trying to maintain tension in the shape, quickly lift it into the prepared loaf pan, allowing it to stretch to the length of the pan as you remove your hands. If necessary, moisten your hands and tuck the sides of the dough under again to re-establish some tension in the dough. Then use your moistened knuckles to gently press down on the top of the loaf so it fills the pan evenly. Repeat the process with the second piece.

9. Cover the pans with oiled plastic wrap and let them rise until they're approaching the top of the pan. This usually takes about 1 hour and 10 minutes, but it can take up to 20 minutes longer if the dough or the room where it's proofing is very cool. You'll be able to see bubbles of gas forming and rising to the top as the proofing progresses. If any of the bubbles get too large, deflate them with the point of a sharp knife and gently reseal the tiny hole in the dough.

10. Once the dough gets high enough to start sticking to the plastic wrap, remove the plastic wrap. Spray the tops of the loaves lightly with water if the dough begins to dry out after the plastic is removed. When the dough reaches the top of the pan, it's ready to bake. If the tops of the loaves start to look like they're deflating instead of rising, bake them immediately.

11. Thirty minutes before baking, preheat the oven to 450°F. Prepare the oven by placing a cast-iron skillet and a smaller pan (a mini loaf pan) on the floor of the oven or on the lowest possible rack in an electric oven. Place an oven rack two rungs above the cast-iron pan, and if you have one, put a baking stone on the rack. Fill a plastic water sprayer with water. Fill a teakettle with water to be boiled later, and have a metal 1-cup measure with a straight handle available near the kettle.

12. Five to 10 minutes before the loaves are ready to bake, turn the water on to boil, and carefully place two or three ice cubes in the small loaf pan in the bottom of the oven. This helps to create moisture in the oven prior to baking.

13. When the loaves are ready, mist them lightly with water. Quickly but carefully fill the metal 1-cup measure with boiling water, open the oven and slide the bread pans onto the baking stone, leaving several inches between the pans. (If you're baking without a stone simply slide the loaf pans onto the empty oven rack). Quickly but carefully pour the boiling water into the cast-iron pan and immediately close the oven door.

14. Check the loaves after 20 minutes and rotate them if necessary to ensure even browning. The loaves will shrink away from the sides of the pan after about 30 minutes. Bake them for a total of 40 to 45 minutes, until they are golden brown on top and the sides and bottom are browned and feel firm when you tip the loaves out of the pan (an instant-read digital thermometer should register around 210°F). They will not get much if any oven spring, so the tops of the loaves may only be slightly domed, or they may even look flat. They will not sound hollow when you tap them.

15. Cool them completely on a wire rack, then let them sit out at room temperature for at least 10 hours before cutting them to allow the moisture on the inside of the bread to be absorbed evenly into the crumb. This bread has a long shelf life because the crumb is so moist. Let it sit on the counter with the cut side down. Refrigerate or freeze it after the third day.

TIPS AND TECHNIQUES

If the tops of your loaves look streaked with white because you didn't get enough steam in the oven, you can brush them lightly with a little oil or butter to produce an even brown color.

Spelt flour is sometimes tricky to work with because the quality of protein in the flour can vary so much from one brand to another. If the quality of the protein is very good, the first rising times in the recipe can be increased to give the protein more time to develop and strengthen. The resulting loaves may rise higher in the pan and in the oven, so with subsequent bakes it may be necessary to use a 9 x 5-inch loaf pan instead of the size specified in the recipe. On the other hand, if the protein quality is not good, then the rising time after the first turn may need to be shortened or the strength of the gluten may deteriorate during the proofing stage after the loaves have been shaped. In this case, you'll notice that the dough is losing strength and becoming more slack as it rises and proofs, so it will be difficult to get very much volume in the loaf. Only experience and repetition will teach you how best to work with the brand of spelt flour that is available in your area. Don't be discouraged—your loaves will taste wonderful and be very satisfying to eat even if they're not perfect.

BREADS MADE WITH RYE FLOUR

Rye breads are the unsung heroes of the bread world. They have a chewy texture and a denser crumb than breads made with wheat flour. They are usually very flavorful and hearty, and go well with savory, robust meats, cheeses, and fish. The tradition of baking with rye flour comes from Germany and Eastern Europe, where rye grows abundantly and wheat was not always available to bakers. Rye flour is low in protein and does not develop the same stretchy gluten formation that wheat flour does. So breads made with a high proportion of rye flour are denser and heavier, but also extremely satisfying. Because rye flour absorbs more water, the bread is moist with a longer shelf life. Most rye flours are whole grain, so breads with at least 50 percent rye flour contribute to a healthy diet. At Amy's Bread we always offer three or four kinds of bread made with rye flour, and although they will never match the popularity of white bread or whole wheat, they certainly have a devoted fan club.

Amy's Rye with Caraway and Mustard Seeds

MADE WITH FIRM LEVAIN

Makes three 14-ounce loaves

Equipment: baking stone and wooden peel, or 17 x 12-inch sheet pan

This is a wonderfully chewy, tangy, and very flavorful loaf that goes well with cured or smoked meats, poultry, or fish. Amy first came up with this recipe when she was working with chef Tom Colicchio at Mondrian in the early 1990s. He was making an untraditional squab pastrami and wanted the perfect bread to accompany it. The bread was supposed to echo the taste of a New York pastrami sandwich on rye spread with mustard. Amy developed a dense, chewy rye made more interesting with caraway and mustard seeds mixed right into the dough.

In New York we find breads that are labeled "rye" but they're soft and airy because they are made mainly from wheat flour with a little white rye added in. Our rye bread, on the other hand, has a tight crumb because it is made with a high proportion of rye flour, which is low in gluten, so it doesn't rise high in the oven. We have made this bread ever since the first day we opened, and fans of "real" rye bread adore it.

INGREDIENTS	GRAMS	OUNCES	VOLUME
Very warm water (105° to 115°F)	57	2.00	¼ cup
Active dry yeast	1½ teaspoons	1½ teaspoons	1½ teaspoons
Organic rye flour	326	11.50	2½ cups
Unbleached bread flour	150	5.30	1 cup
Cooked organic rye berries (see "Cooking Wheat and Rye Berries," page 110)	75	2.65	½ cup
Mustard seeds	22	0.80	2 tablespoons
Caraway seeds	12	0.40	1 tablespoon plus 2 teaspoons
Kosher salt	12	0.42	1 tablespoon plus 1 teaspoon
Cool water (75° to 78°F)	397	14.00	1¾ cups
Firm Levain (page 63), at room temperature	255	9.00	1¼ cups
Cornmeal or polenta, for sprinkling	as needed	as needed	as needed

1. Combine the very warm water and yeast in a measuring cup and stir with a fork to dissolve the yeast. Let stand for 3 minutes.

2. Combine the rye flour, bread flour, rye berries, mustard seeds, caraway, and salt in a large mixing bowl. Pour in the cool water and the yeast mixture and stir with your fingers to combine. Bring the dough together into a rough mass and knead and fold it over onto itself in the bowl for 2 minutes. If the dough seems too stiff, knead in up to 3 tablespoons of cool water, 1 tablespoon at a time. (The dough should be very sticky and gloppy, almost like clay, through most of the kneading process.)

3. Place the dough on a lightly floured work surface and spread it slightly, then press the levain starter on top of the dough and gently knead them to blend the two together. Continue to knead until the dough becomes smooth and supple, 6 to 7 minutes. Put the dough back into the mixing bowl, cover with oiled plastic wrap, and let rest for 20 minutes to smooth out and develop elasticity.

4. On a lightly floured surface, knead the dough again for 2 to 3 minutes, until it feels gluey, airy, and supple. It should still feel slightly firm, almost like aerated modeling clay.

5. Shape the dough into a loose ball and place it in a lightly oiled bowl. Cover the bowl with oiled plastic wrap and let the dough rise at room temperature (75° to 78°F) for 1½ to 2 hours, until doubled in bulk. (This dough will not develop and rise as well at cooler temperatures).

6. Sprinkle a peel generously with cornmeal or polenta or cover the back of a baking sheet with parchment and dust it generously with cornmeal. Place the dough on a lightly floured surface and divide it into 3 equal pieces about 425 grams/ 15 ounces each. Shape each piece of dough into a log (see page 34). Place the loaves seam side down on the peel or pan, leaving 2 to 3 inches between them for rising. These loaves are small, so they should all fit on one baking stone. Cover them with oiled plastic wrap and allow to rise at room temperature for 45 minutes to 1½ hours, until doubled in bulk. (Rye bread lacks gluten and the dough has the tendency to crack. If the loaves start to split or tear, they have become too acidic and have risen too long. They should be baked right away. Don't worry—they will still be good but will have a tangier flavor.)

7. Thirty minutes before baking, preheat the oven to 450°F. Prepare the oven by placing a cast-iron skillet and a smaller pan (a mini loaf pan) on the floor of the oven or on the lowest possible rack in an electric oven. Place an oven rack two rungs above the cast-iron pan, and if you have one, put a baking stone on the rack. Fill a plastic water sprayer with water. Fill a teakettle with water to be boiled later, and have a metal 1-cup measure with a straight handle available near the kettle.

8. Five to 10 minutes before the loaves are ready to bake, turn the water on to boil, and carefully place two or three ice cubes in the small loaf pan in the bottom of the oven. This helps to create moisture in the oven prior to baking.

9. Sprinkle a little rye flour on top of each loaf, then gently score the top of each loaf with a razor blade, making four to five shallow cuts across the loaf, being careful not to deflate them. Open the oven door and gently slide the bread onto the stone. (If you're baking without a stone simply put the pan onto the empty oven rack.) Quickly mist the loaves with water 6 to 8 times, pour 1 cup of boiling water into the skillet, and immediately shut the oven door. After 1 minute, quickly mist the loaves with water again, then shut the oven door.

10. Bake for 20 minutes, then reduce the oven temperature to 400°F and bake for 15 to 20 minutes longer, until the loaves are a rich reddish brown and sound hollow when tapped on the bottom. Transfer the bread to a rack to cool completely. (Make sure the loaves are completely cool before slicing, or they will be gummy inside.) This bread is great on the second day.

TIPS AND TECHNIQUES

We used unbleached bread flour with a protein content of 12.7% for this dough.

French Rye

Makes two 1¼-pound log-shaped loaves

Equipment: baking stone and wooden peel; one 17 x 12-inch sheet pan; baker's linen or heavy smooth cotton towel

This unique little rye loaf was the result of a request from one of our upscale restaurant wholesale customers. They wanted a dense, mild-flavored rye bread, like the ones they'd had in Parisian brasseries, that they could cut into thin rounds to serve with their *Plateaux de Fruits de Mer* (shellfish platters). Amy knew exactly what they were talking about and thought it would be fun to create a bread made almost totally from rye flour, not only for the restaurant but also for our retail customers to enjoy. The bread has a complex flavor that comes from the fruitiness of the organic rye flour and the savory, almost meat-like flavor of the rye salt sour starter. It's delicious plain or spread with a thin layer of lightly salted butter (as it's eaten in Paris), and it makes a perfect base for hors d'oeuvres or open-face mini sandwiches like the ones on page 228.

Working with bread dough that has a lot of rye flour in it is a little like working with modeling clay. Rye flour absorbs a lot of water, but does not have the ability to create an extensible, elastic gluten structure to trap the gases produced by yeast fermentation, so the dough (and the bread) will be dense and heavy. It also ferments very easily so the proofing times are short and the dough has to be watched very carefully to avoid overproofing. Don't be intimidated by these unusual qualities because if you master the techniques of handling high percentage rye dough, you'll be rewarded with a unique and wonderful bread tasting experience. This is a small batch of dough so all of the mixing is best done by hand. The sourdough starter in this bread is used more for its flavor qualities than for its leavening power.

INGREDIENTS	GRAMS	OUNCES	VOLUME
Sponge			
Very warm water (105°F to 115°F)	57	2.00	¼ cup
Active dry yeast	1¼ teaspoons	1¼ teaspoons	1¼ teaspoons
Organic rye flour	130	4.60	1 cup
Cool water (75° to 78°F)	78	2.75	⅓ cup
Rye Salt Sour Starter (see page 66)	68	2.40	¼ cup (full)

Dough

Very warm water (105°F to 115°F)	57	2.00	¼ cup
Active dry yeast	2¼ teaspoons	2¼ teaspoons	2¼ teaspoons
Cool water (75° to 78°F)	312	11.00	1⅓ cups
Organic rye flour	300	10.58	2⅓ cups
Unbleached bread flour	230	8.11	1½ cups
Kosher salt	16	0.56	1 tablespoon plus 2 teaspoons
Medium cornmeal or polenta, for sprinkling	as needed	as needed	as needed

1. To make the sponge: combine the very warm water and yeast in a measuring cup and stir to dissolve the yeast. Let stand for 3 minutes.

2. In a small mixing bowl, combine all the ingredients for the sponge, including the yeast mixture, and mix them vigorously with a rubber spatula for 30 to 40 seconds, until the flour is completely moistened and everything is well combined. The sponge will be like very thick paste. Scrape down the sides of the bowl and use your hand, moistened with cool water, to scrape the dough off of the spatula. Wet the spatula and smooth the top surface of the sponge. The temperature of the sponge should be 78°F to 80°F. Cover the bowl with plastic wrap and let it sit for 1 hour. Do not let it sit for longer than 1 hour or it will become too sour. If you see it start to deflate before the hour is up, mix the dough immediately.

3. To make the dough: About 5 minutes before the sponge is ready, combine the very warm water with the yeast for the dough in a measuring cup and stir to dissolve the yeast. Let stand for 3 minutes.

4. In a medium mixing bowl, combine the prepared sponge, the yeast mixture, cool water, rye flour, bread flour, and salt and stir with your hand or a rubber spatula until the flour is well moistened. This dough will be very heavy and sticky like soft wet clay. Continue mixing and kneading the dough for 3 to 5 minutes in the mixing bowl until the dough becomes a little smoother and more compact. It will not be springy and stretchy. Use a rubber spatula to scrape down the sides of the bowl and use your hand, moistened with cool water, to scrape the dough off the spatula. Wet the spatula and smooth the top surface of the dough. The dough temperature should be around 80°F. Let it rise for 30 minutes. If the dough is very warm or it's rising in a very warm room, you may need to shape it before the end of the 30 minutes. Look for little holes and bubbles developing in the dough. Don't let it overproof or the shaped loaves won't rise properly.

5. While the dough rises, prepare a proofing pan by lining a 17 × 12-inch sheet pan with baker's linen so it overlaps the sides and sprinkle it with a moderate amount of flour; or a heavy smooth cotton towel sprinkled generously with flour; or just line the pan with parchment paper and sprinkle the parchment with a moderate amount of flour.

6. Just before shaping the loaves, preheat the oven to 460°F. Prepare the oven by placing a cast-iron skillet and a smaller pan (a mini loaf pan) on the floor of the oven or on the lowest possible rack in an electric oven. Place an oven rack two rungs above the cast-iron pan, and if you have one, put a baking stone on the rack. Fill a plastic water sprayer with water. Fill a teakettle with water to be boiled later, and have a metal 1-cup measure with a straight handle available near the kettle.

7. Scrape the dough out onto a lightly floured work surface, and divide it equally into two pieces weighing about 620 grams/21.87 ounces each. Keeping your hands lightly floured, pat the pieces of dough into rectangles. Using a dough scraper to assist in lifting the dough from the work surface, roll them gently into compact little logs that are 11 inches long. This is going to be more like molding clay than shaping bread dough. The dough is very sticky, so handle it lightly with floured hands but try not to use too much flour on the table. When the logs have been formed, place the first one on the prepared pan, right up against one edge of the pan. Be sure the cloth is covering the side of the pan. Pull up a 2-inch pleat of cloth to separate the two loaves and place the second loaf on the pan next to the first loaf. Pull up another pleat of cloth on the outside of the second loaf to support it while it rises. If you're using a parchment-lined pan, place the loaves about 2 inches in from the sides and leave 3 to 4 inches between the two loaves. Cover the loaves with oiled plastic wrap and let them rise for 25 to 30 minutes. They will expand slightly and spread a little but they won't double. The proofing time may be even less if the dough is very warm or they are proofing in a warm room, so keep a close eye on them. If you start to see holes or cracking in the dough, bake them right away.

8. Five to 10 minutes before the loaves are ready to bake, turn the water on to boil, and carefully place two or three ice cubes in the small loaf pan in the bottom of the oven. This helps to create moisture in the oven prior to baking.

9. Sprinkle the wooden peel generously with medium cornmeal or polenta. When the loaves are ready, remove the plastic wrap and carefully lift them onto the peel, leaving space between the loaves to allow for spreading in the oven (or leave the loaves on the parchment-lined pan.) Mist the loaves evenly with water. Carefully fill the metal 1-cup measure with boiling water, open the oven and slide the rye loaves onto the baking stone (if you're baking without a stone simply slide the sheet pan with the loaves onto the empty oven rack), then quickly pour the boiling water into the cast-iron pan and immediately close the oven door.

10. After 5 minutes, use a small metal baking cup or a metal spoon to prop the oven door open for 5 minutes to vent any residual moisture from the oven. Don't forget to use a pot holder when you remove the spoon or cup!

11. Bake the rye for a total of 30 to 35 minutes or until the loaves feel firm and they are a nice golden reddish brown color. Cool them completely on a wire rack before cutting them.

TIPS AND TECHNIQUES

We used unbleached bread flour with 12.7% protein for this dough.

Some bakers find it easier to work with this dough using lightly moistened hands and a lightly moistened work surface instead of flour. This method works better on wood than it does on Formica, which gets too slippery.

If cracks form in the loaves while they are baking, the dough may not have been mixed long enough, or it may have been mixed too long, or the loaves may have been overproofed, or they may not have gotten enough steam, or may have gotten too much steam, or the moisture in the oven may not have been vented soon enough. With this bread, experience and observation are your best teachers. Take notes about your results each time you make the bread. It's a very tricky bread to make, but if you can master it, it's well worth the effort.

Chewy Pumpernickel

Makes two 9 x 5-inch loaves, or 4 smaller oval loaves

Equipment: two 9 x 5-inch loaf pans, oiled, or 17 x 12-inch baking sheet

In our version of a dark pumpernickel bread, the rye salt sour starter is used more for its taste than for its leavening power. Traditionally coffee, molasses, cocoa powder, or caramel color gives pumpernickel its characteristic dark brown color. We tried them all and finally decided the caramel color achieved the almost-black bread we desired—but we left all the others in for the depth of flavor they added. (The caramel color can be made well ahead of time and stored.) We add sunflower seeds to the dough for a nutty flavor and extra crunch, and we've also included the option of adding raisins. In the bakery we make this bread into pan loaves, rustic ovals, and dinner rolls. It's a versatile and flavorful bread that is good for sandwiches or to accompany a meal. We think you'll be pleased by how closely this formula duplicates sophisticated pumpernickel bread made in the best bakeries.

INGREDIENTS	GRAMS	OUNCES	VOLUME
Very warm water (105° to 115°F)	57	2.00	¼ cup
Active dry yeast	1 teaspoon	1 teaspoon	1 teaspoon
Unbleached all-purpose flour	435	15.35	3 cups
Pumpernickel flour	290	10.25	2¼ cups
Kosher salt	15	0.53	1 tablespoon plus 2 teaspoons
Unsweetened cocoa powder	9	0.30	1½ tablespoons
Biga (page 56)	340	12.00	1½ cups
Rye Salt Sour Starter (page 66)	127	4.50	½ cup
Cool water (75° to 78°F)	312	11.00	1¼ cups plus 2 tablespoons
Brewed strong coffee	85	3.00	¼ cup plus 2 tablespoons
Caramel Color (recipe follows)	35	1.25	2 tablespoons
Honey	30	1.00	1½ tablespoons
Molasses	30	1.00	1½ tablespoons
Dark raisins (optional)	255	9.00	1 ¾ cups
Raw shelled sunflower seeds	142	5.00	1 cup
Cornmeal, for sprinkling (optional)	as needed	as needed	as needed

1. Combine the very warm water and yeast in a large bowl and stir with a fork to dissolve the yeast. Let stand for about 3 minutes.

2. Whisk the all-purpose flour, pumpernickel flour, salt, and cocoa powder together in a medium bowl. Set aside.

3. Add the biga, rye salt sour, cool water, coffee, caramel color, honey, and molasses to the yeast mixture. Mix the ingredients with your fingers for 1 to 2 minutes, just long enough to break up the starters. The mixture should be cloudy, but not chunky. Add the flour mixture and stir with your fingers to incorporate the flour, scraping the sides of the bowl and folding the dough over itself until it gathers into a shaggy mass.

4. Move the dough to a lightly floured surface and knead it for 5 to 6 minutes, until it becomes supple and somewhat elastic. The dough will have a heavy, sticky consistency because of the pumpernickel flour in it, but it should not be hard to knead. If necessary, add additional cool water 1 tablespoon at a time until you have a soft but not mushy, pliable dough. Put the dough back into the mixing bowl, cover with oiled plastic, and let rest for 20 minutes to smooth out and develop elasticity.

5. If you are using raisins, soak them by placing them in a measuring cup with warm water to just below the surface of the raisins. Don't use too much water or you will wash away the flavor of the raisins.

6. Dump the dough onto a lightly floured surface, then flatten and stretch it slightly with your fingers to form a rectangle about an inch thick. Spread the sunflower seeds evenly over the rectangle, and if you are adding raisins, drain the raisins and spread them over the dough as well. Fold the dough like a business letter, with the top edge down and the bottom edge up, then knead and fold it gently until the seeds and/or raisins are well distributed, 2 to 3 minutes. Some of the seeds and raisins may pop out, but they can easily be incorporated again after the first rise, when the dough has softened.

7. Shape the dough into a loose ball and place it in a lightly oiled bowl, along with any loose sunflower seeds or raisins. Cover the bowl with oiled plastic wrap. Let the dough rise at room temperature (75° to 77°F) for 1½ to 2 hours, or until it looks puffy and has almost doubled in volume. When it's ready it will still feel heavy, but you will be able to see that it has risen enough.

8. Gently remove the dough from the bowl and place it on a lightly floured surface. Divide it into two equal pieces about 905 grams/32 ounces each without raisins, or 1030 grams/36 ounces with raisins. This dough is very malleable and the loaves are easy to shape. Shape each piece into a log (see page 34) and place each log seam side down in an oiled 9 X 5-inch loaf pan. Or, divide the dough into four equal pieces and form them into small oval loaves by shaping a bâtard (see page 35) and

Chewy Pumpernickel, top; Chewy Pumpernickel with Raisins and Sunflower Seeds, bottom tucking the ends under to make them more rounded. Cover the back of a sheet pan with parchment and sprinkle with cornmeal. Place the 4 loaves on the pan leaving 3 inches between them for rising, and make a thick line of flour down the length of each loaf. Cover the loaves with oiled plastic wrap and allow them to rise for about 1½ to 2 hours, until they have doubled in size (a finger pressed into the dough will leave an indentation).

9. Thirty minutes before baking, preheat the oven to 450°F. Prepare the oven by placing a cast-iron skillet and a smaller pan (a mini loaf pan) on the floor of the oven or on the lowest possible rack in an electric oven. Place an oven rack one or two rungs above the cast-iron pan, and if you have one, put a baking stone on the rack, making sure to allow space for the pan loaves to rise without touching the top of the oven. Fill a plastic water sprayer with water. Fill a teakettle with water to be boiled later, and have a metal 1-cup measure with a straight handle available near the kettle.

10. Five to 10 minutes before the loaves are ready to bake, turn the water on to boil, and carefully place two or three ice cubes in the small loaf pan in the bottom of the oven. This helps to create moisture in the oven prior to baking.

11. When the loaves have doubled, gently place the pans on the stone in the oven, then quickly mist the loaves with water 6 to 8 times; or score the smaller loaves with one cut running down the length of each loaf, then slide the paper with the loaves onto the baking stone, and mist with water 6 to 8 times. (If you're baking without a stone simply slide the bread pans onto the empty oven rack.) Carefully pour 1 cup of boiling water into the skillet, and immediately shut the oven door. After 1 minute, quickly mist the loaves with water again, then shut the oven door.

12. Bake for 20 minutes, then reduce the oven temperature to 375°F and bake for 15 to 20 minutes longer, until the loaves sound slightly hollow when removed from the pan and tapped on the bottom. (The small oval-shaped loaves will take a total of 30 to 35 minutes to bake.) The sides and bottoms of the loaves should feel firm and slightly crusty; if the tops are browned but the sides are still some-what soft, remove them from the pans and place the loaves directly on the stone to bake for 5 to 10 minutes longer. Transfer the loaves to a rack and allow to cool completely before slicing.

Caramel Color

Makes about ⅓ cup

INGREDIENTS	GRAMS	OUNCES	VOLUME
Sugar	57	2.00	4½ tablespoons
Cold water	21	0.75	1½ tablespoons
Cream of tartar	pinch	pinch	pinch
Boiling water	57	2.00	¼ cup

1. Combine the sugar and cold water in a small heavy saucepan and heat over medium-low heat, stirring with a wooden spoon until the sugar has almost dissolved. Increase the heat to medium-high and bring the syrup to a full boil. Use a pastry brush moistened with water to wash down any sugar crystals sticking to the sides of the pan.

2. Boil for about 2 minutes. Using a clean wooden spoon, stir in the cream of tartar. Continue boiling the syrup until it is almost black in color—for at least 3 to 5 minutes or more. It will begin to smoke because the sugar is actually burning, but don't be afraid to let it get really dark. If you don't cook it dark enough at this stage, your bread will not be as dark as you like, and it won't develop that deep, slightly bitter flavor that is characteristic of pumpernickel.

3. Take the pan from the heat and allow it to cool slightly, about 2 to 3 minutes. Gradually add the boiling water, stirring to dissolve the caramel. Be very careful, because the syrup will bubble up and splatter. Let cool completely, then store it at room temperature in an airtight container such as a glass jar. It will last indefinitely.

TIPS AND TECHNIQUES

We used unbleached all-purpose flour with a protein content of 11.7% for this bread.

It is not easy to find pumpernickel flour in most supermarkets, but it is available by mail order from King Arthur Flour (see page 270). It's essentially whole rye flour with the germ and bran intact. If you are unable to find it, you can substitute rye flour and add a little extra bran to get the coarser texture found in pumpernickel flour. Use 280 grams/10 ounces/2¼ cups minus 2 tablespoons of rye flour and add ¼ cup/ 17 grams/0.5 ounces of bran as a substitute—the bran most likely being wheat bran.

In the bakery we add caraway to our pumpernickel bread. If you like that flavor, add 1 tablespoon caraway seeds to the dough as you begin to mix it together.

Onion and Parmesan Bread with Caraway

MADE WITH BIGA STARTER

Makes two 9 × 5-inch loaves

Equipment: two 9 × 5-inch loaf pans, oiled

This wonderful savory bread has a dense but light-textured crumb and a rich cheese flavor that can only be achieved if you use a high-quality imported Parmesan. Mild prepackaged cheese will produce disappointing results. The onions in the dough release their juices while the bread is baking, adding moisture as well as flavor. This bread may not even last long enough to make sandwiches out of it, but if it does, try a "fresh green salad" filling: Moisten mixed baby lettuces (mesclun) with your favorite vinaigrette and pile between two pieces of toasted Parmesan bread along with some slices of ripe tomato, salt, and a grind of fresh pepper. It's a delicious way to eat your greens. This bread lasts for several days wrapped in plastic and tastes great toasted. With toasting each slice gets a crisp, tender surface, and the full flavor of the cheese comes through.

INGREDIENTS	GRAMS	OUNCES	VOLUME
Very warm water (105° to 115°F)	57	2.00	¼ cup
Active dry yeast	1½ teaspoons	1½ teaspoons	1½ teaspoons
Unbleached bread flour	450	15.90	3 cups
Rye flour	282	10.00	2¼ cups
Imported Parmesan cheese, grated	177	6.25	1½ cups
Caraway seeds	12	0.40	1 tablespoon
Kosher salt	18	0.64	2 tablespoons
Biga (page 56)	510	18.00	2¼ cups
Cool water (75° to 78 °F)	510	18.00	2¼ cups
Onion, cut into ¼-inch dice	170	6.00	1½ cups

1. Place the very warm water and yeast in a medium bowl and stir with a fork to dissolve the yeast. Allow to stand for about 3 minutes.

2. Whisk the bread flour, rye flour, Parmesan, caraway seeds, and salt together in a medium bowl. Set aside.

3. Add the biga and cool water to the yeast mixture and mix with your fingers for 2 minutes, breaking up the starter. The mixture should look milky and slightly foamy.

4. Add the flour mixture and stir with your fingers to incorporate the flour,

scraping the sides of the bowl and folding the dough over itself until it gathers into a shaggy mass.

5. Move the dough to a lightly floured surface and knead it for 7 to 10 minutes, until it becomes supple and elastic. The dough will feel somewhat sticky because it contains rye flour; it should be moist but not mushy. If it feels too stiff to knead, add cool water 1 tablespoon at a time until you have a soft, pliable dough. Put the dough back into the mixing bowl, cover with oiled plastic wrap, and let rest for 20 minutes to smooth out and develop elasticity.

6. Lightly flour the work surface. Flatten the dough and stretch it gently with your fingers to form a rectangle about an inch thick. Spread the diced onions evenly over the rectangle and press them in. Fold the top edge of the rectangle down and the bottom edge up like a business letter, then knead and fold it gently until the onions are well distributed, 2 to 3 minutes. If the dough resists, let it rest for 5 minutes and then continue kneading it again. Some of the onions may pop out of the dough, but they can easily be incorporated again after the first rise, when the dough has softened.

7. Shape the dough into a loose ball and place it in a lightly oiled bowl, along with any loose onions. Cover the bowl with oiled plastic wrap. Let the dough rise at room temperature (75° to 77°F) until it has doubled in volume, about 1¼ to 2 hours. When the dough is fully risen, an indentation made by poking your finger deep into the dough should not spring back.

8. When the dough has doubled, loosen it from the bowl with lightly floured hands and gently pour it onto a floured work surface. Press any loose onions into the dough, and divide it into two equal pieces about 1050 grams/37 ounces each. Shape each piece into a log (see page 34), and place each one seam side down in a prepared pan. Cover them with oiled plastic wrap and allow to rise for about 1 to 1½ hours, or until they have doubled in size (a finger pressed into the dough will leave an indentation).

9. Thirty minutes before baking, preheat the oven to 450°F. Prepare the oven by placing a cast-iron skillet and a smaller pan (a mini loaf pan) on the floor of the oven or on the lowest possible rack in an electric oven. Place an oven rack one or two rungs above the cast-iron pan, and if you have one, put a baking stone on the rack, making sure to allow space for the loaves to rise without touching the top of the oven. Fill a plastic water sprayer with water. Fill a teakettle with water to be boiled later, and have a metal 1-cup measure with a straight handle available near the kettle.

10. Five to 10 minutes before the loaves are ready to bake, turn the water on to boil, and carefully place two or three ice cubes in the small loaf pan in the bottom of the oven. This helps to create moisture in the oven prior to baking.

11. When the loaves have doubled, mist the surface with water, then gently place the pans on the stone in the oven. (If you're baking without a stone simply slide the bread pans onto the empty oven rack.) Pour 1 cup of boiling water into the skillet and immediately shut the oven door. After 1 minute, quickly mist the loaves with water again, then shut the oven door.

12. Bake for 20 minutes, then reduce the oven temperature to 375°F and bake for 16 to 20 minutes longer, until the loaves sound slightly hollow when removed from the pan and tapped on the bottom. Transfer the loaves to a rack to cool, and allow to cool completely before slicing. This bread stays moist for two to three days and tastes good sliced and toasted when it begins to get dry.

TIPS AND TECHNIQUES

We used unbleached bread flour with a protein content of 12.7% in this dough. The biga was made with unbleached all-purpose flour with a protein content of 11.75%.

FULL-FLAVORED BREADS

When we first opened the bakery we offered several kinds of bread beyond plain white or whole wheat. Breads like Rosemary, Black Olive, and Potato Onion Dill developed a large following and were especially popular with our wholesale customers. We hoped they would order a basic bread like our Country Sourdough because it was more economical to make. But they had enough plain bread, and said our specialty breads set us apart. Being purists we did not want to be known only for breads with things "mixed in," however this became our niche. The difference between ours and the specialty breads made by some other bakeries was that we used restraint and a chef's palate to make our breads sophisticated without being too busy. We usually add one or two full-flavored components to enhance the dough, but making a bread with a moist crumb, a chewy texture, and a great crust are just as important as what has been mixed in.

Fresh Rosemary Bread with Olive Oil

MADE WITH POOLISH

Makes two 20-ounce round loaves

Equipment: Baking stone and wooden peel, or one 17 × 12-inch sheet pan

Fresh rosemary is a pungent and sturdy herb that is well suited for bread making. Some herbs turn black and lose their potency when chopped and heated, but rosemary stays green and flavorful throughout the baking process. We make lots of rosemary bread at the bakery and are still surprised by its versatility. We love it toasted for breakfast and served with orange marmalade. It is also delicious toasted and rubbed with fresh garlic, then drizzled with a little more extra virgin olive oil. The beauty of this bread is that it tastes great with a fresh green salad, or a pasta dish, or in a chicken sandwich, but it's also wonderful eaten by itself.

This dough can be made directly, but we think it has a moister, chewier crumb and a deeper flavor if you let the dough rest in the refrigerator overnight.

INGREDIENTS	GRAMS	OUNCES	VOLUME
Very warm water (105° to 115°F)	57	2.00	¼ cup
Active dry yeast	1 teaspoon	1 teaspoon	1 teaspoon
Poolish (page 54)	397	14.00	2 cups
Cool water (75° to 78°F)	227	8.00	1 cup
Extra virgin olive oil	43	1.50	3 tablespoons
Fresh rosemary leaves, chopped	16	0.55	¼ cup
Unbleached all-purpose flour	435	15.30	3 cups
Organic whole wheat flour	80	2.80	½ cup
Kosher salt	16	0.56	1 tablespoon plus 2 teaspoons
Cornmeal, for sprinkling	as needed	as needed	as needed
Extra virgin olive oil, for brushing (optional)	as needed	as needed	as needed

1. Combine the very warm water and yeast in a large bowl and stir with a fork to dissolve the yeast. Let stand for 3 minutes.

2. Add the poolish, cool water, olive oil, and rosemary to the yeast mixture and mix with your fingers for about 2 minutes, breaking up the sponge. The mixture should look milky.

3. Add the all-purpose flour, whole wheat flour, and salt and mix with your fingers to incorporate the flour, scraping the sides of the bowl and folding the dough over itself until it gathers into a mass. When sticky strands of dough begin to cling to your fingers, gather the dough into a ball and move it to a lightly floured surface. If the dough feels too firm, add cool water 1 tablespoon at a time until the dough is very soft and moist.

4. Knead the dough for about 7 minutes, until it becomes smooth and supple. Put the dough back into the mixing bowl, cover with oiled plastic wrap, and let rest for 20 minutes to smooth out and develop elasticity.

5. Return the dough to the lightly floured surface and knead it for 2 to 3 minutes. The dough will already feel stretchy, but will become smoother and develop strength with kneading. Do not knead extra flour into the dough. It should be soft and loose.

6. Place the dough in a lightly oiled bowl. Cover the dough with oiled plastic wrap and allow it to rise at room temperature (75° to 78°F) for 1 hour. After one hour, turn the dough while it is still in the mixing bowl. Gently deflate the dough in the middle of the bowl with your fingertips, then fold the left side over the middle, and the right side over the middle. Fold the dough in half, gently pat it down, and then turn it over so the seam is underneath. Cover the dough tightly with plastic wrap or a large plastic bag, and place it in the refrigerator to chill for at least 8 hours or preferably overnight.

7. Take the dough from the refrigerator and let it warm up until it begins to rise again, 1½ to 2 hours.

8. Cover a peel or the back of a sheet pan with parchment paper, then sprinkle with cornmeal. Place the dough on a well-floured surface and divide it into two equal pieces about 625 grams/22 ounces each; the dough may be quite sticky. Shape each piece into a boule (see page 37). Don't work the dough too long or make the ball too tight, or the skin will tear; you want surface tension, but you also want to leave some of the medium air holes in the dough. Flour the seam of each boule and place the loaves seam side down on the peel or pan, leaving 3 to 4 inches between them for rising. These loaves are moist and will spread. Cover with oiled plastic wrap and let rise for 1¼ to 1¾ hours, until doubled in bulk.

9. Thirty minutes before baking, preheat the oven to 450°F. Prepare the oven by placing a cast-iron skillet and a smaller pan (a mini loaf pan) on the floor of the oven or on the lowest possible rack in an electric oven. Place an oven rack two rungs above the cast-iron pan, and if you have one, put a baking stone on the rack. Fill a plastic water sprayer with water. Fill a teakettle with water to be boiled later, and have a metal 1-cup measure with a straight handle available near the kettle.

10. Five to 10 minutes before the loaves are ready to bake, turn the water on to boil, and carefully place two or three ice cubes in the small loaf pan in the bottom of the oven. This helps to create moisture in the oven prior to baking.

11. Mist the tops of the loaves with water, then using a lame or a razor blade, cut a shallow tic-tac-toe pattern on the top of each loaf (see page 258), being careful not to tear the dough or score it too deeply. Gently slide the loaves from the parchment onto the baking stone. (If you're baking without a stone simply slide the sheet pan with the scored and misted loaves onto the empty oven rack.) Pour 1 cup of boiling water into the cast-iron pan and immediately shut the oven door. After about 1 minute, quickly mist the loaves 6 to 8 times, then shut the oven door.

12. Bake for 20 minutes, then reduce the oven temperature to 400°F and bake for 10 to 15 minutes longer, until the loaves are light golden brown and sound hollow when tapped on the bottom. If you would like a rich, aromatic crust, brush the loaves with olive oil just as they are removed from the oven. Place them on a rack to cool, and enjoy them while they're still slightly warm and crusty.

TIPS AND TECHNIQUES

We used unbleached all-purpose flour with a protein content of 11.7% for this dough. Unbleached all-purpose flour with a protein content of 11.7% was also used in the poolish. Organic or conventional whole wheat flour can be used.

We have given instructions for retarding this dough overnight. This process gives it a wetter crumb, bigger holes, and a fuller flavor. If you don't have time to wait, you can make the loaf using a direct process. Instead of chilling the dough in step 6, let it rise again for 1 to 1½ hours, until it doubles in volume. Then proceed with dividing and shaping the loaves in step 8.

Rustic Black Olive with Sweet Red Pepper

MADE WITH POOLISH STARTER

Makes three 13-ounce oval loaves

Equipment: baking stone and wooden peel; one or two 17 x 12-inch sheet pans

On a trip to Italy many years ago, Amy and her sister, Sally, spent some time in Venice. Since they were on a limited budget, they made their meals of small tastes from the local food shops. One day, as they were buying provisions for a picnic, they passed a bakery window where they saw a chewy-looking white bread that was studded with olives and stripes of bright red peppers. The loaf was tall and dense and it looked so tempting they bought a wedge. After hiking along twisting alleyways, they came to some docks on the far edge of town where they spread their feast: Yes, the cheeses were tasty, the salami appealing, and the wine pleasant, but the bread! It was the best thing they had ever tasted. The crust was hard and crunchy, the inside chewy and moist. The olives were robust and, in true Italian style, came complete with their pits. But the best part of the loaf was the sweet, tender strips of fresh red pepper. The soft bread around each strip was filled with sweet juices that perfectly balanced the salty olives. That loaf lives on in our memory, and this version is a close approximation. Buon appetito!

INGREDIENTS	GRAMS	OUNCES	VOLUME
Very warm water (105° to 115°F)	57	2.00	¼ cup
Active dry yeast	¾ teaspoon	¾ teaspoon	¾ teaspoon
Poolish (page 54)	340	12.00	1¾ cups
Cool water (75° to 78°F)	227	8.00	1 cup
Unbleached all-purpose flour	472	16.65	3¼ cups
Kosher salt	12	0.42	1 tablespoon plus 1 teaspoon
Large red bell pepper	212	7.50	1 pepper
Imported black olives (see Tips and Techniques)	170	6.00	1 cup
Cornmeal, for sprinkling	as needed	as needed	as needed

1. Combine the very warm water and yeast in a large bowl and stir with a fork to dissolve the yeast. Let stand for 3 minutes.

2. Add the poolish and cool water to the yeast mixture and mix with your

fingers for 2 minutes, breaking up the sponge. The mixture should look milky and slightly foamy.

3. Add the flour and salt and mix with your fingers to incorporate the flour, scraping the sides of the bowl and folding the dough over itself until it gathers into a mass. The dough will be sticky, with long strands hanging from your fingers.

4. Move the dough to a lightly floured surface and knead for about 7 minutes, until the dough becomes smooth, supple, and elastic, using as little additional flour as possible. The dough should feel slightly firm. Put the dough back into the mixing bowl, cover with oiled plastic wrap, and let rest for 20 minutes to smooth out and develop elasticity.

5. Meanwhile, drain the black olives well on paper towels. Pit them (crush them gently with your hand to loosen the pits) and chop them very roughly, leaving some whole olives. Cut the red pepper in half lengthwise, then in quarters, and remove the core and seeds. Place the pepper quarters skin side down and, using a serrated knife, cut crosswise into very thin strips. It is important to cut the strips as thin as possible, or they will steam inside the bread, leaving open air pockets.

6. Spread the olives and red pepper on top of the dough in the mixing bowl, fold the dough over the ingredients, and begin to knead the dough gently in the bowl until the olives and peppers are mostly incorporated, about 2 minutes. Lift the dough with one hand, oil the bowl, and place the dough back in the bowl. Cover with oiled plastic wrap and allow it to rise at room temperature (75° to 78°F) for 1 hour.

7. After 1 hour, turn the dough while it is still in the mixing bowl. Gently deflate the dough in the middle of the bowl with your fingertips, then fold the left side over the middle, and the right side over the middle. Fold the dough in half, gently pat it down, and then turn it over so the seam is underneath. Let it rise again for 1 to 1½ hours, until it doubles in volume. When the dough is fully risen, an indentation made by poking your finger deep into the dough should not spring back.

8. Gently dump the dough onto a well-floured surface and spread it into a rectangle, then fold it in thirds, as if you were folding a business letter, making sure the peppers and olives are evenly distributed. The dough will be very sticky. Divide it into three equal pieces, about 454 grams/16 ounces each. Place each piece on a lightly floured surface, gently press out the large air bubbles, and form it into an oval, like shaping a bâtard (see page 35), but don't make the ends of the loaf too tapered. Generously sprinkle a peel or the back of a baking sheet with cornmeal and line another sheet pan with parchment paper. (These loaves spread, so you will need to place two on the peel and one on a separate pan. If you're working without a peel, use two parchment-lined pans). Dust the seams of the loaves with flour

and place the loaves seam side down on the prepared surface. Spread a small layer of flour on top of the loaves (this will give them a rustic appearance), cover with oiled plastic wrap, and allow to rise for 1¼ to 1¾ hours, or until almost doubled in bulk.

9. Thirty minutes before baking, preheat the oven to 450°F. Prepare the oven by placing a cast-iron skillet and a smaller pan (a mini loaf pan) on the floor of the oven or on the lowest possible rack in an electric oven. Place an oven rack one rung above the cast-iron pan, and place another rack two rungs above that. If you have one, put a baking stone on the top rack. Fill a plastic water sprayer with water. Fill a teakettle with water to be boiled later, and have a metal 1-cup measure with a straight handle available near the kettle.

10. Five to 10 minutes before the loaves are ready to bake, turn the water on to boil, and carefully place two or three ice cubes in the small loaf pan in the bottom of the oven. This helps to create moisture in the oven prior to baking.

11. Use a lame or razor to score a long but shallow line from end to end on top of each loaf, then open the oven door and gently slide two loaves onto the stone and place the third loaf on the sheet pan on the rack below. (If you're baking without a stone simply slide the sheet pan with the two scored loaves onto the other empty oven rack.) Quickly mist the loaves with water 6 to 8 times trying not to spray directly on the floured area, pour 1 cup of boiling water into the skillet, and immediately shut the oven door. After 1 minute, quickly mist the loaves with water again, then shut the oven door.

12. Bake for 15 minutes, then rotate the loaves from one shelf to the other and reduce the oven temperature to 400°F. Bake for 12 to 18 minutes longer, until the loaves sound slightly hollow when tapped on the bottom. Transfer the bread to a rack to cool for at least 45 minutes before serving. (This bread is rather sticky if cut too soon.) These loaves are still very nice the second day.

TIPS AND TECHNIQUES

We used unbleached all-purpose flour with a protein content of 11.7% for this dough. Unbleached all-purpose flour with a protein content of 11.7% was also used in the poolish.

We use fleshy black olives such as Kalamatas or other large full-flavored black olives. If you can buy them pitted, all the better!

Wands of Walnut Scallion Bread

Makes three 12-ounce loaves

Equipment: one 17 × 12-inch sheet pan

This is delicious bread that is loved by everyone who tastes it. We used to make it at the bakery as an occasional special, but it became too labor intensive to make big batches because we had to clean and slice so many scallions. When we do make Walnut Scallion, it is gone in a moment. Making a small batch at home is much easier, and this recipe comes out great in a home oven. It is one bread that we recommend most highly to our serious home baker friends. Try it warm from the oven on its own, or with a soft, rich cheese. We like it as an appetizer with thinly sliced prosciutto and wedges of ripe cantaloupe. Between the crunch of the walnuts with their toasty, nutty flavor and the mild taste of scallion, we know you'll fall in love with this bread, too.

INGREDIENTS	GRAMS	OUNCES	VOLUME
Very warm water (105° to 115°F)	57	2.00	¼ cup
Active dry yeast	½ teaspoon	½ teaspoon	½ teaspoon
Biga (page 56)	227	8.00	I cup
Cool water (75° to 78°F)	200	7.00	¾ cup plus 2 tablespoons
Walnut oil	25	0.90	I tablespoon plus 1½ teaspoons
Honey	20	0.70	I tablespoon
Unbleached bread flour	369	13.00	2½ cups plus I tablespoon
Kosher salt	9	0.30	I tablespoon
Walnut halves and pieces, toasted (see "Toasting Nuts," page 111)	170	6.00	1½ cups
Scallions, thinly sliced, just the green part	75	2.65	¾ cup (2 small bunches)

1. Combine the very warm water and yeast in a large bowl and stir with a fork to dissolve the yeast. Let stand for 3 minutes.

2. Add the biga, cool water, walnut oil, and honey to the yeast mixture and mix with your fingers for 2 minutes, breaking up the biga. The mixture should look milky and slightly foamy.

3. Add the flour and salt and mix with your fingers to incorporate the flour, scraping the sides of the bowl and folding the dough over itself until it gathers into a mass. The dough will be wet and sticky, with long strands hanging from your fingers.

4. Move the dough to a very lightly floured surface and knead for 5 to 6 minutes, until it becomes supple and elastic, using as little additional flour as possible. If the dough feels too stiff, knead in cool water, 1 tablespoon at a time. This dough should be very sticky and wet. Sprinkle a little flour on the work surface and pat the dough gently into a rectangle. Allow the dough to rest, covered with a towel, for 15 minutes to relax and develop elasticity.

5. Stretch the dough into a larger rectangle. Spread the walnuts and scallions evenly over the dough and gently press them into it. Fold the dough in thirds, as if you were folding a business letter. Roll up the dough and gently knead for 1 to 2 more minutes to incorporate the nuts and scallions. Some may pop out of the dough, but they can easily be incorporated after the dough has rested.

6. Shape the dough into a loose ball and place in a lightly oiled bowl, along with any loose nuts or scallions. Cover the bowl with oiled plastic wrap and let the dough rise at room temperature (75° to 77°F) for about 1 hour, until it looks slightly puffy but has not doubled.

7. After one hour, turn the dough while it is still in the mixing bowl. Gently deflate the dough in the middle of the bowl with your fingertips, then fold the left side over the middle, and the right side over the middle. Fold the dough in half, gently pat it down, and then turn it over so the seam is underneath. Let it rise again for 1½ to 2 hours, until it doubles in volume. When the dough is fully risen, an indentation made by poking your finger deep into the dough should not spring back.

8. While the dough is rising, prepare a proofing pan for the loaves by lining a 17 X 12-inch sheet pan with parchment, and sprinkle it with a moderate amount of flour.

9. Gently dump the dough onto a lightly floured surface, pressing in any loose nuts or scallions. Divide the dough into three equal pieces, about 360 grams/12.6 ounces each. Gently flatten each piece of dough into a rectangle and shape it into a rough-looking cylinder or wand about the length of a baking sheet, as if you were shaping a baguette (see page 36). These loaves look nice when left a bit irregular in shape.

10. Place the loaves side by side on the prepared sheet pan, leaving at least 3 inches between them. Sprinkle the loaves with a little flour to give them a rustic appearance,

then cover with oiled plastic wrap and allow to rise for 1 to 1½ hours, until doubled in bulk. These loaves get flat if allowed to rise too long, so watch them closely, and bake them before they begin to spread out.

11. Thirty minutes before baking, preheat the oven to 425°F. Prepare the oven by placing a cast-iron skillet and a smaller pan (a mini loaf pan) on the floor of the oven or on the lowest possible rack in an electric oven. Place an oven rack two rungs above the cast-iron pan, and if you have one, put a baking stone on the rack. Fill a plastic water sprayer with water. Fill a teakettle with water to be boiled later, and have a metal 1-cup measure with a straight handle available near the kettle.

12. Five to 10 minutes before the loaves are ready to bake, turn the water on to boil, and carefully place two or three ice cubes in the small loaf pan in the bottom of the oven. This helps to create moisture in the oven prior to baking.

13. Mist the loaves with water, then open the oven and place the pan of bread inside. Pour 1 cup of boiling water into the skillet, and immediately shut the oven door. After 1 minute, quickly mist the loaves with water again, then shut the oven door.

14. Bake for 15 minutes, then reduce the oven temperature to 375°F and bake for 18 to 23 minutes longer, until the loaves are a glossy purple brown and sound slightly hollow when tapped on the bottom. After the first 20 minutes, you may need to flip the loaves over so they brown evenly on the top and bottom. Transfer the bread to a rack to cool slightly before serving. This bread tastes delicious when it's still warm from the oven. It freezes well too, wrapped tightly in aluminum foil and then in a heavy-duty freezer bag.

TIPS AND TECHNIQUES

We used unbleached all-purpose flour with a protein content of 11.7% for this dough. Unbleached all-purpose flour with a protein content of 11.7% was also used for the biga.

You can substitute olive or vegetable oil for the walnut oil, but your bread won't have quite such a deep, nutty flavor.

Picholine Olive Bread

MADE WITH POOLISH

Makes two 1-pound bâtard-shaped loaves

Equipment: electric stand mixer with dough hook; baking stone and wooden peel;
one 17 × 12-inch sheet pan; baker's linen or heavy smooth cotton towel

This bread is a big favorite among the Amy's Bread staff. We love it when there are loaves left in the retail store at the end of the day so we can take them home to enjoy. Amy created this bread when the chef from a well-known upscale Manhattan restaurant asked her to make an olive bread using picholine olives. Amy of course loved the challenge (not to mention the new wholesale business!) and this bread was the result. With a thin crunchy crust, a moist and tender open-textured crumb, and big savory chunks of salty green olives, it seemed like the perfect partner for a juicy roast beef sandwich (page 229.) When it's not being used for sandwiches, we scatter a little coarse sea salt on the top of the loaves just before they're loaded into the oven.

INGREDIENTS	GRAMS	OUNCES	VOLUME
Picholine olives, cut in half and pitted	150	5.30	1¼ cups
Very warm water (105° to 115°F)	57	2.00	¼ cup
Active dry yeast	1¼ teaspoons	1¼ teaspoons	1¼ teaspoons
Unbleached bread flour	445	15.70	3 cups
Poolish (page 54)	266	9.38	1 cup
Very cool water (65° to 70°F)	210	7.40	⅞ cup
Kosher salt	12	0.42	1 tablespoon plus 1 teaspoon
Coarse cornmeal or polenta, for sprinkling	as needed	as needed	as needed
Coarse sea salt, for topping loaves (optional)	as needed	as needed	as needed

1. In a colander or a strainer, rinse the olives with cool water to remove any excess brine. Set them aside to drain.

2. Combine the very warm water and yeast in a measuring cup and stir to dissolve the yeast. Let stand for 3 minutes.

3. In the bowl of an electric stand mixer fitted with a dough hook, combine the yeast mixture, flour, poolish, cool water, and kosher salt and mix on low speed for

1 minute. Scrape down the sides of the bowl, increase the speed to medium-low and continue mixing for 3 minutes, until all the flour is moistened and gathers into a loose mass of dough. Slide the dough down from the top of the hook (to be sure all of the dough will be evenly kneaded), increase the speed to medium and knead the dough for 3 to 4 more minutes, until the dough begins to slap the sides of the bowl and is beginning to pull up from the bottom of the bowl but does not clean the bottom of the bowl. The dough should be about 90 percent developed at this point. It should have strength and elasticity but it will be soft and a little sticky and you will not be able to pull a transparent sheet without having it tear at the end. Let the dough rest in the bowl for 15 minutes.

4. Add the olives, pressing them down into the dough, tucking some of them around the sides and under the dough. Mix on low speed for 1 minute to begin incorporating the olives. The dough will start to look shredded. Slide the dough down from the neck of the hook and increase the speed to medium for 2 minutes. Slide the dough down from the hook again, increase the speed to medium-high and continue kneading the dough for 4 to 5 minutes, until the dough slaps the side and cleans the bottom of the bowl. Remove the dough from the bowl and finish kneading it by hand on a very lightly floured surface for two or three turns, just to be sure the olives are evenly distributed. The dough should be very supple and elastic, covering the olives smoothly without shredding. If some of the olives pop out, just tuck them back into the bottom of the dough. The temperature of the dough should be around 79°F.

5. Put the dough in an oiled bowl that is large enough to allow it to almost double, cover it with oiled plastic wrap, and allow it to rise for 50 minutes. It should feel very puffy but it will not have doubled.

6. Gently fold the dough in from the sides to the middle to deflate it, turn it over so the smoother bottom side is up, cover it and let it rise again for 30 minutes. The dough will almost double during this second rest. Let it rest again for 20 minutes to relax before you begin the shaping process.

7. Pour the dough out onto a lightly floured work surface and divide it into two equal pieces, about 550 grams/19.4 ounces each. With lightly floured hands, pre-shape each piece by gently patting it into a rectangle. Exact dimensions are not important; just don't stretch it too thin. You want to maintain the network of gas bubbles that have developed in the dough. Position the rectangle so the short sides are at the top and the bottom of the rectangle. If the dough sticks to the work surface, lift it gently with a dough scraper and lightly flour the surface. Also keep your hands lightly floured so the dough doesn't stick to them and tear. Starting with the upper edge of the dough, gently fold the top third down and the bottom third up, like a business letter, so you have three equal layers. Gently but firmly seal the seam at the top edge, give the dough a quarter turn so the short side is at the top again and repeat the folding process. Seal the seam again and roll the dough over so the seam is on the bottom. Repeat with the second piece of dough. Cover the pieces with oiled plastic wrap and let them rest until they're starting to rise and feel puffy. This could take 20 to 30 minutes or more depending on the temperature of the dough and whether the pre-shaping was tight or loose.

8. While the dough rests, prepare a proofing pan for the loaves by lining a 17 X 12-inch sheet pan with baker's linen so it overlaps the sides, and sprinkle it with a moderate amount of flour; or a heavy smooth cotton towel sprinkled generously with flour; or just line the pan with parchment and sprinkle it with a moderate amount of flour.

9. Use a dough scraper to lift one of the pieces of dough and gently flip it over onto the lightly floured work surface. With lightly floured hands, pat the dough gently into a rectangle that is almost square, with the long edge facing you. (Don't be too heavy-handed with the patting; you want to preserve some of the gas bubbles in the dough so you'll have a nice airy crumb in your finished loaf). Shape each piece into a bâtard (see page 35). The bâtards should be about 11 inches long. Place one loaf lengthwise on the prepared pan touching against the edge of the pan (be sure the edge of the pan is covered by part of the floured cloth). Pull up a 3-inch pleat of cloth to separate the two loaves and place the second loaf on the pan next to the first loaf. Pull up another pleat of cloth on the outside of the second loaf to support it while it rises. If you're using a parchment-lined pan, place the loaves about 2 inches in from the sides and leave 3 to 4 inches between the two loaves. Cover the loaves with oiled plastic wrap and let them rise until they have almost doubled. They should look large and plump and hold a slight indentation when pressed lightly with your finger. This could take 1 hour or more depending on the temperature of the dough and how tightly the bâtard is shaped. Baking them when they're slightly underproofed guarantees more oven spring, which contributes to a more open, airy crumb in the finished loaf.

10. Thirty minutes before baking, preheat the oven to 450°F. Prepare the oven by placing a cast-iron skillet and a smaller pan (a mini loaf pan) on the floor of the oven or on the lowest possible rack in an electric oven. Place an oven rack two rungs above the cast-iron pan, and if you have one, put a baking stone on the rack. Fill a plastic water sprayer with water. Fill a teakettle with water to be boiled later, and have a metal 1-cup measure with a straight handle available near the kettle.

11. Five to 10 minutes before the loaves are ready to bake, turn the water on to boil, and carefully place two or three ice cubes in the small loaf pan in the bottom of the oven. This helps to create moisture in the oven prior to baking.

12. At the same time, 5 to 10 minutes before the loaves are ready to bake, sprinkle the wooden peel with coarse cornmeal or polenta and gently lift each loaf from the proofing pan onto the peel. (If using a sheet pan, leave the loaves on the pan used for proofing.) The easiest way to do this is to put one hand under each end of the loaf and gently scoot them in toward the center so the middle will be supported during the move. Try not to stretch the loaves, and leave enough space between them to allow for spreading in the oven. Cover them again with the oiled plastic wrap.

13. When the loaves are ready, mist the top of each loaf with water, sprinkle them lightly with coarse sea salt, if desired, and use a lame or a sharp razor blade to score the loaves by making one long cut down the center of each bâtard. The cut should run from one end of the loaf to the other leaving 1 to 2 inches unscored at each end. Use the plastic water sprayer to mist the loaves lightly with water. Open the oven and slide the bâtards onto the baking stone, being mindful not to stretch them too much. (If you're baking without a stone simply slide the sheet pan with the scored and misted loaves onto the empty oven rack.) Quickly pour the boiling water into the skillet and immediately close the oven door. After 3 minutes, pour in another ½ cup of boiling water.

14. Check the loaves after 20 minutes and rotate them if necessary to insure even browning. Bake them for a total of 40 to 45 minutes, until they are uniformly golden brown in color and sound hollow when tapped on the bottom. Cool them completely on a wire rack before cutting them.

TIPS AND TECHNIQUES

We used unbleached bread flour with a protein content of 12.7% for this dough. Unbleached all-purpose flour with a protein content of 11.7% was used in the poolish.

We like to halve the olives with our fingers rather than cutting them with a knife, but either way works fine and also ensures that you'll find any stray pits before they end up in the bread. You can also leave the olives whole if you prefer.

Potato Onion Dill Bread

....

MADE WITHOUT A STARTER

Makes two 1-pound boules

Equipment: wooden peel and baking stone, or one 17 x 12-inch sheet pan

We have been making this popular bread at the bakery since we opened, but the recipe did not appear in the first version of our cookbook *Amy's Bread*. Now we have decided to include it, but the dough is a little tricky to make. It contains potato flakes, which make it sticky and starchy. As you are kneading, the dough almost seems to break down. Then roasted diced potatoes and onions are added, and they make the dough even slipperier. Once you bring the dough together, the gluten in the wheat flour takes over and helps to create a stretchy and elastic dough. Just don't give up during the mixing process because the bread you make will be worth it. It's delicious with almost any meal, from breakfast with bacon and eggs, to dinner of roasted meat and vegetables. It also goes nicely with a vegetarian meal. It is very moist, full flavored, and satisfying, and it has a long shelf life. It toasts beautifully and makes a terrific grilled ham and Swiss—one of the signature sandwiches in our bakery café!

INGREDIENTS	GRAMS	OUNCES	VOLUME
Very warm water (105° to 115°F)	57	2.00	¼ cup
Active dry yeast	1 teaspoon	1 teaspoon	1 teaspoon
Unbleached bread flour	450	15.90	3 cups
Potato flakes	40	1.41	½ cup plus 2 tablespoons
Kosher salt	12	0.42	1 tablespoon plus 1 teaspoon
Dill seed	1 teaspoon	1 teaspoon	1 teaspoon
Ground black pepper	½ teaspoon	½ teaspoon	½ teaspoon
Cool water (75° to 78°F)	369	13.00	1½ cup plus 2 tablespoons
Medium red potato, cooked, diced (see Tips and Techniques)	100	3.53	⅔ cup
Small onion, cut into small dice	70	2.47	½ cup
Cornmeal, for sprinkling	as needed	as needed	as needed

1. Combine the very warm water and yeast in a measuring cup and stir with a fork to dissolve the yeast. Let stand for 3 minutes.

2. Mix the flour, potato flakes, salt, dill, and pepper together in a large mixing bowl. Add the yeast mixture and cool water, then mix the ingredients with your fingers to form a sticky mass, 1 to 2 minutes.

3. Gather the dough into a ball and move it to a lightly floured surface. If the dough feels too firm, add cool water 1 tablespoon at a time, until the dough is soft and moist.

4. Knead the dough for 6 to 7 minutes, until it becomes smooth and elastic. Put the dough back into the mixing bowl, cover with oiled plastic wrap, and let rest for 20 minutes to smooth out and develop elasticity.

5. With the dough still in the mixing bowl, flatten it out, spread the diced potatoes and onions on top of the dough, and press them into the surface. Fold the dough in from the sides of the bowl towards the middle, and knead the dough in the bowl for 1 minute to incorporate the chunky ingredients. Return the dough to the lightly floured surface and knead for 1 more minute. Some of the onions and potatoes will pop out of the dough, but they will stay in it after it rises. Do not knead extra flour into the dough. It should be soft and loose.

6. Place the dough in a lightly oiled bowl, and turn it to coat it with oil. Cover the bowl with oiled plastic wrap and allow the dough to rise at room temperature (75° to 78°F) for 1½ to 2 hours, until it doubles in volume. When the dough is fully risen, it will feel very soft and sticky, and an indentation made by poking your finger into the dough will not spring back.

7. Cut a piece of parchment paper to cover the top of a wooden peel, or line a sheet pan with parchment, then sprinkle the paper generously with cornmeal. Place the dough on a well-floured surface, and with floured hands divide it into two equal pieces, about 515 grams/18.2 ounces each; the dough will be quite sticky. Shape each piece into a boule (see page 37.) Don't work the dough too long or make the ball too tight, or the skin will tear; you want surface tension, but this dough is very delicate and cannot tolerate being overworked. If the loaves are too sticky to handle, lift them with a dough cutter, flour the bottom of each boule, and place the loaves seam side down on the peel or pan, leaving 3 to 4 inches between them for rising. These loaves are moist and will spread. Cover with oiled plastic wrap and let rise for 45 minutes to 1 hour, until nearly doubled in volume. It is better to bake these loaves slightly underproofed, or they will spread and flatten out in the oven.

8. Thirty minutes before baking, preheat the oven to 450°F. Prepare the oven by placing a cast-iron skillet and a smaller pan (a mini loaf pan) on the floor of the oven or on the lowest possible rack in an electric oven. Place an oven rack two rungs above the cast-iron pan, and if you have one, put a baking stone on the rack. Fill a plastic water sprayer with water. Fill a teakettle with water to be boiled later, and have a metal 1-cup measure with a straight handle available near the kettle.

9. Five to 10 minutes before the loaves are ready to bake, turn the water on to boil, and carefully place two or three ice cubes in the small loaf pan in the bottom of the oven. This helps to create moisture in the oven prior to baking.

10. Mist the tops of the loaves with water, then using a lame or a razor blade, cut a shallow *T* that stretches to the edges of the loaf (see page 40), being careful not to tear the dough or score it too deeply. Slide the loaves on the parchment paper onto the baking stone. (If you're baking without a stone simply slide the sheet pan with the scored and misted loaves onto the empty oven rack.) Pour 1 cup of boiling water into the water pan and immediately shut the oven door. After about 1 minute, quickly mist the loaves 6 to 8 times, then shut the oven door.

11. Bake for 20 minutes, then reduce the oven temperature to 375°F and bake for 14 to 18 minutes longer, until the loaves are golden brown and sound hollow when tapped on the bottom. If you have the option of convection in your oven, turn on the convection fan for the last 5 minutes of baking to help crisp and brown the crust. Place the loaves on a rack to cool, and allow them to cool completely before cutting, or the crumb will be sticky and starchy. These loaves age well and are actually better to eat the day after they were baked.

TIPS AND TECHNIQUES

We used unbleached bread flour with a protein content of 12.7% for this dough.

To prepare the potato, cut it in quarters leaving the skin on, and place it in a small pot with enough water to almost cover it. Salt the water, bring to a simmer, and cook until the potato is still slightly firm. Drain, let cool, then cut into ¼-inch dice.

Orlando Roman

Starting a small business is an adventure filled with unknown outcomes. You may be able to imagine your product line, how your business will look, and who your customers will be. Beyond that you are never quite sure how long your business will be open, although you hope for a long-running success. When it comes to employees, they are the most difficult to predict. It's hard to guess who will stay, who will go, and which ones will influence the business in their own unique way. When Amy first opened the bakery, she had no idea how it would evolve or who would be working with her over the many years ahead. In the early days she always needed extra employees to fill in on the busiest days of the week. When people

with baking experience applied for part-time jobs, she would happily have them work on weekends to cover holes in the schedule. In fact, back then things were so relaxed that applying for a part-time job meant writing your name and phone number on a piece of paper and trying out shaping bread for an hour or two. When good ones came along, they would pick up a day here and there, and over time might eventually join the full-time staff.

When Orlando Roman showed up, he was an architecture student in his early twenties, who wanted to earn extra money while attending college. He had grown up in the Dominican Republic, and had worked as a bread baker there. He offered to work a few days per week, but he had lots of commitments, juggling school, marriage, family, work, and living in New York. Although we didn't know how often we would see him, we appreciated his skills on the days he was there. Over the years he continued to work at the bakery and began to go to school less and work more, until one day he decided he wanted to be a professional bread baker. That was our lucky day! Ever since then Orlando has worked his way through the bakery, shaping dough, supervising the shaping team, making baguettes, making organic breads, and finally working as a full-time mixer. Now he is our Mix Manager, responsible for training and supervising all the mixers and mix assistants. Making the dough is the first and most crucial step in the bread-making process. Orlando pays attention to all the details, including the condition of the starters and the current shipment of flour and how it's working in the formulas, and he teaches the other mixers how to make gorgeous, supple, silky dough every day. When his coworkers are not performing up to his standards, he is not shy about saying something. But when the team is working smoothly and professionally, he couldn't be happier or prouder.

Alfredo Vicuna turned up a year before Orlando, and arrived in much the same way. A twenty-something man of Mexican descent, he was working full-time at another bakery, but wanted to pick up extra work on his days off. After a brief tryout, he was hired and was immediately a huge asset to our weekend team. He had excellent training at Ecce Panis, and was very professional and conscientious. Alfredo always shaped the bread, and had a good sense of humor about the repetitive nature of the work. He liked making consistent loaves, made them quickly, and took pleasure in the process. Eventually it became too much for him to work two jobs, so he left for a brief time. But when Ecce Panis moved to New Jersey, he called Amy for a full-time job. She welcomed him with open arms and was very pleased to have him back in the Amy's Bread kitchen. He picked up where he left off shaping bread, and today is our Head Shaping Supervisor. Of course he is still interested in making sure that the loaves are well shaped, but that is usually the least of his worries. His job is to count every piece of bread that is shaped by the eight-person shaping team to be sure we have what was ordered by our wholesale customers—totaling thousands of pieces each day. Since we have trouble saying "no" to any customer, this count includes a few pieces of seeded-this and seeded-that, scored and unscored twists, stencil boules, random ficelles from every kind of dough, and hundreds of dozens of rolls. He knows how many of each kind of roll goes on a pan, some being spaced 7 X 9, or 6 X 9, or 4 X 6, and which kinds get covered with oiled plastic wrap or a rack cover. He monitors whether each shaped loaf is placed on a pan, a cloth, a board, or a basket, and where it rises after it has been shaped. He takes the heat if bread is ugly, misshapen, or missing for some reason. If something is wrong with a loaf of bread and you ask Alfredo what happened, he will know exactly what went on with the dough, even if it was a few days before. "That dough was very wet, and they turned off the ventilation system in the oven room so it got too hot, and we had to put it in the walk-in because the oven was full." He has great insight into what systems work best for each kind of dough, and his knowledge is critical to the success of our bread-making process. Even after a difficult day, you will still see him smile, chuckle, and make a little joke about how they got through the day.

Orlando, Alfredo, and Amy are no longer twenty- or thirty-something but are now forty-something and have known each other and worked together for a very long time. The ideas and the efforts of Orlando and Alfredo, along with those of many other long-time employees, are woven into the very fabric of the bakery. What the bakery is today—our products, our spirit, and our workplace—are all due to the commitment and energy of the wonderful people who are part of the Amy's Bread family.

Alfredo Vicuna

GOLDEN SEMOLINA BREADS

When Amy's Bread opened in 1992, we had two semolina breads on our menu. Both breads, made from durum wheat, have a beautiful golden crumb, a chewy, dense texture, and a wonderful flavor. One was Semolina with Black Sesame Seeds, made daily, and the other was Semolina with Golden Raisins and Fennel. The latter was a bread that Amy had perfected working at Mondrian. We felt it was rather unusual and something that people would not order very often, so we planned to make it only on weekends. Our customers had another idea. They loved it and wanted it every day! Soon we complied and added it to our daily menu. Over the years it became our signature bread—the bread the bakery is best known for around New York City.

Here we have shared recipes for three semolina breads that you can make at home. Although it is very easy to mix up a batch of any of these breads in your home kitchen, you may find it quite difficult to find the right flour to make them. Semolina bread is made from patent durum flour. If you buy a product labeled semolina, that is durum wheat which is ground too coarsely for bread making. It will make heavy, dense loaves that are unappealing. You need patent durum flour that is creamy yellow in color, and soft and silky in feel. It can be ordered from several mail-order companies (see page 270) or purchased from a local bakery, but you won't find it in your local supermarket. Don't let that discourage you. These breads have a lovely, moist crumb and a really nice flavor that comes from using this mild flour in your dough.

Golden Italian Semolina Loaves

MADE WITHOUT A STARTER

Makes two 15-ounce loaves

Equipment: wooden peel and baking stone, or 17 x 12-inch sheet pan

Italian bread" has its own definition in New York City. When we first opened the bakery, people often came in and asked for Italian bread. We would say, "Our Semolina Black Sesame Bread is inspired by an Italian recipe, and we have this beautiful focaccia today." "*No*, I want Italian bread," they would insist. Eventually we realized that the bread they wanted was a pointed white loaf with a soft, plain crumb and a medium-thick, golden crust. It had become a staple of local bakeries because of the large number of Italian immigrants in New York who grew up on this bread. It can still be found in every area supermarket in a red, white, and green paper bag. We find that version of Italian bread cottony and uninteresting. Having traveled in Italy, we know that Italians make hundreds of kinds of breads based on centuries-old baking traditions. For us, these robust, sophisticated, and delicious semolina breads are real Italian bread. Our semolina version of the New York loaf is moist, chewy, and delightfully different from the supermarket variety.

INGREDIENTS	GRAMS	OUNCES	VOLUME
Very warm water (105° to 115°F)	57	2.00	¼ cup
Active dry yeast	2 teaspoons	2 teaspoons	2 teaspoons
Patent durum flour	520	18.35	4 cups
Kosher salt	1 tablespoon	1 tablespoon	1 tablespoon
Cool water (75° to 78°F)	368	13.00	1½ cups plus 2 tablespoons
Sesame seeds, for topping (optional)	28	1.00	3 tablespoons
Cornmeal, for sprinkling	as needed	as needed	as needed

1. Mix the very warm water and yeast together in a small bowl and stir with a fork to dissolve the yeast. Let the mixture stand for 3 minutes.

2. Mix the flour and salt together in a large mixing bowl. Add the yeast mixture and the cool water and, using your fingers, mix the dough into a shaggy mass.

3. Move the dough to a lightly floured work surface and knead for 4 minutes. If the dough feels stiff or dry, gradually knead in more cool water 1 tablespoon at a time. The dough should feel stretchy, and very smooth and supple.

4. Put the dough back into the mixing bowl, cover with oiled plastic wrap, and let rest for 20 minutes to smooth out and develop elasticity.

5. Very lightly flour the work surface and knead the dough for 5 to 7 minutes. At first the dough will be sticky, then it will become stretchy and supple. Don't be tempted to add extra flour; the dough will become soft and smooth without it.

TIPS AND TECHNIQUES

For information about buying patent durum flour, see page 269.

6. Place the dough in a lightly oiled bowl, covered with oiled plastic wrap, and allow it to rise at room temperature (75° to 78°F) for 1 to 1½ hours, until it has doubled in volume.

7. Lift the dough onto a very lightly floured surface and divide it into two equal pieces, about 460 grams/16.25 ounces each. Shape each piece into a bâtard (see page 35). If desired, mist or lightly brush the loaves with water and spread the sesame seeds on top.

8. Line a peel or cover the back of a sheet pan with parchment paper, then sprinkle with cornmeal. Place the loaves on the peel or pan, cover with oiled plastic wrap, and let rise at room temperature for 45 minutes to 1 hour, until they have almost doubled. These loaves should be baked slightly underproofed; if they are rising too quickly, place them in the refrigerator for 20 to 30 minutes to slow the rise.

9. A few minutes after shaping the loaves, preheat the oven to 425°F. Prepare the oven by placing a cast-iron skillet and a smaller pan (a mini loaf pan) on the floor of the oven or on the lowest possible rack in an electric oven. Place an oven rack two rungs above the cast-iron pan, and if you have one, put a baking stone on the rack. Fill a plastic spray bottle with water. Fill a teakettle with water to be boiled later, and have a metal 1-cup measure with a straight handle available near the kettle.

10. Five to 10 minutes before the loaves are ready to bake, turn the water on to boil, and carefully place two or three ice cubes in the small loaf pan in the bottom of the oven. This helps to create moisture in the oven prior to baking.

11. Use a lame or a sharp razor blade to score each loaf gently three times, with cuts running from tip to tip, holding the blade at a 30-degree angle (cutting at this angle will result in a ridge on the edge of each cut as the loaves bake) being careful not to cut too deep. Mist the loaves with water, then gently slide the loaves onto the baking stone. (If you're baking without a stone simply slide the sheet pan with the scored and misted loaves onto the empty oven rack.) Pour 1 cup of boiling water into the skillet, and immediately shut the oven door. After 1 minute, quickly mist the loaves with water again, then shut the oven door.

12. Bake for 15 minutes, then reduce the oven temperature to 400°F and bake for about 25 minutes longer, until the loaves are a golden yellow-brown and sound hollow when they are tapped on the bottom. Place the loaves on a wire rack to cool. Serve with extra virgin olive oil for dipping.

Semolina Rounds with Black Sesame Seeds

Makes two 20-ounce loaves

Equipment: baking stone and wooden peel, or 17 x 12-inch sheet pan

We make this beautiful golden loaf every day at the bakery. We shape the loaves into a distinctive S shape, but we also like this pretty spiraled round shape. The yellow bread is studded with black sesame seeds, which provide an interesting textural contrast and a delicious nutty flavor. We use it to make the very popular tuna sandwich we sell in our three retail cafés. Of all our breads, this one is the favorite of several of our employees. It goes well with so many foods, and it is so easy to mix up a batch that you will want to make it again and again.

INGREDIENTS	GRAMS	OUNCES	VOLUME
Very warm water (105° to 115°F)	57	2.00	¼ cup
Active dry yeast	1 teaspoon	1 teaspoon	1 teaspoon
Cool water (75°F)	354	12.50	1½ cups plus 1 tablespoon
Biga (page 56)	283	10.00	1¼ cups
Patent durum flour	520	18.35	4 cups
Medium yellow cornmeal	57	2.00	⅓ cup
Black sesame seeds	37	1.30	¼ cup
Kosher salt	12	0.42	1 tablespoon plus 1 teaspoon
Extra cornmeal, for sprinkling	as needed	as needed	as needed

1. Combine the very warm water and yeast in a medium bowl and stir with a fork to dissolve the yeast. Let the mixture stand for 3 minutes.

2. Add the cool water and biga to the yeast mixture and mix with your fingers for about 2 minutes, breaking up the starter. The mixture should look milky and slightly foamy.

3. Whisk the flour, cornmeal, 2 tablespoons of the sesame seeds, and the salt together in a large bowl. Pour the yeast mixture on top and mix with your fingers until the dough forms a sticky mass.

4. Move the dough to a lightly floured surface and knead for 5 to 7 minutes, until smooth and elastic, using as little additional flour as possible. The dough should feel soft and supple. If it feels stiff or dry, add cool water 1 tablespoon at a time.

5. Put the dough back into the mixing bowl, cover with oiled plastic wrap, and let rest for 20 minutes to smooth out and develop elasticity.

6. Return the dough to the lightly floured surface and knead it for 2 to 3 minutes. The dough will already feel stretchy, but will become smoother with kneading. Do not knead extra flour into the dough. It should be soft.

7. Place the dough in a lightly oiled bowl. Cover the dough with oiled plastic wrap and allow it to rise at room temperature (75° to 78°F) for 1 to 1½ hours, until nearly double in volume.

8. Divide the dough into two equal pieces, about 638 grams/22.5 ounces each. On a lightly floured surface, gently flatten one piece of dough into a rectangle, then shape it into a cylinder by rolling it up tightly from left to right, as if you were shaping a baguette (see page 36). Seal the seam well. Place both hands over the center of the cylinder and roll it back and forth from the center out to the ends to elongate it until you have a rope about 32 inches long. Roll the rope lightly in flour and shape it into a coil, following the instructions on page 254. Repeat with the second piece of dough.

9. Line a peel or cover the back of a baking sheet with parchment paper and generously sprinkle it with cornmeal. (If your baking stone is small, you may need both a peel and a pan for rising because these loaves are so large.) Place the loaves seam side down on the peel and/or baking sheet; if they are placed side by side, leave 3 to 4 inches between them for rising. With a plant mister, spray a stream of water into the groove of each coil, not over the surface of the whole loaf. Using the remaining 2 tablespoons of sesame seeds, hold them in your hand and pour the seeds in a stream into the groove of each coil. The neater your seeds, the nicer the loaves will look. Cover the loaves with oiled plastic wrap and allow them to rise for 45 minutes to 1½ hours, until almost doubled in bulk but still slightly underproofed. (If you must bake the loaves in two batches, refrigerate one loaf after the first 30 minutes of rising to stop the rising process, then let the loaf finish rising at room temperature while the other one bakes.)

10. Thirty minutes before baking, preheat the oven to 425°F. Prepare the oven by placing a cast-iron skillet and a smaller pan (a mini loaf pan) on the floor of the oven or on the lowest possible rack in an electric oven. Place an oven rack two rungs above the cast-iron pan, and if you have one, put a baking stone on the rack. Fill a plastic spray bottle with water. Fill a teakettle with water to be boiled later, and have a metal 1-cup measure with a straight handle available near the kettle.

11. Five to 10 minutes before the loaves are ready to bake, turn the water on to boil, and carefully place two or three ice cubes in the small loaf pan in the bottom of the oven. This helps to create moisture in the oven prior to baking.

12. Mist the loaves with water, then open the oven and gently slide them onto the baking stone with the parchment paper underneath. (If you're baking without a stone simply slide the sheet pan with the misted loaves onto the empty oven rack.) Pour 1 cup of boiling water into the skillet and immediately shut the oven door. After 1 minute, quickly mist the loaves 6 to 8 times, then quickly shut the oven door.

13. Bake for 20 minutes, then reduce the oven temperature to 375°F and bake for 15 to 20 minutes longer, until the loaves are golden yellow and sound slightly hollow when tapped on the bottom. Transfer the bread to a rack to cool completely before slicing. (If necessary, let the baking stone reheat for 5 minutes, then bake the second loaf).

TIPS AND TECHNIQUES

Unbleached all-purpose flour with a protein content of 11.7% was used in the biga.

For information about patent durum flour see "Tips for Working with Durum Flour," below; and about medium cornmeal, see the Tips and Techniques for Semolina Bread with Apricots and Sage on page 200.

Japanese black sesame seeds are available at natural food stores and Asian markets. If you can't find them, you can always use regular sesame seeds for the same flavor but a slightly different look.

TIPS FOR WORKING WITH DURUM FLOUR

Dough made with durum wheat flour ferments and rises very quickly. The dough can become sticky if it gets too warm and rises too fast. In our previous book we suggested retarding these doughs before baking, and we still believe the retarding method enhances the quality of our semolina breads. If you want to slow down the rising process and would like to have a moister crumb in your finished bread, we suggest the following technique for retarding the dough: After the dough has risen for one hour, give it a turn and fold in the bowl. Then move it into a large oiled plastic bag with room to rise, or cover the mixing bowl with a large plastic bag, and place in your refrigerator. Allow the dough to chill for at least eight hours, or overnight. Take it out of the refrigerator, let it warm up and rise for one to two hours until it's puffy, and then proceed with the rest of the instructions for dividing, shaping, rising, and baking the bread.

Semolina Bread with Apricots and Sage

....

MADE WITH BIGA STARTER

Makes three 1-pound round loaves

Equipment: baking stone and wooden peel, one 17 x 12-inch sheet pan

This lovely golden bread is both sweet and savory. Apricots sweeten the loaves and chopped fresh sage adds an earthy, grassy flavor. It is very similar to our Semolina with Golden Raisins and Fennel in shape, color, and texture. We form and cut the bread into a sunflower—a special shape we make for all the holidays. It also makes a unique gift because it looks so pretty. We like to serve this Semolina with Apricots and Sage with fish or poultry, and we've even diced it to add to Thanksgiving turkey stuffing. With its crunchy cornmeal crust and dense, almost cakelike interior, this bread is sure to please.

INGREDIENTS	GRAMS	OUNCES	VOLUME
Dried apricots, diced	227	8.00	1½ cups
Very warm water (105° to 115°F)	57	2.00	¼ cup
Active dry yeast	1 teaspoon	1 teaspoon	1 teaspoon
Cool water (75°F)	355	12.50	1½ cups plus 1 tablespoon
Biga (page 56)	284	10.00	1¼ cups
Patent durum flour	520	18.35	4 cups
Medium yellow cornmeal	170	6.00	1 cup
Kosher salt	16	0.56	1 tablespoon plus 2 teaspoons
Fresh sage leaves, chopped	7	0.25	3 tablespoons
Extra cornmeal, for sprinkling	as needed	as needed	as needed

1. Place the apricots in a large measuring cup, and add warm water to come just below the top of the fruit. Set aside to soak.

2. Combine the very warm water and yeast in a medium bowl and stir with a fork to dissolve the yeast. Let the mixture stand for 3 minutes.

3. Add the cool water and biga to the yeast mixture and mix with your fingers for about 2 minutes, breaking up the starter. The mixture should look milky and slightly foamy.

4. Whisk the flour, ½ cup of the cornmeal, and the salt together in a large bowl. Pour in the yeast mixture and mix with your fingers until the dough forms a sticky mass. If the dough feels too stiff, add cool water 1 tablespoon at a time.

5. Move the dough to a very lightly floured surface and knead for 5 to 8 minutes, until it is smooth, elastic, supple, and somewhat resilient. The dough will still be somewhat firm. Put the dough back into the mixing bowl, cover with oiled plastic wrap, and let rest for 20 minutes to smooth out and develop elasticity.

6. Drain the apricots. Spread out the dough in the mixing bowl and evenly sprinkle on the chopped sage and diced apricots. Press them into the dough, then pull the dough from the edges of the bowl and fold it in toward the middle. Knead the dough in the bowl until the fruit and sage are incorporated, 1 to 2 minutes.

7. Gather the dough into a loose ball, lift it up and oil the bowl, then place it back in the bowl, along with any loose apricots. Turn the dough to coat with oil, cover the bowl with oiled plastic wrap, and let it rise at room temperature (75° to 77°F) for 1 hour.

8. After 1 hour, turn the dough while it is still in the mixing bowl. Gently deflate the dough in the middle of the bowl with your fingertips, then fold the left side over the middle, and the right side over the middle. Fold the dough in half, gently pat it down, and then turn it over so the seam is underneath. Let it rise again for 40 minutes to 1 hour, until it doubles in volume. When the dough is fully risen, an indentation made by poking your finger deep into the dough should not spring back.

9. Divide the dough into three equal pieces, about 510 grams/18 ounces each. Shape each piece into a boule (see page 37).

10. Place the remaining ½ cup cornmeal in a bowl. Using a plant mister, spray each loaf generously, then roll the loaves in the cornmeal, coating them completely. Place the loaves on the work surface and press down gently to flatten them into disks about 8 inches in diameter.

11. Line a peel and cover a baking sheet with parchment paper and sprinkle with cornmeal. Place one disk on the peel and the others on the baking sheet, leaving at least 4 inches between each loaf. If you don't have a baking stone, place one loaf on one baking sheet, and two on the other to rise. Let the loaves rise for 45 minutes to 1 hour.

12. Thirty minutes before baking, preheat the oven to 425°F. Prepare the oven by placing a cast-iron skillet and a smaller pan (a mini loaf pan) on the floor of the oven or on the lowest possible rack in an electric oven. Place an oven rack two rungs above the cast-iron pan, and if you have one, put a baking stone on the rack. Place another oven rack on the rung just below the stone. Fill a plastic spray bottle with water. Fill a teakettle with water to be boiled later, and have a metal 1-cup measure with a straight handle available near the kettle.

Golden Italian Semolina Loaves and Semolina Bread with Apricots and Sage

13. Five to 10 minutes before the loaves are ready to bake, turn the water on to boil, and carefully place two or three ice cubes in the small loaf pan in the bottom of the oven. This helps to create moisture in the oven prior to baking.

14. Place an inverted mug or glass with a 3- to 4-inch opening in the center of one disk. Press it gently into the dough, and use a dough cutter to cut the dough into 4 wedges, starting at the edge of the glass. Cut those wedges in half, then in half again, so you have 16 segments. Give each cut segment a quarter-turn so a cut side is facing upward. If the dough feels too sticky, don't twist the segments—just leave them flat and separate each one slightly from the one next to it. Remove the glass, leaving an uncut area in the center of the loaf. Repeat the procedure with the other 2 disks. Let the loaves rest for 10 minutes before baking.

15. Make sure the parchment is not sticking to the peel, open the oven door, and gently slide the bread onto the stone. Place the pan of bread on the rack below. Or if using two baking sheets, place one on the upper rack and one on the rack below that. Quickly mist the loaves with water 6 to 8 times, pour 1 cup of boiling water into the skillet, and immediately shut the oven door. After 1 minute, quickly mist the loaves with water again, then shut the oven door.

16. Bake for 10 minutes, then reduce the oven temperature to 375°F and bake for 15 to 18 minutes longer, until the loaves are a golden yellow-brown and sound hollow when tapped on the bottom. The crust should be firm but not too dark; watch the bread carefully—it will brown quickly during the last few minutes of baking. Place the loaves on wire racks and cool completely before serving.

TIPS AND TECHNIQUES

Unbleached all-purpose flour with a protein content of 11.7% was used in the biga.

For information on patent durum flour, see page 196.

We recommend using medium cornmeal for this dough. Fine cornmeal does not produce a contrasting texture, and coarse cornmeal is too rough and makes the bottom crust very tough. Bob's Red Mill produces medium cornmeal and corn grits (polenta). Both work well for this dough.

BAKERY FAVORITES: PIZZA AND FOCACCIA

Pizza and focaccia are beloved snack foods at Amy's Bread and around the world. Although most people think that what's on top of the pizza or focaccia is the focal point, at the bakery we put just as much effort into developing the recipes for pizza crust and focaccia dough as we put into creating our signature breads. If you start out with an incredible base, you can create a masterpiece by putting even the simplest fresh ingredients on top. Both of these recipes are easy to make and turn out beautifully in a home oven.

A Versatile Pizza Crust with Simple Toppings

MADE WITHOUT A STARTER

Makes four 9-inch round pizzas

Equipment: baking stone and wooden peel, or two 17 x 12-inch sheet pans if making rectangular pizzas

I n Manhattan, pizza is practically a way of life. You can't walk two blocks without seeing at least one "famous" quick-service establishment where you can run in (we're always running in Manhattan) and buy fresh, hot pizza by the slice. Long-time New Yorkers experience culture shock when they find themselves in a town where the only way they can get a slice of pizza is to purchase an entire pie! In recent years, pizza making has been embraced by well-known chefs and bakers like Mario Batali, Nancy Silverton, and Jim Lahey, joining long-time pizza pros like Chris Bianco. They have opened pizza restaurants where small pizzas with amazing crusts and simple, fresh toppings are all the rage. This trend toward well-crafted pizzas is one we are happy to indulge. In fact, our pizza recipe can help you to create this kind of pizza at home. The only equipment you need is a hot oven and a pizza stone. The rest is up to your technique and your own personal taste.

Making pizza in your own kitchen can be fun and rewarding from start to finish. Amy began making pizza at home with her son when he was two and a half. At that time she wanted to find a very simple and forgiving bread dough that was easy to knead and required a very short rise, so that even a young child could help. This pizza dough was just that. After the kneading and rising, it takes only a few minutes to stretch the crust, add toppings, and then bake your beautiful creation. In the world of baking, that's almost immediate gratification. All you need is good-quality bread dough for the crust, a selection of vegetables and/or meat, some freshly grated cheese, and some herbs for extra flavor. Tomato sauce is a good option, but we also like to use sliced or diced ripe fresh tomatoes when they're in season, or make pizza without tomatoes.

The secret to great pizza is to use fresh ingredients and to use them sparingly. Keep it simple and try to keep it small. While the idea of creating a big, beautiful sixteen-inch pizza is appealing, the reality is often a culinary disaster if you're inexperienced or lack all the necessary professional equipment. We've found the easiest size to work with in a home kitchen is a disk no larger than ten inches in diameter or a 17 x 12-inch rectangle to fit a baking sheet. A baking stone is mandatory if you want to achieve that satisfying crackly crust.

If you are baking with children, let them take turns mixing and kneading the dough, then once it has risen for at least forty-five minutes, they can help stretch the rounds of dough, spread them with tomato sauce, and top them with their favorite toppings and cheese. You can slide the pizza onto the baking stone for them, and within fifteen minutes, their freshly baked masterpiece will be out of the oven and ready to eat.

INGREDIENTS	GRAMS	OUNCES	VOLUME
Very warm water (105° to 115°F)	312	11.00	1¼ cups plus 2 tablespoons
Active dry yeast	1¼ teaspoons	1¼ teaspoons	1¼ teaspoons
Unbleached all-purpose flour	435	15.35	3 cups
Olive oil	28	1.00	2 tablespoons
Kosher salt	2½ teaspoons	2½ teaspoons	2½ teaspoons
Medium cornmeal, for peel	57	2.00	¼ cup
Olive oil, for brushing	as needed	as needed	as needed
Tomato sauce	340	12.00	1½ cups
Fresh mozzarella cheese, grated	454	16.00	5 cups
Parmesan cheese, grated	123	4.30	1 cup
Toppings of your choice (see below)	to taste	to taste	to taste

1. For the dough: Combine the very warm water and yeast in a large bowl and stir to dissolve the yeast. Add the flour, olive oil, and salt and mix with your fingers to bring the wet and dry ingredients together.

2. When the dough becomes a shaggy mass, move it to a very lightly floured surface and knead until it becomes smooth and somewhat elastic, 5 to 7 minutes. This dough should not be too dry, or it will be difficult to stretch when you're shaping the pizza, so don't knead in any extra flour. If necessary, add warm water 1 tablespoon at a time until you have a soft, pliable dough.

3. Gently shape the dough into a loose ball. Put it in a lightly oiled bowl, turn to coat with oil, and cover it with oiled plastic wrap. Let it rise at room temperature (75° to 77°F) until it has doubled in volume, 45 minutes to 1 hour.

4. About 30 minutes before baking, preheat the oven to 450°F and place a baking stone on the top rack in the oven.

5. When the dough has doubled, loosen it from the bowl with lightly floured hands and gently pour it onto a floured work surface. Divide it into four equal pieces, about 180 grams/6.35 ounces each if making round pies, or two equal pieces of about 360 grams/12.7 ounces, if making large rectangular pizzas. Shape each piece into a tight ball, dip them in flour, place them on the work surface, and cover with plastic wrap to rest for 10 minutes. (This allows the dough to relax so it's easier to shape.)

6. To make round pies: Place a dough ball on a lightly floured work surface and press down to flatten slightly. From the center, use your fingertips to gently press the dough out to a 9- or 10-inch circle of uniform thickness (about ¼ inch), leaving it slightly thicker around the edge. Do not tear the dough; you may have to lift the edges gently and shake the dough slightly to encourage the stretching. (You can also use a rolling pin; flour the table and the top of the dough lightly and lift and turn the disk frequently as you roll to be sure the dough doesn't stick.) If the dough resists stretching, let it rest again for 2 to 5 minutes—or until it will let you stretch it again. Keep letting the dough rest as necessary until you achieve the size you want.

Line a peel or the bottom of a baking sheet with parchment paper, then sprinkle with cornmeal. Gently move the dough onto the paper on the peel or sheet pan and stretch again. If you are making four pies, assemble and bake them in two batches; don't start shaping and topping the second batch until the first one is in the oven. You can bake one pizza on the baking stone and one on a pan, or just bake them one by one on the stone and eat them as they come out of the oven. Once they are on parchment paper, you can slide them where you need to until the peel or baking stone are ready to use.

To shape large rectangular pizzas: Line two 17 by 12 inch sheet pans with parchment paper, and oil the paper. Place a 360-gram/12.7-ounce piece of dough on each pan and oil the dough too. Starting at the middle of the dough piece, pat it gently with your fingertips, pushing and stretching it outward toward the edges of the pan. Do not stretch or force the dough until it tears. Just let it relax for a few minutes and go back to patting it with your fingertips until it stretches to the edges of the pan. The pressing and relaxing process may take about 10 minutes.

7. Lightly brush the edges of each round or rectangle of dough with olive oil. Place about 85 grams/3 ounces/6 tablespoons of the tomato sauce on the first 9-inch round crust and spread it evenly over the dough with the rounded bottom of a ladle or a spoon. Top evenly but sparingly with any additional ingredients such as sliced mushrooms, quickly cooked spinach or broccoli, cooked sausage or pepperoni, sliced or diced ham, imported pitted black olives, and fresh basil, then top each pizza with about 113 grams/4 ounces/1¼ cups of the grated fresh mozzarella and 28 grams/1 ounce/¼ cup of the grated Parmesan, sprinkling them evenly over the top of the pizza.

8. For the round pies: Slide the pizza with the parchment onto the baking stone. If only one disk fits on your stone,

---

MORE TOPPING SUGGESTIONS

At home we top our pizza with whatever ingredients are desired by those who will be enjoying it that day. We always make one plain pizza with tomato sauce and cheese for the people that like it simple. Then we use the following ingredients divided among the remaining three pizzas: 12 ounces of sliced fresh mushrooms; 12 ounces of diced ham or cooked sausage; 10 to 12 leaves of fresh basil, roughly chopped; a few pitted Kalamata olives; cooked spinach or broccoli; anything else that suits your taste. We usually start our pizzas with tomato sauce or fresh tomatoes, and finish them with grated fresh mozzarella and Parmesan. The only thing to remember is that these are small pizzas with a thin crust, so don't top them too heavily or the crust won't bake through and will become soggy.

bake the second pie on a parchment–lined pan on an oven rack below the baking stone, or bake each pizza one at a time on the stone. For the rectangular pizzas in the pan, place the pan in the oven once the pizzas have been topped.

9. Bake the 9-inch pizzas for 12 to 14 minutes and the 17 × 12-inch pizzas for 14 to 16 minutes, until the crust is crisp and golden and the cheese is completely melted and bubbly but not browned. Too much browning will make the cheese stringy and tough.

10. Use the peel or a flat baking sheet to remove each round pizza from the oven and slide it onto a cutting surface. Use a pizza wheel or a long chef's knife to cut each pie into four to six wedges, to eat immediately. Or let the pan pizzas cool on a rack for about 5 minutes. Use a sturdy metal spatula to loosen the crust of each pizza from the edges of the pan, then slide the pie out of the pan onto a cutting surface, parchment and all. Discard the parchment and use a pizza wheel or a long chef's knife to cut the pizza into eight to ten pieces. Serve immediately.

TIPS AND TECHNIQUES

We used unbleached all-purpose flour with a protein content of 11.7% for this dough.

At the bakery we make our own tomato sauce with fresh tomatoes, canned Italian San Marzano plum tomatoes, garlic, herbs, and spices. But when we make pizza at home, we like to simplify the process by purchasing high-quality premade sauce. One of our favorites is Eden Organic Pizza and Pasta sauce, sold in 15-ounce cans. It has a nice balance of tomato, herbs, and spices, is convenient to use, and is just enough to top four pies. We always buy our mozzarella in fresh 1-pound balls from a local dairy. Luckily, the Italian influence around New York City still makes that possible. Fresh mozzarella adds a creamy, rich note to the pizza without being too oily.

OUR TOPPINGS AT THE BAKERY

At Amy's Bread we feature a different pizza every day. We use our baguette dough to make the crust, press it out to ½-inch thickness, and when it's baked, serve it in large squares. These are some of the toppings we offer:

Monday: Roasted potatoes, roasted diced onions, and Swiss cheese (no tomatoes)
Tuesday: Chopped fresh tomato sauce, basil pesto, fresh mozzarella, and Parmesan
Wednesday: Chopped fresh tomato sauce with fresh basil, spinach, fresh mozzarella, and Parmesan
Thursday: Sliced plum tomatoes, Kalamata olives, goat cheese, and Parmesan
Friday: Chopped fresh tomato sauce with herbs and 4 cheeses: Swiss, Cheddar, provolone, and fresh mozzarella

Focaccia with Fresh Rosemary

MADE WITH BIGA STARTER

Makes one 17 × 12-inch rectangle

Equipment: one 17 × 12-inch sheet pan, lined with parchment paper and lightly oiled with olive oil

Our focaccia is the ideal bread to bake in your home oven. It doesn't require a stone hearth to give it a beautiful color or crust, and it's easy to spread the dough out onto the pan without doing any special shaping. In the early years after the bakery opened, focaccia was found in every bread basket and on every menu around New York. Just like other things that we see too much of, it fell out of favor for a few years because chefs became bored with it. But recently we have seen a resurgence of interest in this delicious and versatile flat bread. Chefs around the city are using it in bread baskets, as croutons with antipasto, and as wonderful sandwich bread.

Unlike our pizza dough, our focaccia includes a little milk to keep it tender and moist, and it is allowed a second rise to get a thicker, more breadlike texture. Just before baking, the dough is given the traditional "dimpling." The dimples, made by firmly pressing your fingertips into the dough, help flavor and moisten the bread by capturing some of the olive oil that is brushed over the surface; they also keep the dough from puffing up and forming a domed center as the focaccia bakes. Traditionally, only a single ingredient is used as a topping for focaccia, spread sparsely over the top or sprinkled in a decorative pattern. The bread is the focal point, the topping an accent.

Focaccia can be eaten like pizza as a meal, sliced in strips and served in a bread basket, or cut into squares, split it in half, and filled to make a sandwich. It can be served warm or at room temperature, but it is best eaten the same day it was baked.

INGREDIENTS	GRAMS	OUNCES	VOLUME
Warm water (85° to 90°F)	425	15.00	1¾ cups plus 2 tablespoons
Active dry yeast	½ teaspoon	½ teaspoon	½ teaspoon
Biga (page 56)	340	12.00	1½ cups
Unbleached bread flour	638	22.50	4½ cups
Milk	42	1.48	2 tablespoons plus 2 teaspoons
Extra virgin olive oil	36	1.27	2 tablespoons plus 2 teaspoons
Kosher salt	13	0.45	1 tablespoon plus 1¼ teaspoons

| Fresh rosemary, about 2½ branches, chopped | 10 | 0.35 | 2 tablespoons plus 1 teaspoon |
| Additional olive oil and kosher salt, for topping | as needed | as needed | as needed |

1. Place the warm water and yeast in a large bowl. Stir with a fork to dissolve the yeast and allow to stand for about 3 minutes. If you are working in a cool kitchen on a cool day, increase the water temperature to 105°F to give the dough a warmer start.

2. Add the biga to the yeast mixture and mix with your fingers for 1 to 2 minutes to break it up. The mixture should look milky and foamy. Add the flour and mix it in with your hands, lifting the wet mixture over the flour to incorporate it. When the dough becomes a shaggy mass, move to a very lightly floured surface and knead until it becomes smooth and somewhat elastic, about 5 minutes. Place the dough back into the mixing bowl, cover with oiled plastic, and let rest for 20 minutes to smooth out and develop elasticity.

3. After the rest period add the milk, oil, and salt to the dough in the mixing bowl and knead it in the bowl until it is all incorporated.

4. Move the dough to a lightly floured work surface and knead until it is very smooth, silky, and elastic, 7 to 10 minutes. The dough will be sticky, but don't use too much flour for kneading. The finished dough should be wet but supple and springy.

5. Put the dough in a lightly oiled bowl, turn it to coat with oil, and cover it tightly with oiled plastic wrap. Let the dough rise at room temperature (75° to 77°F) for 1 hour.

6. Turn the dough while it is still in the mixing bowl. Gently deflate the dough in the middle of the bowl with your fingertips, then fold the left side over the middle, and the right side over the middle. Fold the dough in half, gently pat it down, and then turn it over so the seam is underneath. Let it rise again for 1 to 1½ hours, until nearly doubled in volume.

7. When the dough has risen, loosen it from the bowl and gently pour it onto the center of the oiled baking sheet. Pat it gently with your fingertips to stretch it evenly out to the edges of the pan. Be careful not to tear the dough. If the dough resists stretching, let it rest for 2 to 5 minutes, until it becomes supple enough to stretch again, then continue to press it out to the edges of the pan. (If the dough is dry, you may have to repeat the resting/stretching procedure several times.) Brush the top of the dough lightly with olive oil, cover with lightly oiled plastic wrap, and let rise for 1 to 2 hours, until the dough has doubled and fills the pan (a finger pressed into the dough will leave an indentation).

8. Thirty minutes before baking, preheat the oven to 425°F and prepare the oven by placing a cast-iron skillet and a smaller pan (a mini loaf pan) on the floor of the oven or on the lowest possible rack in an electric oven. Place an oven rack two rungs above the cast-iron pan. Fill a plastic spray bottle with water. Fill a teakettle with water to be boiled later, and have a metal 1-cup measure with a straight handle available near the kettle.

9. Five to 10 minutes before the focaccia is ready to bake, turn the water on to boil, and carefully place two or three ice cubes in the small loaf pan in the bottom of the oven. This helps to create moisture in the oven prior to baking.

10. Brush and dot the surface of the dough gently with olive oil, dimple it in several spots with your fingertips to prevent air pockets from developing underneath, and sprinkle the surface lightly with kosher salt. Sprinkle with chopped rosemary all the way to the edges.

11. Quickly but carefully fill the metal 1-cup measure with boiling water, open the oven, and place the pan of focaccia on the oven rack, then using the plastic spray bottle, quickly mist it 6 to 8 times. Quickly but carefully pour the boiling water into the cast-iron skillet and immediately close the oven door.

12. Bake for 15 minutes, then reduce the oven temperature to 350°F and bake for 15 to 20 minutes longer, until golden brown and crusty but still very soft inside.

13. Remove the focaccia from the oven and immediately brush it lightly with olive oil. Cool in the pan 10 minutes, then carefully slide it onto a cooling rack. Remove the parchment (to prevent steam from softening the bottom crust) and let cool. Serve warm or at room temperature, cut into squares.

TIPS AND TECHNIQUES

We used unbleached bread flour with a protein content of 12.7% for this dough. The biga was made with unbleached all-purpose flour with a protein content of 11.7%.

SANDWICHES

The current marketplace abounds with prepared food and take-out options that provide immediate gratification. Today people expect to walk in the door of a bakery to pick up breakfast and coffee, a loaf of bread, a snack at any hour of the day, *and* a great selection of sandwiches as well. At Amy's Bread it's no different. Luckily we have a wide variety of terrific breads that make the perfect canvas for all of our sandwich creations. Ever since we expanded to Chelsea Market around our fourth anniversary, we have been able to prepare sandwiches for our customers every day.

When Amy started working in restaurant kitchens, her first job was cooking savory food. She has always loved pairing bread with different toppings to create interesting sandwiches. As she developed each of our sandwiches, she had a specific goal in mind. She wanted to offer some small sandwiches for a snack or light meal, some bigger and heartier sandwiches, some options for vegetarians, and some that were great toasted on our sandwich press. She is still inventing new sandwiches, and as she creates each one, she tests them many times and gives tastes to the kitchen and office staff until they all approve of the new combination. When the response is "Delicioso! Muy rico!" she knows she has a winner.

Every morning long before the sun rises, our sandwich makers—four dedicated women who put their passion into their work—begin to assemble our repertoire of nearly twenty different sandwiches. Each kind is made with a precise formula using carefully prepped ingredients. The daily production is usually over

450 sandwiches. Each one is wrapped meticulously in its own unique package that complements its shape and size. Some are rolled neatly in a small sheet of waxed butcher paper that shows off only the tip of the sandwich, and others are enveloped in a clear sheet of cellophane that lets all the abundant ingredients show through around the edges. All of the Sandwich Ladies—as they are fondly called—have worked at the bakery for at least five and up to eleven years, and they work together as a finely tuned team. They know how to season the sauces, how to slice the meats and cheeses accurately, and how to mix up a mean batch of tuna salad that keeps regular customers coming back for more. In fact, the tuna salad has become such a labor of love that it was hard to measure the ingredients precisely for the Tuna Melt in this chapter. One day it needs a little more lemon juice, and the next it might take another spoonful of mayo and three more grinds pepper. We hope that as you make our sandwiches, you use your taste and intuition to make them your own.

In this chapter we have given recipes for making many of the sandwiches we prepare every day for our retail cafés. Each one calls for a specific bread, and we've given the recipes for all the sandwich breads within this book, but if you want to simplify the process, you can buy a similar type of bread from your local bakery.

Tuna Melt

Makes 4 sandwiches

Tuna sandwiches can be found on nearly every sandwich menu in New York, if not the United States. They are a popular standby, and they're always satisfying when nothing else sounds appealing. We have such a large following for our tuna sandwiches and salads that they are now our #1 best seller. We use white albacore tuna and fresh crunchy celery, a little bit of fresh chives, some mayo, lemon, and Dijon mustard to make our tuna salad zesty and delicious. Here we have shared the recipe for our Tuna Melt, which is tuna salad topped with a slice of cheddar cheese and served on our soft sandwich roll. Almost any large, soft roll will do, but we recommend using our challah dough—the recipe can be found in *The Sweeter Side of Amy's Bread*—to make a great sandwich roll. We "melt" the sandwich for just a couple of minutes in our sandwich press. If you don't have a press at home, you can toast the sandwiches in a toaster oven or a nonstick pan on the stove for a minute or two. The main goal is to crisp the bread, to melt the cheese, and to warm the tuna just a little.

INGREDIENTS	GRAMS	OUNCES	VOLUME
Tuna, packed in water	340	12.00	two 6-ounce cans
Mayonnaise	113	4.00	½ cup
Celery, cut in small dice	62	2.20	heaping ½ cup
Chives, fresh, cut very fine	1 tablespoon	1 tablespoon	1 tablespoon
Dijon mustard	2 teaspoons	2 teaspoons	2 teaspoons
Lemon juice	1½ teaspoons	1½ teaspoons	1½ teaspoons
Freshly ground pepper	to taste	to taste	to taste
Soft sandwich rolls	4 rolls	4 rolls	4 rolls
Aged sharp cheddar cheese, sliced in 28-gram/1-ounce slices	113	4.00	4 slices

1. Drain the tuna well, but do not press it until it is bone dry. In a medium bowl combine the tuna, mayonnaise, celery, chives, mustard, lemon juice, and pepper and stir well. Do not overmix it or the tuna will break down too much.

2. Slice the sandwich rolls in half. Divide the tuna salad evenly into four portions, about 113 grams/4 ounces each, and place it on the bottom half of each roll. Top the tuna with a slice of cheddar cheese and cover with the top half of each roll.

Tuna Melt (*continued*)

3. Preheat a toaster oven, broiler, or sandwich press for a few minutes, then place the sandwiches inside to toast and melt for 2 to 3 minutes. Watch them very carefully so the tops of the rolls do not burn. The bread should be toasted, the cheese beginning to melt, and the tuna salad slightly warm when they are finished. Serve immediately.

THE POWER WORKOUT: WORKING IN A BREAD BAKERY

Every job in a bread bakery requires skill and strength. Imagine making 8,000 pounds of dough a day. The people who mix all the dough start the process by taking fifty-pound bags of flour, adding at least 65 to 75 percent more weight in the form of water, and mixing in other ingredients to form beautiful, supple dough. Besides possessing the skills required to measure accurately and the intuition to know if the amount of moisture and the degree of kneading are correct, the mixer has to hunch over a high bowl, cutting, lifting, pulling, scraping, and moving large amounts of living dough from one place to another. This is great for upper body development and forearm strength!

After the dough has risen, the pans and tubs each containing fifteen to twenty-five pounds of dough are lifted and dumped into a twenty-part dough divider or onto a table, to be cut and weighed into individual pieces to fulfill customers' orders. This is excellent for shoulder and biceps development: lift, dump, cut, round, move the board. With more than 1,000 repetitions a day, dividing dough is a fantastic toning exercise.

After the dough is portioned, it is shaped into loaves. If you are shaping, you must have very strong hands. After pressing, rounding, stretching, and rolling for seven to eight hours a day, the hands and forearms develop tremendous dexterity, tone, and definition. Look at all those hand, wrist, and forearm muscles you never noticed before! (Remember, through all of this you are supported by two legs that must stand, pivot, flex, and walk for those seven or eight hours. This work cannot be done from a sitting position.)

Now comes the total body workout: working at the deck oven. Here you must lift each and every loaf of the day's bread, along with the pans, boards, baskets, and cloths that the loaves are rising on, onto the loader, then move the loaves off the boards and baskets and into and out of the oven. You place the breads on a cloth-covered metal loader that is elevated up to the oven, pushed inside, and then retracted. After that you must lower the loader and push it back to its starting position. When the loaves are baked, they are pulled out eight at a time on a wooden peel, and placed on wire cooling racks to cool. Talk about hips, calves, biceps, lower back, ankles, shoulders, and forearms: They're all screaming! When the pan loaves are finished baking, you lift the hot strapped 4-loaf pans—weighing ten to twelve pounds each—flip them onto a table, move the loaves to the cooling rack, and put the heavy pans away. Repeat 100 or more times. (Did I mention that you are doing this total body workout at a room temperature of 80° to 100°F? It's a great way to sweat it out.)

Finally, the people bagging bread for deliveries move every loaf of cooled bread from the cooling racks to brown satchel bags. Then they carry the bags, thirty pounds at a time, on extended arms to the area of the packing room where that delivery route is stacked, and return to where they started. Each trip is ten to twenty feet each way—this job is for track stars only. Packers have been known to log four to six miles a day.

Given the nature of the work, you might guess that most people working in the bakery are trim and strong, with nicely toned muscles. They are sustained by plenty of cool water and snacks of bread. No wonder we always laugh when people say, "Doesn't working in a bakery make you fat?"

Goat Cheese with Black Olive and Roasted Vegetables on a French Baguette

Makes 4 sandwiches

Equipment: two 17 × 12-inch sheet pans

Fresh goat cheese, ripe tomatoes, and black olives are a winning combination, and for lovers of goat cheese, this sandwich is a favorite. First we roast tomatoes and eggplant in our oven to concentrate their flavor and make them soft and juicy. Next we prepare our own black olive tapenade from robust Greek olives. Then it's all put together on a freshly baked French Baguette. When the sweetness of the tomatoes, the salty olives, the silky eggplant, and the creamy goat cheese come together on a crusty baguette, it's a match made in heaven.

INGREDIENTS	GRAMS	OUNCES	VOLUME
Eggplant, fresh	454	16.00	I large or 2 small
Tomatoes, fresh	382	13.47	2 medium
Extra virgin olive oil	60	2.11	4 tablespoons
Salt and freshly ground pepper	to taste	to taste	to taste
Imported black olives such as Kalamata, pitted and roughly chopped	57	2.00	⅓ cup
Garlic, finely minced	½ small clove	½ small clove	½ small clove
Fresh goat cheese (not aged)	240	8.46	12 slices
Thyme, fresh	I small branch	I small branch	I small branch
French Baguette (page 79)	one 24-inch loaf or two 12-inch loaves	one 24-inch loaf or two 12-inch loaves	one 24-inch loaf or two 12-inch loaves

1. Preheat the oven to 350°F. Line two 17 × 12-inch sheet pans with parchment paper.

2. Wash and trim the eggplant and the tomatoes. Slice each kind of vegetable crosswise about ¼-inch thick, into 12 slices. Place the eggplant slices on one prepared sheet pan and the tomato slices on the other. Brush the eggplant slices with 2½ tablespoons of the olive oil, and the tomatoes with ½ tablespoon of the olive oil and season them with salt and pepper. Roast the vegetables in the oven until they begin to brown and become somewhat dehydrated, the tomatoes about 25 minutes, and the eggplant about 45 minutes. Place the pans on wire racks to cool.

3. Make the olive tapenade: With a mortar and pestle or food processor, grind the olives and garlic together. Add 1 tablespoon of olive oil and blend to make a smooth paste.

4. Slice the goat cheese into twelve ⅜-inch-thick slices, about 20 grams/¾ ounce each, and top each slice with a few leaves and leaf clusters of fresh thyme.

5. To assemble the sandwich, cut the French Baguette(s) into 4 equal lengths. Slice the pieces in half lengthwise. Place the bottom half of each sandwich on the work surface and spread it with about one quarter of the olive tapenade. Place 3 slices of goat cheese on each base. Top the cheese with 3 slices of roasted eggplant and 3 slices of roasted tomato. Place the top half of the bread on each sandwich. Serve at room temperature, or toast lightly in a toaster oven to begin to melt the cheese.

TIPS AND TECHNIQUES

To save time you can purchase premade black olive tapenade.

We like to place a few leaves of fresh thyme on each slice of goat cheese, but it can be omitted if it's not available.

The baguettes in this book are not as long as traditional baguettes because that length would not fit into a home oven. If you make your own bread you'll use two short baguettes, or purchase one 24-inch baguette to make four sandwiches.

Goat Cheese with Black Olive and Roasted Vegetables on a French Baguette and Brie and Tomatoes Vinaigrette on Baguette (page 220)

Turkey and Avocado on Country White Bread

Makes 4 sandwiches

Turkey Avocado" was created when our retail managers requested a sandwich that could be wrapped, refrigerated for several hours, and served in the evening. Most bread does not survive well in the refrigerator, but this combination of bread and filling seemed to work just fine. Our customers love this sandwich because they enjoy the soft rich avocado in contrast to the sweet tomato, crisp lettuce, and tender turkey.

The secret to the most delicious sandwich is to use fresh, soft bread; a perfectly ripe avocado; juicy, flavorful tomatoes; and natural turkey that is not highly processed. We dress the bread with mayonnaise to moisten it and wrap the whole sandwich tightly in cellophane. If you're going on a picnic or a road trip, you can make the sandwiches ahead of time and keep them cool until you're ready to enjoy them several hours later. When you board an airplane and pull out this sandwich, all the nearby passengers will be jealous.

INGREDIENTS	GRAMS	OUNCES	VOLUME
Tomato, ripe	284	10.00	1 medium to large
Avocado, ripe, whole	218	7.70	1 medium
Country White Bâtard (page 85), sliced ¾ inch thick	8 slices (one 1½-pound loaf)	8 slices (one 1½-pound loaf)	8 slices (one 1½-pound loaf)
Mayonnaise	40	1.41	4 tablespoons
Turkey, thinly sliced	340	12.00	12 to 16 slices
Romaine lettuce, washed and dried	68	2.40	4 small leaves

TIPS AND TECHNIQUES

We cut the bread in ¾-inch-thick slices; to get a wider slice, we cut the bread at an angle. The surface of our slices is about 6 inches wide and 3 inches high.

At the bakery we use natural turkey that is minimally processed, with less salt and no nitrates, and you can really taste the difference.

1. Slice the tomato in 8 to 12 slices that are ⅜ inch thick. Cut the avocado into quarters, remove the skin and pit, and cut each quarter lengthwise into 3 slices.

2. Place 4 slices of bread on the work surface. Spread each slice with 1½ teaspoons of mayonnaise. Place 85 grams/3 ounces/ 3 or 4 slices of turkey on each sandwich. Top the turkey with 2 or 3 slices of tomato, 3 slices of avocado, and a leaf of lettuce. Spread 1½ teaspoons of mayonnaise on the top slice of bread and close each sandwich. Cut the sandwiches in half and serve immediately, or wrap tightly in plastic, chill, and serve within 6 hours.

Turkey and Avocado on Country White Bread

Brie and Tomatoes Vinaigrette on Baguette

Makes 4 sandwiches

At Amy's Bread we make this sandwich on a Baguettine roll that's a miniature version of our French Baguette. It's a small sandwich that makes a perfect snack or accompaniment to soup or a salad. Here we've suggested using a whole wheat baguette to create your sandwich. If you don't bake your own, select a wheat baguette that is slender, or remove some of the bready crumb from the middle of the loaf so the taste of the sandwich ingredients comes through. At the bakery we prefer to use plum tomatoes because they have narrower slices. We dress them with a bit of vinaigrette to perk up their flavor. We round out the sandwich with soft, rich Brie that's perfectly ripe. It makes a delicious flavor combination.

INGREDIENTS	GRAMS	OUNCES	VOLUME
Extra virgin olive oil	24	0.80	2 tablespoons
Red wine vinegar	1 teaspoon	1 teaspoon	1 teaspoon
Dijon mustard	2½ teaspoons	2½ teaspoons	2½ teaspoons
Kosher salt	to taste	to taste	to taste
Freshly ground black pepper	to taste	to taste	to taste
Ripe plum tomatoes	195	6.88	2 medium
Imported Brie cheese	227	8	four ⅜-inch-thick slices
Organic Wheat Baguette (page 101) or French Baguette (page 79),	1 long or 2 short loaves	1 long or 2 short loaves	1 long or 2 short loaves

TIPS AND TECHNIQUES

The wheat baguettes in this book are not as long as traditional baguettes because that length would not fit into a home oven. If you make your own bread you'll use two short baguettes, or purchase one 20-inch baguette to make four sandwiches.

1. To prepare the vinaigrette: In a medium bowl, whisk together the olive oil, vinegar, ½ teaspoon of the mustard, and salt and pepper.

2. Slice the tomatoes into 12 to 16 slices, season them with salt and pepper, and place them in the bowl of vinaigrette to marinate. Cut the Brie into 4 equal pieces, 57 grams/2 ounces each.

3. Cut the baguette(s) into 5-inch lengths and slice each piece in half lengthwise. Place the bottom halves on the work surface and spread each one with ½ teaspoon of Dijon mustard. Place a slice of Brie on each sandwich, and top with 3 to 4 slices of marinated tomato that are still wet with dressing. Place the top on each sandwich. Serve immediately.

Jorge Grande is the "stats man" at Amy's Bread. He walks around every day with a clipboard and a thermometer, and takes note of the time each batch of dough is mixed and the dough temperature at the end of mixing. He knows that if a certain batch comes out three degrees too warm, he will need to put it in our big walk-in refrigerator early, and if the dough is on the cool side, he will move it to the warmest spot in the bakery to rise. He works with the people dividing the dough to let them know when the dough is ready, and with the shapers to alert them of any dough that needs special attention. He is the bridge from the early morning Mix Shift to the afternoon Shape Shift. Making good bread is all about controlling the dough by watching time and temperature, and Jorge is our control person.

Besides knowing the finer details about every dough, Jorge also orders all the ingredients for our breads and sandwiches. He keeps track of the best prices, which ingredients are running low, what is in season, and which company is delivering at what time each day. He manages the flow of 30,000 pounds of flour arriving at the bakery (in fifty-pound bags) each week, and keeps an eye on a vast array of ingredients, including fruits, nuts, vegetables, olives, dairy products, and meat.

Jorge is also our "resident chef." When it's time for our monthly birthday party, Jorge makes four kinds of pizza, including his spicy pineapple and ham pizza—popular with our Latin employees—and his delicious tomato, basil, and mozzarella with his homemade sauce. For our staff Thanksgiving meal he helps Amy make the feast and masterfully prepares his famous chicken for everyone. This year he broke down forty-six whole chickens, marinated them in freshly squeezed orange juice, garlic, and a blend of secret spices, then roasted them to perfection in our rotating rack oven. Some people think Jorge's job is easy, just strolling around with a clipboard, but if you spend ten minutes trying to talk to him, you will see what his day is really like. As you are talking he gets two phone calls, is interrupted by two employees who need certain ingredients, checks the temperature of one dough, turns and folds another kind of dough, greets a delivery man, signs for a delivery, and talks to you at the same time. That's just a small slice of Jorge's day. He joined us in 1996, becoming our stats man about ten years ago, and we have not looked back. Without Jorge's calm demeanor, warm smile, attention to detail, and great pride in his work, Amy's Bread would not be what it is today. We are grateful that Jorge is on our team and has his eye on the dough.

Vegetarian Hummus on Organic Miche

Vegetarian Hummus on Organic Miche

Makes 4 sandwiches

Fondly known as "Veggie Miche," this sandwich is one of our healthy options. It's a vegetarian sandwich that's satisfying and easy to prepare. It is made on our Organic Miche, a large round loaf that's a mild sourdough, made from organic wheat and rye flours. The chewy bread is topped with a tahini sauce, freshly made hummus, grated carrots, and broccoli sprouts. It's colorful and crunchy, and fills you up without being rich. We like to use broccoli sprouts because they have a pleasant flavor but don't taste musty like some other sprouts. We've given our formula for homemade hummus, but you can save time by buying a container at your local grocery store. It's a good sandwich year round because the ingredients are always available, and they can be assembled into a tasty sandwich in no time.

INGREDIENTS	GRAMS	OUNCES	VOLUME
Hummus			
Garbanzo beans, cooked or canned, drained, liquid reserved	238	8.40	one 15-ounce can, drained and liquid reserved (2 cups beans)
Bean cooking liquid	42	1.50	3 tablespoons
Extra virgin olive oil	42	1.50	3 tablespoons
Sesame tahini	1 tablespoon	1 tablespoon	1 tablespoon
Lemon juice	1 tablespoon	1 tablespoon	1 tablespoon
Fresh garlic, finely minced	½ small clove	½ small clove	½ small clove
Kosher salt	to taste	to taste	to taste
Paprika or freshly ground black pepper	to taste	to taste	to taste
Tahini Sauce			
Sesame tahini	68	2.40	3 tablespoons
Plain, full-fat yogurt	31	1.10	1½ tablespoons
Lemon juice	1 tablespoon	1 tablespoon	1 tablespoon
Water	1 teaspoon	1 teaspoon	1 teaspoon
Kosher salt	to taste	to taste	to taste
Sandwich Assembly			
Organic Miche (page 139), sliced ½ inch thick	8 slices	8 slices	8 slices
Hummus	250	8.80	1 cup
Carrots, fresh, trimmed and grated	102	3.60	1 large (1 cup grated)
Broccoli sprouts	57	2.00	⅓ of a 6-ounce box
Tahini Sauce	132	4.65	5 tablespoons plus 1 teaspoon

1. Prepare the hummus: In a blender or food processor combine the cooked garbanzo beans, bean cooking liquid, olive oil, tahini, lemon juice, garlic, salt, and paprika or pepper. Blend or process on high speed until a smooth puree has formed. Taste and season it to your liking.

2. Prepare the tahini sauce: In a small bowl whisk together the tahini, yogurt, lemon juice, water, and salt.

3. To assemble the sandwiches, place 4 slices of bread on the work surface. Place 62 grams/2.2 ounces/¼ cup of hummus on each slice. Top each one with ¼ cup of grated carrots, and 14 grams/½ ounce/¹⁄₁₂ box broccoli sprouts. Spread each of the 4 remaining slices of bread with 33 grams/1.1 ounces/1 tablespoon plus 1 teaspoon of tahini sauce and place on the sandwiches. Serve immediately.

TIPS AND TECHNIQUES

At the bakery we soak and cook our own garbanzo beans, but to save time you can purchase the canned variety. We like to buy canned organic beans, but any kind of good-quality canned garbanzo beans will be fine. To make the process even easier, you can purchase premade hummus instead of making your own.

We season our hummus with paprika for a warm, spicy flavor, but freshly ground black pepper can be substituted. Both the hummus and tahini sauce can be made several hours ahead and refrigerated until ready to use.

If you are unable to find bread similar to our Miche, we suggest using a mild whole wheat sourdough bread as an alternative. Make sure your bread is sliced thinly and evenly or the bread will overwhelm the sandwich. Our large Miche weighs about 4 pounds and it yields 16 large slices of bread.

We use broccoli sprouts in this sandwich, but if they are not available, other mild-tasting sprouts can be used.

Grilled New York State Cheddar Cheese Sandwich

Makes 4 sandwiches

This sandwich is a big favorite here at the bakery. Here is a letter we received from one of our many grilled cheese fans.

Subject: ABSOLUTELY THE BEST . . . Grilled cheese sandwich!
    Whenever I want a taste of comfort, I go straight to your Hell's Kitchen location and order the grilled cheese with tomato, cilantro and red onions! Today I went there with a friend from work and we absolutely floated back to the office after we finished our meal. We've decided to make a visit every Wednesday from now on! Keep up the fantastic work! And your staff at Hell's Kitchen also adds to the atmosphere of comfort.

Thanks, Amy!
—Debbie Whyte

. . . .

Thank *you,* Debbie. We couldn't have said it better ourselves. Here's our recipe for the ultimate comfort food, as only Amy's Bread can make it, until now—because now we're sharing it with you.

For this sandwich we use our Country Sourdough bread baked in a traditional pan loaf shape, but you can use any good-quality mild-flavored sourdough cut into ¾-inch-thick slices.

When selecting ingredients, we use nice fresh cilantro, flavorful tomatoes, and a good-quality sharp cheddar cheese for the best-tasting sandwich. We spread the bread with a spicy sauce made from chipotle peppers, and that's what sets it apart from the rest. The way we construct the sandwich is also rather special. We put the sliced cheese next to the bread, then the other ingredients on top of that, and we finish with more sliced cheese. When the sandwich is grilled the cheese melts completely, enclosing the other fillings. To get the right texture, you'll need a sandwich grill that compresses the sandwiches as they cook, or one large skillet and a heavy pot that will fit inside the skillet to sit on top of the sandwiches. Serve them hot off the grill to enjoy them while the cheese is still soft and the bread is still crusty.

INGREDIENTS	GRAMS	OUNCES	VOLUME
Tomato paste	85	3.00	½ of 6-ounce can
Chipotle pepper in adobo sauce (canned)	20	0.70	1 pepper
Adobo sauce from peppers	1½ teaspoons	1½ teaspoons	1½ teaspoons
Molasses	1½ teaspoons	1½ teaspoons	1½ teaspoons
Country Sourdough Pan Loaf (page 121), sliced ¾-inch thick	8 slices	8 slices	8 slices
Sharp cheddar cheese	227	8.00	10 slices
Tomatoes, fresh	227	8.00	1 large, or 3 or 4 small
Red onion	40	1.41	4 very thin slices
Cilantro leaves, fresh, washed and picked	28	1.00	½ cup

1. Put the tomato paste, chipotle pepper, adobo sauce, and molasses in a blender or food processor and puree until smooth.

2. Taste the pepper spread so you'll know how spicy it is, and spread each slice of bread with as much of the pepper mixture as you'd like. We use about 1 tablespoon per slice.

3. Slice the tomato(es) into ¼-inch slices. Roughly chop the cilantro leaves.

4. On each of 4 slices of bread, place 28 grams/1 ounce/1¼ slices of cheddar cheese, then place 2 to 3 tomato slices on the cheese. Top with a few thin rings of sliced red onion and a tablespoon of chopped cilantro. Place 28 grams/1 ounce/1¼ more slices of cheese on each sandwich. Put another slice of bread, pepper spread side down, on top of the sandwich.

5. If you have a sandwich grill, grill the sandwiches following the manufacturer's instructions until the bread is toasted and the cheese has begun to melt. If not, place a large skillet or sauté pan over medium-high heat to preheat for 30 seconds. Put the sandwiches in the pan and weight them down with a clean, heavy pot. When the bread has begun to toast and brown, 1 to 2 minutes, flip the sandwiches over and toast the other side. Serve immediately.

TIPS AND TECHNIQUES

Canned chipotle peppers in adobo sauce can be found in stores that carry a selection of authentic Latin ingredients. They are very spicy so a little goes a long way. After you have opened the can, you can freeze the remaining peppers for later use.

Presliced sharp cheddar is packed with ten slices per 8-ounce package. Use 1¼ slices per bread slice to get the proper proportion.

We suggest slicing the bread in thicker slices so that when the sandwich is pressed on the grill the bread still has some body. Thinner slices of bread will be paper thin after they have been pressed.

Grilled New York State Cheddar Cheese Sandwich

Open-Face Mini Smoked Salmon Sandwiches on French Rye

Makes 24 mini open-face sandwiches

These little open-face sandwiches make nice hors d'oeuvres, and are easy to eat without utensils while mingling with friends. For these sandwiches we use our French Rye, a simple rye bread without caraway or other spices. It's a narrow loaf with slices about 2½ inches wide. In place of this bread you can substitute cocktail rye and cut the little slices in half on the diagonal with good results. Here we have suggested using smoked salmon, but we also enjoy making the sandwiches with gravlax (cured salmon without the smoky flavor). The milder-tasting fish allows the flavor of the sauce and the bread to shine through. Once you have assembled these little sandwiches, it is best to serve them right away. Otherwise the bread and the toppings will dry out.

INGREDIENTS	GRAMS	OUNCES	VOLUME
Crème fraîche	142	5.00	½ cup plus 2 tablespoons
Plain full-fat yogurt	57	2.00	4 tablespoons
Capers, drained, chopped	20	0.70	1 tablespoon plus 1 teaspoon
Red onion, minced	14	0.50	1 tablespoon plus 1 teaspoon
Kosher salt and freshly ground pepper	to taste	to taste	to taste
French Rye (page 135)	300	10.58	½ loaf
Smoked salmon or gravlax	340	12.00	eight 1½-ounce slices
Fresh dill	3 branches to yield 24 small "leaves"	3 branches to yield 24 small "leaves"	3 branches to yield 24 small "leaves"

TIPS AND TECHNIQUES

If you toast the bread, be sure that the toaster oven has been preheated or the bread will get dried out and lose some of its flavor. If the slices of bread are too wide, trim them to fit the size of the salmon slice.

1. To make the sauce: Combine the crème fraîche, yogurt, capers, and onion. Season the sauce with salt and pepper to taste.

2. Slice the bread into 24 thin slices, about ⅛ inch thick. Toast the bread very lightly in a preheated toaster oven if desired.

3. Cut the slices of salmon into thirds to make 24 narrow strips of salmon, about 14 grams/½ ounce each.

4. Place a scant tablespoon of sauce on each slice of bread. Top with a strip of salmon that has been rolled up to fit neatly on the bread. Garnish with a little frond or "leaf" of fresh dill. Serve immediately.

Rare Roast Beef with Sautéed Onions on Picholine Olive Bread

Makes 4 sandwiches

This is a rather exotic and delicious sandwich, and it's one we like to make at home. We use our Picholine Olive Bread—a crusty, chewy bread with big holes and a mild-tasting crumb that's studded with whole green olives. The bread is lightly dressed with a mayo-horseradish spread, and then topped with sautéed sweet onions and rare roast beef. The combination of sweet, salty, and chewy is very satisfying. We like to serve these sandwiches with pickles, salty potato chips, and a crunchy chopped salad to satisfy all our senses.

INGREDIENTS	GRAMS	OUNCES	VOLUME
Sweet yellow onion	200	7.00	½ large onion
Unsalted butter	14	0.50	1 tablespoon
Mayonnaise	40	1.41	4 tablespoons
Prepared horseradish	1½ teaspoons	1½ teaspoons	1½ teaspoons
Picholine Olive Bread (page 179)	8 slices (1 loaf)	8 slices (1 loaf)	8 slices (1 loaf)
Rare roast beef, thinly sliced	226	8.00	12 to 16 thin slices

1. Slice the onion thinly. Put it, with the butter, into a skillet and cook over low heat, stirring, until the onion is softened and light golden brown.

2. In a small bowl stir together the mayonnaise and horseradish.

3. Toast the bread lightly if desired. Spread a little mayo-horseradish on all 8 slices of bread. On 4 slices place 57 grams/2 ounces/3 or 4 slices of roast beef. Place a quarter of the sautéed onions evenly on each sandwich, and top with the remaining 4 slices of bread. Serve immediately.

TIPS AND TECHNIQUES

Picholine Olive Bread is very special and adds a unique dimension to this sandwich. If you can't find it and don't have time to make your own, you can substitute black olive bread or a crusty loaf of country white bread instead. We slice the bread at an angle to get wider slices.

Sweet onions such as Vidalia taste delicious on this sandwich.

When we don't have prepared horseradish on hand, we substitute Dijon mustard in the same proportion to make our mayo spread.

You can prepare your own roast beef or purchase good-quality rare roast beef that is sliced to order at your local deli counter.

BRIOCHE AND SWEET SPECIALTY BREADS

The breads in this chapter are sweeter and richer than the other breads in this book. They rely on the addition of special ingredients like chocolate, pumpkin, cherries, butter, eggs, and maple syrup to provide unique flavor and texture elements to otherwise basic bread dough. Dough that has a high ratio of one or more special ingredients like these can present a bread baker with some interesting challenges in dough handling, as it is often very soft and sticky. But don't let that discourage you from giving these recipes a try. You'll learn some valuable new techniques and the rewards you'll reap when you eat and share these sweet, tender breads will be so worth the effort! Some of them, like the Hot Cross Buns and the Autumn Pumpkin Pecan Loaf, are made at the bakery on holidays but our customers beg for them year round. The others—Chocolate Cherry Rolls, Maple Walnut Fig Bread, and the Brioche Pan Loaf—are part of our regular menu. They're perfect for breakfast, snacks, and weekend brunch. Though our first love is for breads that are high in nutrition and low in fat, we sympathize with our customers' cravings for sweet delights and are pleased to offer these rich, sweet specialty breads for their enjoyment. We hope you'll enjoy them, too.

Chocolate Cherry Rolls

Makes 12 rolls

Equipment: two 17 x 12-inch baking sheets

These moist, plump, glossy little treats were inspired by the recipe for chocolate bread in Carol Field's wonderful book *The Italian Baker*. For variety, you can replace the dried cherries with Reese's peanut butter chips. These take about four hours from start to finish. If you're an early riser, you can have them warm from the oven in time for a mid-morning coffee break or weekend brunch. They're also great in picnic baskets and lunch boxes. Don't overbake them, or their flavor will be greatly diminished.

INGREDIENTS	GRAMS	OUNCES	VOLUME
Very warm water (105° to 115°F)	57	2.00	¼ cup
Active dry yeast	2 teaspoons	2 teaspoons	2 teaspoons
Sugar	67	2.36	scant ⅓ cup plus ¼ teaspoon
Unbleached bread flour	397	14.00	2⅔ cups
Unsweetened cocoa powder (see Tips and Techniques)	¼ cup	¼ cup	¼ cup
Kosher salt	1½ teaspoons	1½ teaspoons	1½ teaspoons
Warm brewed coffee (90°F)	250	8.80	1 cup plus 2 tablespoons
Egg yolk	20	0.71	1 large
Unsalted butter, softened	14	0.50	1 tablespoon
Dried cherries	135	4.76	1 scant cup
Semisweet chocolate chips	135	4.76	¾ cup
Egg white, for egg wash	30	1.06	1 large
Salt, for egg wash	pinch	pinch	pinch

1. Combine the very warm water, yeast, and ¼ teaspoon sugar in a large bowl. Stir with a fork to dissolve the yeast. Let stand for 3 minutes.

2. Whisk the flour, cocoa powder, the remaining scant ⅓ cup sugar, and the salt together in a medium bowl. Set aside.

3. Using a wooden spoon or your hand, stir the coffee, egg yolk, and butter into the yeast mixture. Gradually add the flour mixture, stirring until a shaggy mass forms and all of the flour is moistened.

4. Move the dough to a lightly floured surface and knead for 7 to 8 minutes, until it is silky-smooth and elastic. This dough should be nice and moist, so add flour sparingly as you work. Shape the dough into a loose ball, cover it with oiled plastic wrap, and let it rest for 15 minutes to relax the gluten strands.

5. Flatten the dough and stretch it gently with your fingers to form a rectangle about ¾ inch thick. Spread the dried cherries and chocolate chips evenly over the rectangle. Fold the dough into an envelope (see page 29) and knead gently for 2 to 3 minutes, until the cherries and chips are well distributed. The dough should be soft, smooth, and springy. If it resists, let it rest for 5 minutes and then continue kneading it. Some of the chips may pop out of the dough, but they can easily be incorporated again after the first rise, when the dough has softened. Shape the dough into a loose ball and place it in a lightly oiled bowl, along with any loose chips. Turn to coat the dough with oil, and cover the bowl tightly with oiled plastic wrap. Let rise at room temperature (75° to 77°F) until the dough has doubled in volume, about 2 hours.

6. Line two 17 X 12-inch baking sheets with parchment paper. Gently pour the dough onto the floured work surface, pressing any loose cherries and chips into the dough. Flour your hands lightly and divide the dough into 12 equal pieces, weighing about 85 grams/3 ounces each. Shape the pieces into rolls (see page 38) and place 6 rolls on each prepared baking sheet, leaving several inches between them so they won't grow together as they rise. Cover loosely with oiled plastic wrap and let them rise for 1 to 1½ hours or until almost doubled in volume. A finger pressed lightly into the dough will leave a slight indentation.

7. Whisk the egg white with a pinch of salt to make an egg wash. Cover with plastic wrap and set aside.

8. Thirty minutes before baking, preheat the oven to 400°F, and prepare the oven by placing a cast-iron skillet and a smaller pan (a mini loaf pan) on the floor of the oven or on the lowest possible rack in an electric oven. Place one oven rack in the top third of the oven and another in the bottom third. Fill a plastic water sprayer with water. Fill a teakettle with water to be boiled later, and have a metal 1-cup measure with a straight handle available near the kettle.

9. Five to 10 minutes before the rolls are ready to bake, turn the water on to boil, and carefully place two or three ice cubes in the small loaf pan in the bottom of the oven. This helps to create moisture in the oven prior to baking.

10. When the rolls are ready, lightly brush them with the egg wash, being careful not to deflate them. Place the pans in the oven. Pour 1 cup of boiling water into the skillet and immediately shut the oven door. After 2 minutes, quickly pour another ½ cup of boiling water into the skillet, then shut the oven door.

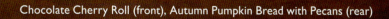
Chocolate Cherry Roll (front), Autumn Pumpkin Bread with Pecans (rear)

11. After 10 minutes, reduce the oven temperature to 350°F and rotate the pans if necessary to ensure even browning. Bake for another 10 to 12 minutes, until the tops of the rolls feel firm but not hard when you press them slightly and the bottoms are very lightly browned. They should have a thin soft covering, not a hard, crunchy crust. It's better to underbake them than overbake them.

12. Transfer the rolls to a wire rack and to cool. They can be served warm or at room temperature and are best eaten the day they are baked. They can also be frozen, wrapped tightly in aluminum foil and a heavy-duty plastic freezer bag. Thaw them at room temperature, then pop them in a 350°F oven for 5 to 7 minutes to revive the moist crumb and chocolate flavor.

TIPS AND TECHNIQUES

We used unbleached bread flour with a protein content of 12.7% for this dough.

Instead of weighing the cocoa powder for this recipe, we're showing only a volume measurement. The weight of cocoa powders varies so dramatically from one brand to the next that it's safer in this case to use the volume measurement.

If you want to sleep in a little later in the morning, make the dough the night before: Put it in a lightly oiled nonmetal bowl, cover the bowl tightly with oiled plastic wrap, and let the dough sit out at room temperature (75° to 77°F) for 1 hour, or until it looks slightly puffy. Then refrigerate it overnight. First thing in the morning, take it out, divide it, and shape it into rolls. Let the rolls rise as described in the recipe, until they have completely doubled in volume (about 2 hours), then bake them. The only difference is that the rolls will be a little more densely textured than they would be if you made them all in one day.

Maple Walnut and Fig Bread

....

A QUICK BREAD MADE WITHOUT YEAST

Makes two 9 × 5-inch loaves

Equipment: two 9 × 5-inch loaf pans, oiled

At the bakery we make a dozen different kinds of quick bread, taking advantage of seasonal ingredients and changing the selection throughout the week to offer our customers variety. This one is Amy's personal favorite, and a favorite of many of our regular customers, too. One customer gets quite upset when she sees that we've used our figs to make something other than her beloved maple walnut bread! The recipe was created in the winter when Amy wanted to make a breakfast bread that was homey and comforting, with the goodness of dried fruit, maple syrup, and oatmeal. Eat it plain, lightly toasted, or spread with a thin layer of cream cheese.

INGREDIENTS	GRAMS	OUNCES	VOLUME
Dried figs, diced	298	10.51	2 cups
Warm water (85° to 90°F)	113	4.00	½ cup
Unbleached all-purpose flour	340	12.00	2⅔ cups
Cake flour	184	6.50	1⅔ cups
Old-fashioned rolled oats	148	5.25	1¾ cups
Baking powder	28	1.00	2 tablespoons
Kosher salt	½ teaspoon	½ teaspoon	½ teaspoon
Maple syrup	312	11.00	1⅓ cups
Whole milk	312	11.00	1⅓ cups
Eggs, lightly beaten	200	7.05	4 large
Egg yolks	40	1.41	2 large
Canola oil	170	6.00	¾ cup
Walnut pieces, toasted (see "Toasting Nuts," page 111)	227	8.00	2 cups
Additional maple syrup, for glazing	80	2.82	⅓ cup

1. Position a rack in the center of the oven and preheat the oven to 350°F.

2. Put the diced figs in a medium bowl and add the warm water. Let soak until softened.

3. Whisk the all-purpose flour, cake flour, oats, baking powder, and salt together in a large bowl. Set aside.

4. Put the maple syrup, milk, eggs, egg yolks, and oil in a medium bowl and stir with the whisk to combine. Add the mixture to the dry ingredients, stirring with a spoon just until all of the flour is moistened. This should be a wet batter, because the oats will absorb a lot of the liquid during baking.

5. Fold the walnuts and figs into the batter (the figs do not need to be drained). Divide the batter evenly between two oiled 9 X 5-inch loaf pans. Bake for about 1 hour, until a toothpick inserted in the center comes out clean. (If your oven bakes unevenly, rotate the pans about halfway through the baking time.)

6. Remove the pans from the oven and use a pastry brush to glaze the tops of the loaves generously with maple syrup. Set them on a rack to cool for about 10 minutes. Turn the loaves out of the pans and set them on the rack to cool completely before serving.

7. Wrap any leftovers tightly in plastic wrap and store at room temperature. They may also be frozen, wrapped first in aluminum foil and then in plastic wrap or a heavy-duty freezer bag.

TIPS AND TECHNIQUES

We used unbleached all-purpose flour with a protein content of 11.5% for this dough.

Brioche Pan Loaf

Makes two 1½-pound pan loaves

Equipment: electric stand mixer with dough hook; two 9 × 5-inch loaf pans

These big, beautiful loaves of brioche are baked in a regular bread pan so they can be cut into thick slices to make luscious almond brioche toast (recipe in our book *The Sweeter Side of Amy's Bread*) or French toast that's to die for. Unlike most brioche recipes, this one has no milk or water in it except for the small amount needed to dissolve the yeast and the water contained in the poolish starter. Eggs are the primary liquid. The amount of yeast we use is also fairly small for such a rich, heavy dough. The result is slow-proofing times. We believe this improves the flavor and texture of the bread because the flour has more time to be fully hydrated. You won't get the yeasty aftertaste that is often found in some brioche breads. So if you want to make your own brioche loaves using the Amy's Bread formula, you have to be a patient soul. But once you taste it we think you'll agree it's well worth the wait. This is an all-day process, as it is when we make it in the bakery, so be sure to plan ahead and start the dough early in the day.

INGREDIENTS	GRAMS	OUNCES	VOLUME
Very warm water (105° to 115°F)	57	2.00	¼ cup
Active dry yeast	1½ teaspoons	1½ teaspoons	1½ teaspoons
Unbleached bread flour	565	20.04	3⅔ cups
Eggs, cold	340	12.00	7 large
Poolish (page 54), cold if possible	140	4.94	½ cup
Sugar	70	2.50	⅓ cup
Kosher salt	14	0.49	1 tablespoon plus 1½ teaspoons
Unsalted butter, cold	282	10.00	1¼ cups
Softened butter or nonstick cooking spray, for the pans	as needed	as needed	as needed
Egg, for egg wash	50	1.76	1 large

1. Combine the very warm water and yeast in a measuring cup and stir to dissolve the yeast. Let stand for 3 minutes.

2. In the bowl of an electric stand mixer fitted with a dough hook, combine the yeast mixture, flour, cold eggs, poolish, sugar, and salt and mix on medium-low

speed for 3 minutes, scraping down the sides and bottom of the bowl after the first minute if necessary. Increase the speed to medium and continue mixing for 2 minutes until all the flour is moistened and gathers into a ball of dough. Slide the dough down from the top of the hook (to be sure all of the dough will be evenly kneaded), increase the speed to medium-high and knead the dough for 10 minutes or until the dough slaps the side of the bowl, is very strong, and cleans the bottom of the bowl. If the dough tries to climb up over the top of the dough hook, you may have to periodically stop the mixer and slide the dough down from the hook again. Keep a close eye on the mixer, as it may vibrate at this high speed with this heavy dough and dance its way off of the counter.

3. While the dough is mixing, remove the butter from the refrigerator, place it in a heavy-duty plastic bag, and pound it vigorously with a wooden mallet or rolling pin to make it malleable. It should still be cold but take an impression easily when you press it with your finger. When the dough is ready, with the mixer on medium-high speed, gradually begin adding the butter in silver dollar–size chunks. You don't have to wait until one piece is absorbed to add another one, just steadily keep tossing them into the bowl until all of the butter has been added. At first the butter will clump around the sides of the bowl. If it gets too close to the top of the bowl, just stop the mixer and push it down with a rubber spatula. Eventually—as unlikely as it seems in the beginning—the butter will start to be incorporated into the dough mass. The dough will shred but then come back together. Continue mixing at medium-high speed for 6 to 8 minutes, until the dough slaps the side and cleans the bottom of the bowl. At this point it will be very smooth and satiny looking, and strong enough so you can pull a transparent square window of dough without having it tear. Hopefully the dough temperature will be no higher than 82°F. The ideal temperature is 77°F to 80°F but it's difficult to achieve that with such long and vigorous mixing.

4. Put the dough in an oiled bowl that is large enough to allow it to double, cover it with oiled plastic wrap, and allow it to rise for 1 hour to 2 hours, until it has almost doubled.

5. Refrigerate the dough for 1½ to 2 hours to cool it down and make it easier to handle. After the first 30 minutes or once it has actually doubled, gently deflate the dough in the middle of the bowl with your fingertips, then fold it in half, pat it down, and turn it over so the seam is underneath. Return it to cool in the refrigerator.

6. While the dough is cooling, prepare the two loaf pans by greasing them thoroughly with soft butter, or spraying them with nonstick cooking spray, paying particular attention to the corners. Grease the top edges of the pans, too.

7. Pour the dough out onto a lightly floured work surface and gently pat it into a 11½ × 10-inch rectangle. Divide it in half so you have two rectangles that are 10 × 5¾ inches, weighing approximately 700 grams/24.7 ounces each. Gently flip one of the rectangles over so the smooth side of the dough is down on the table and the short sides are at the top and bottom of the rectangle. If the dough sticks to the work surface, lift it gently with a dough scraper and lightly reflour the surface. Starting with the upper edge of the dough, gently fold the top third down and the bottom third up, like a business letter, so you have three equal layers. Press along the top edge to seal the seam and gently roll the dough back and forth on the table to make a loose log shape that is about the length of the loaf pan. Do not shape these loaves too tightly or they will blow out the top on one side when they are baking. Press gently to seal the ends of the log and place it in one of the prepared loaf pans, pressing down firmly with your knuckles along the length of the dough so it fills the pan evenly. Repeat this shaping process with the second piece of dough. Cover the loaves with oiled plastic wrap and let them rise at room temperature until they are approaching the top of the pan. This may take up to 3 hours or more, depending on the temperature of the dough. Remove the plastic covering.

8. In a small bowl, mix 1 egg with 1 teaspoon of water to make an egg wash. When the proofing loaves have risen about ½ inch above the top of the pan, gently brush the tops of the loaves with egg wash. Try not to let the egg wash puddle around the edges of the pan too much, or the cooked egg will make it difficult to get the loaf out of the pan after baking. Let the loaves continue to rise until they are about 1 inch above the top of the pan. A finger pressed into the dough should leave an indentation.

9. Thirty minutes before baking, preheat the oven to 375°F. Prepare the oven by placing a cast-iron skillet and a smaller pan (a mini loaf pan) on the floor of the oven or on the lowest possible rack in an electric oven. Place an oven rack in the middle of the oven. Fill a plastic water sprayer with water. Fill a teakettle with water to be boiled later, and have a metal 1-cup measure with a straight handle available near the kettle.

10. Five to 10 minutes before the loaves are ready to bake, turn the water on to boil, and carefully place two or three ice cubes in the small loaf pan in the bottom of the oven. This helps to create moisture in the oven prior to baking.

11. When the loaves are ready, place the loaf pans on the oven rack, leaving several inches of space between them. Pour 1 cup of boiling water into the skillet and immediately shut the oven door. After about 2 minutes, pour another ½ cup of boiling water into the skillet, then shut the oven door.

12. Check the loaves after 20 minutes and rotate them if necessary to ensure even browning. Continue baking for 15 more minutes. The loaves will be very dark brown in color. Remove one of the pans from the oven and tip the loaf out of the pan. If the sides of the loaf are also dark brown and feel firm, not soft and doughy, the loaf is done. If the sides are too soft, return the loaf to the pan and bake it for another 5 minutes. Repeat the procedure for the second pan. When the loaves are done, remove them from the pans and cool them completely on a wire rack. Store the loaves in a plastic bag. They should be used or frozen within three days.

TIPS AND TECHNIQUES

We used unbleached bread flour with a protein content of 12.7% for this dough. The poolish was made with unbleached all-purpose flour with a protein content of 11.5%.

This dough can also be made in the evening, proofed at room temperature for 1½ to 2 hours until it starts to rise and get slightly puffy, and put in the refrigerator overnight. If the dough is very active, you may have to deflate it before you go to bed. In the morning, remove the dough from the refrigerator. Let it sit at room temperature for an hour or so to soften slightly, then shape the loaves, proof them, and bake them as described in the recipe steps. It may take up to 5 hours for the cold dough to rise completely in the loaf pans.

This dough is mixed vigorously for a long time, which generates a lot of heat. To keep the dough temperature from climbing into the high 80s, which melts the butter and makes the dough very sticky and difficult to work with, keep all the ingredients as cold as possible for as long as possible. It's even good if you can chill the poolish and the metal mixing bowl and dough hook.

If the loaves consistently blow out one side on top, the next time you bake them try using a lame or a sharp razor blade to score the top of each loaf with three evenly spaced diagonal slashes or one long slash down the middle. It's not as pretty as the smooth domed top but it will help to prevent the blowout.

To make brioche hamburger buns, weigh out pieces of dough at 85 grams/3 ounces each, shape them into rolls (see page 38), and place up to six of them on a parchment lined 17 × 12-inch sheet pan to double in size. Shorten the baking time to 15 to 20 minutes.

Hot Cross Buns

Makes 18 small buns

Equipment: two 17 × 12-inch baking sheets

We like to make at least one special bread to celebrate each holiday throughout the year. For Easter we always make hot cross buns. These little currant-filled rolls are slightly sweet, mildly spicy, and richly tender with milk and eggs. In the pre-Christian era, these buns were served to honor the goddess of spring. Later, the cross was cut in the top to symbolize the Christian religion. Hot cross buns are traditionally sold in England on Good Friday. We sell them on Good Friday and the following Saturday, too, as a special treat for our customers' Easter Sunday breakfasts. Don't wait until Easter season to try this recipe, however—once you've made them, you'll want them all year round. Be careful not to overbake them, or their delicate flavor will be lost.

INGREDIENTS	GRAMS	OUNCES	VOLUME
Very warm water (105° to 115°F)	113	4.00	½ cup
Active dry yeast	9	0.32	1 tablespoon plus ¾ teaspoon
Unbleached all-purpose flour	485	17.10	3⅓ cups
Kosher salt	1½ teaspoons	1½ teaspoons	1½ teaspoons
Ground cinnamon	½ teaspoon	½ teaspoon	½ teaspoon
Grated nutmeg	½ teaspoon	½ teaspoon	½ teaspoon
Eggs, lightly beaten	150	5.29	3 large
Canola oil	106	3.74	½ cup
Granulated sugar	64	2.26	⅓ cup
Warm milk (90°F)	57	2.00	¼ cup
Dried currants	85	3.00	⅔ cup
Egg white, for egg wash	30	1.06	1 large
Powdered sugar	85	3.00	¾ cup
Vanilla extract	¼ teaspoon	¼ teaspoon	¼ teaspoon

1. Place the very warm water and yeast in a large bowl and stir with a fork to dissolve the yeast. Allow to stand for 3 minutes.

2. Whisk the flour, salt, cinnamon, and nutmeg together in a medium bowl. Set aside.

3. Using a wooden spoon or your hand, stir the beaten eggs, oil, sugar, and warm milk into the yeast mixture. Gradually add the flour mixture, stirring until a shaggy mass forms and all of the flour is moistened.

4. Move the dough to a lightly floured surface and knead for 6 to 8 minutes, until it is silky-smooth and elastic. The dough is wet and sticky at first, but it becomes easier to work with as the gluten forms to make it springy and give it strength. Keep your hands and the table very lightly floured, using a dough scraper to lift the dough as needed. Shape the dough into a loose ball, cover it with oiled plastic wrap, and let it rest for 20 minutes to relax the gluten strands.

5. Flatten the dough and stretch it gently with your fingers to form a rectangle about ½ inch thick. Spread the dried currants evenly over the rectangle. Fold the dough into an envelope (see page 29) and knead gently for 2 to 3 minutes, until the currants are well distributed. The dough should be soft, smooth, and springy. If it resists, let it rest for 5 minutes and then continue kneading it. Some of the currants may pop out of the dough, but they can easily be incorporated again after the first rise, when the dough has softened.

6. Shape the dough into a loose ball and place it in a lightly oiled bowl, along with any loose currants. Turn to coat the dough with oil, and cover the bowl tightly with oiled plastic wrap. Let rise at room temperature (75° to 77°F) for 1½ to 2 hours, or until the dough has doubled in volume. A finger pressed into the dough should leave an indentation that won't spring back.

7. Line two 17 × 12-inch baking sheets with parchment paper. Gently pour the dough onto the floured work surface, pressing any loose currants into the dough. Flour your hands lightly and divide the dough into 18 equal pieces weighing about 57 grams/2 ounces each. Shape them into rolls (see page 38) and place 9 buns on each prepared baking sheet, leaving several inches between them so they won't grow together as they rise. Cover loosely with oiled plastic wrap and let them rise about 1 hour or until almost doubled in volume. A finger pressed lightly into the dough will leave a slight indentation.

8. Whisk the egg white with a pinch of salt to make an egg wash. Cover with plastic wrap and set aside.

9. Thirty minutes before baking, preheat the oven to 400°F, and prepare the oven by placing a cast-iron skillet and a smaller pan (a mini loaf pan) on the floor of the oven or on the lowest possible rack in an electric oven. Place one oven rack in the top third of the oven and another in the bottom third. Fill a plastic water sprayer with water. Fill a teakettle with water to be boiled later, and have a metal 1-cup measure with a straight handle available near the kettle.

10. Five to 10 minutes before the buns are ready to bake, turn the water on to boil, and carefully place two or three ice cubes in the small loaf pan in the bottom of the oven. This helps to create moisture in the oven prior to baking.

11. When the buns are ready, use a lame or a pair of kitchen scissors to cut a shallow cross on the top of each one. Lightly brush them with the egg wash, being careful not to deflate them. (Reserve the remaining egg wash.) Place the pans in the oven. Pour 1 cup of boiling water into the skillet and immediately shut the oven door. After 2 minutes, quickly pour another ½ cup of boiling water into the skillet, then shut the oven door.

12. After 10 minutes, reduce the oven temperature to 375°F and rotate the pans if necessary to ensure even browning. Bake for another 5 to 10 minutes, until the buns have turned a nice golden brown and the surface feels slightly firm but not hard when you press it lightly. These rolls should have a thin soft covering, not a hard, crunchy crust. Transfer the rolls to a rack and let them cool for 10 minutes.

13. Meanwhile, make the frosting: In a small bowl, combine the powdered sugar with the reserved egg wash and the vanilla, and whisk to mix well.

14. While the rolls are still warm, use a pastry bag fitted with a small plain tip, or a teaspoon, to make an *X* of frosting over the cross on each bun. The frosting will harden somewhat as the buns cool. These are best eaten the same day they are baked.

TIPS AND TECHNIQUES

We used unbleached all-purpose flour with a protein content of 11.5% for this dough.

These buns completely lose their delicate texture and flavor if the dough is made too dry. It's very important not to be intimidated by the stickiness of this dough. It should be very soft and moist. If the dough feels too stiff and hard when you're mixing, add more warm (85° to 90°F) water, 1 tablespoon at a time, until you have soft pliable dough to knead.

Autumn Pumpkin Bread with Pecans

MADE WITHOUT A STARTER

Makes two 1¼-pound loaves

Equipment: wooden peel and baking stone, or one 17 × 12-inch baking sheet

The Indians of the Taos Pueblo in New Mexico use their beehive-shaped outdoor adobe ovens to make wonderful addictive little yeast breads they call pumpkin cookies. Toy loved these so much she wanted to duplicate their simple, fresh pumpkin flavor in a larger loaf that could be sold in the retail store during the fall/winter holiday season. Somehow, as the testing progressed, what started out as a relatively plain bread became almost cakelike instead. The pumpkin-gold loaf, flecked with bits of toasty pecans, is shaped in a knot, which makes it especially attractive for gift-giving. Be sure you make enough to eat at your own holiday table, too, because the buttery rich, spicy aromas that fill the house when this bread is baking will drive your family wild.

INGREDIENTS	GRAMS	OUNCES	VOLUME
Very warm water (105° to 115°F)	57	2.00	¼ cup
Active dry yeast	12	0.42	1 tablespoon plus 1 teaspoon
Pumpkin puree	234	8.25	1 cup
Honey	170	6.00	½ cup
Milk, at room temperature	120	4.23	½ cup
Coarse cornmeal or polenta	42	1.48	¼ cup
Egg yolks, at room temperature	40	1.41	2 large
Unbleached bread flour, divided	560	19.75	3¾ cups
Ground cinnamon	1 teaspoon	1 teaspoon	1 teaspoon
Ground ginger	½ teaspoon	½ teaspoon	½ teaspoon
Ground cloves	½ teaspoon	½ teaspoon	½ teaspoon
Kosher salt	2½ teaspoons	2½ teaspoons	2½ teaspoons
Unsalted butter, melted	113	4.00	8 tablespoons
Pecan pieces, toasted (see "Toasting Nuts," page 111)	113	4.00	1 cup
Additional flour or cornmeal, for the peel	as needed	as needed	as needed

1. Combine the very warm water and yeast in a large bowl and stir with a fork to dissolve the yeast. Allow to stand for 3 minutes.

2. Add the pumpkin puree, honey, milk, cornmeal, egg yolks, and 228 grams/ 8 ounces/1½ cups of the flour to the yeast mixture. Stir briskly with a whisk until the ingredients are well combined. Let this sponge rest for at least 15 minutes but no longer than 30 minutes.

3. In a medium bowl, whisk the remaining 332 grams/11.75 ounces/2¼ cups of flour together with the cinnamon, ginger, cloves, and salt to mix well. Add the melted butter to the sponge and stir with your fingers to incorporate, then add the flour mixture, stirring and folding the dough over itself until it gathers into a shaggy mass.

4. Move the dough to a lightly floured work surface and knead until it is very smooth, silky, and elastic, 8 to 9 minutes. The dough will be soft and sticky, so keep the work surface and your hands lightly floured, but don't overdo it. The dough should be soft, supple, and springy. Shape it into a loose ball, cover with plastic wrap, and let it rest for 20 minutes.

5. Flatten the dough and stretch it gently with your fingers to form a rectangle about an inch thick. Spread the toasted pecans evenly over the rectangle. Fold the whole mass into an envelope (see page 29) and knead it gently until the nuts are well distributed, 2 to 3 minutes. If the dough resists, let it rest for 5 minutes and then continue kneading it. Some of the pecans may pop out of the dough, but they can easily be incorporated again after the first rise, when the dough has softened.

6. Shape the dough into a loose ball and place it in a lightly oiled bowl, along with any loose pecans. Turn to coat the top with oil, then cover the bowl with oiled plastic wrap. Let rise at room temperature (75° to 77°F) until it has doubled in volume, about 2 hours. A lightly floured finger pressed into the dough will leave an indentation that does not spring back.

7. When the dough has doubled, gently pour it out of the bowl onto the floured work surface, pressing in any loose nuts. Flour your hands lightly and gently divide the dough into two equal pieces weighing about 680 grams/24 ounces each. Shape each piece into a knot (see page 254). Place the loaves on a peel or the back of a baking sheet that has been lined with parchment and sprinkled generously with cornmeal. Leave several inches between them so they won't grow into each other.

8. Generously dust a peel or the bottom of a baking sheet with flour or coarse cornmeal. Carefully place the shaped loaves on the peel or sheet, leaving several inches between them so they won't grow into each other as they rise. Cover with oiled plastic wrap and allow them to rise at room temperature until just doubled in volume, about 1½ to 2 hours.

9. Thirty minutes before baking, preheat the oven to 425°F. Prepare the oven by placing a cast-iron skillet and a smaller pan (a mini loaf pan) on the floor of the oven or on the lowest possible rack in an electric oven. Place an oven rack two rungs above the cast-iron pan, and if you have one, put a baking stone on the rack. Position another oven rack two rungs above the stone. Fill a plastic water sprayer with water. Fill a teakettle with water to be boiled later, and have a metal 1–cup measure with a straight handle available near the kettle.

10. Five to 10 minutes before the loaves are ready to bake, turn the water on to boil, and carefully place two or three ice cubes in the small loaf pan in the bottom of the oven. This helps to create moisture in the oven prior to baking.

11. Mist the loaves with water, then open the oven and gently slide them onto the baking stone with the parchment paper underneath. (If you're baking without a stone simply put the pan onto the empty oven rack.) Pour 1 cup of boiling water into the skillet and immediately shut the oven door. After 1 minute, quickly mist the loaves again, then shut the oven door.

12. Bake for 15 minutes, then rotate the loaves for even browning, reduce the oven temperature to 375°F, and bake for 20 to 25 minutes longer, until the loaves are golden brown and the surface feels firm but not hard when you press it lightly. These should have a thin soft crust, not a hard, crunchy one. An instant-read digital thermometer will read about 200°F.

13. Transfer the loaves to a metal rack and allow to cool completely before serving. This bread is best eaten the day it is baked, but it also freezes exceptionally well if you wrap it in aluminum foil and then a heavy duty-plastic freezer bag. Thaw at room temperature before serving.

TIPS AND TECHNIQUES

We used unbleached bread flour with a protein content of 12.7% for this dough.

If you have difficulty with shaping a knot, the dough can be made into any of your favorite shapes but the proofing and baking times may need to be adjusted slightly to accommodate that specific shape.

ADDITIONAL TECHNIQUES AND INFORMATION FOR AVID BAKERS

SOURDOUGH INFORMATION

Sourdough is a subject of considerable debate among serious bakers and not one that lends itself to definitive answers. Our purpose in this section is merely to pass along some of the more detailed information we have been able to accumulate from our own experience.

A Little Bit of Chemistry

Baking consistently excellent bread using sourdough as the leavener is the ultimate challenge for the passionate bread baker. Getting consistent results with commercially produced yeast is relatively easy because there are almost 200 billion yeast cells in just a tablespoon of active dry yeast. With that many little microbes madly multiplying, your chances for success are pretty good. On the other hand, a whole cup of sourdough starter often contains well under one billion wild yeast cells. The trick to using a sourdough starter is to coerce those wild yeast cells into a reproductive frenzy so their strength will be equal to that of commercial yeast.

Yeasts are not the only important microbes in sourdough. The unique taste of sourdough bread comes from a variety of organic acids, primarily lactic acid and acetic acid that are produced by bacteria called lactobacilli. These bacteria have a symbiotic relationship with the types of wild yeasts found in sourdough cultures. Unlike commercially processed yeasts, the wild yeasts that thrive in an acid environment cannot metabolize maltose, one of the complex sugars found in flour. The lactobacilli, on the other hand, can't survive without maltose, so you would be unlikely to find them growing in a dough made only with commercial yeast, because the commercial yeasts would have metabolized the maltose. In mature sourdough cultures, these same lactobacilli apparently produce an antibiotic that protects the starter from being contaminated by other harmful bacteria. This partially explains why there are sourdough starters that have been around for decades—perhaps even for centuries.

Once you get a good, strong sourdough starter going, as long as it is either refrigerated or dehydrated, it's pretty difficult to kill it. When their food and water supply has been consumed, and/or they are subjected to cold temperatures, yeast cells go into a dormant state by forming spores. These spores can survive until they encounter favorable conditions for reactivation of the yeast. That's why you can leave a mature starter in the refrigerator for weeks without feeding it. We don't recommend it, but just about every baker has done it. A gray liquid will accumulate on the top of the starter, but you can just pour it off, discard half the starter, feed it with flour and water, and let it sit at room temperature until the bubbling starts all over again (see the section on sourdough starters in Chapter 3, pages 57 to 58). You may have to feed it two or three times to really get it going, but it will work. As long as the starter isn't some unnatural color—green, pink, orange, purple, or black—it's safe to reactivate it. If you have any doubts, though, discard it and start from scratch.

If you're going on a long vacation or you know you won't be baking with sourdough for an extended period of time, you can dehydrate or freeze your starter. To dehydrate it, spread about half a cup of your starter in a very thin layer on a parchment paper–lined baking sheet. Leave it out at room temperature until it has completely dried out, then crumble it into chips and store the chips at room temperature in a waterproof, airtight container, such as a heavy-duty plastic freezer bag with a zip-up closure. They will last indefinitely. To reactive the starter, soak the chips in half a cup of cool water (75° to 78°F) to soften and dissolve them, then begin refreshing the mixture with flour and water as described in Chapter 3. Or you can simply freeze your starter without dehydrating it. Stored in an airtight container, it will retain its potency for at least six months. Thaw it in the refrigerator and feed it as usual to reactive it.

There are many different strains and combinations of yeasts and lactobacilli throughout the world, and that's why the sourdough starters cultivated in different regions produce breads that have unique flavors and textures. Chicago sourdough bread is different from San Francisco sourdough and Parisian *pain au levain*. In fact, there is some question about whether or not you can maintain the integrity of a San Francisco starter if you take it to New York City, where it will be exposed to Big Apple microbes over an extended period of time. We haven't found the answer to that one yet, but we'll keep on trying!

To Yeast or Not to Yeast

Sourdough purists cringe at the idea of adding commercial yeast to sourdough breads. At Amy's Bread, we do add about a pinch of yeast to most of our naturally leavened doughs, though the sourdough starters themselves are free of any commercial yeast. Many noted French bread bakers believe that you can add up to 0.2 percent of its weight in yeast to a sourdough—either the starter or the dough made from the starter—without destroying its flavor or the nature of the controlling microorganisms. Some also feel that this tiny bit of yeast produces a thinner, though still crunchy, crust and a lighter, more chewable crumb. We also use it because it helps us maintain the consistency with our sourdough breads from one day to the next. Performance of sourdough starters can be affected by changes in temperature and humidity. In the bakery, where we don't have a 100% artificially controlled environment, we are often at the mercy of the weather and seasonal changes. So we use commercial yeast to "kick start" our natural starter. We are convinced that by the time the dough has fully matured, the properties of the commercial yeast have dissipated and only the qualities of the natural leavener remain. If you are curious, perform your own experiments with and without added yeast to create the sourdough loaf that gives you the most satisfaction.

Different Ways to Make a Sourdough Starter

In Chapter 3 we explain how to make a starter using organic grapes, water, and unbleached flour. However, if you are a born experimenter, you will want to try some of the variations below. Each produces a starter with unique flavor and fermentation characteristics.

- Make a Rye Sourdough Starter (page 61), adding 1 tablespoon of milk to the rye flour and water mixture in Stage 1.
- Place ½ cup of organic raisins in a covered container, add room-temperature water to cover, and let sit at room temperature for several days, until you begin to see some bubbling action. Drain the raisins, reserving the liquid (discard the raisins). Use this liquid instead of the whole grapes to make the White Sourdough Starter, combining it with an equal measure (by volume) of flour in Stage 1, and proceed from there.
- Use orange juice from a carton (squeezed or reconstituted) as the liquid instead of water in Stage 1. We have also had interesting results using Apple & Eve Cranberry Apple juice instead of water. Any fruit juice you try should be free of added sugar and preservatives.

- Use potato water for the liquid in Stage 1.
- Add 1 tablespoon of mashed ripe banana or mashed potatoes along with the flour in Stage 1.
- Add 1 teaspoon of honey, maple syrup, or barley malt syrup to the flour and water mixture in Stage 1.
- You will discover that some mixtures ferment more quickly than others, so the resulting starters will need to be refreshed more often than our basic sourdough starter.

Some Words of Encouragement

Don't be discouraged if your first attempts at creating a sourdough culture fail miserably. Flours vary dramatically in quality, and the concentration of yeast cells in the air of your home can't compare to the concentration of yeast cells in a commercial bakery. Try different brands and types of flour until you find one that likes to ferment readily. If you don't see any activity within the time frame we describe in Chapter 3, don't be afraid to let the mixture sit a little longer, and keep feeding it. As long as it's not moldy or discolored, chances are you'll eventually get a culture that will double in eight hours. Patience, persistence, and careful attention to detail are the keys to success with sourdough.

SUGGESTIONS FOR BREAD SHAPES

At the bakery we form all our loaves by hand. Besides being gentler on the dough, hand-shaping allows you to leave more air bubbles in the dough, producing lighter, open-holed loaves. Although our loaves are sometimes irregular, our hand-shaped bread is beautiful and more rustic-looking than bread shaped by a machine.

Shaping bread takes repetition and practice, and it's hard to get that kind of experience when working with recipes that yield only two loaves. Here are some guidelines that should help you get better results without the experience of shaping hundreds of loaves a day: Start by gently patting the piece of dough into a small rectangle, lightly pressing out some of the bubbles but leaving some so you'll end up with irregular air holes in the bread. When forming the loaf, your goal is to pull the outer "skin" of the loaf tight without tearing it and without deflating the bubble formation too much. Then seal the seam of the bread very well so it doesn't unroll. The tight skin is important, because it holds in the carbon dioxide gas released as soon as the bread goes into the hot oven. A loaf with a loose skin or an unsealed seam will spread and flatten into a broad flat mass in the oven.

Here we describe some of the more unusual shapes we like.

Coil, Beehive, or Snail

Shape a baguette following the instructions on page 36. Then elongate the rope further, placing your palms over the middle of the loaf, pushing down slightly, and rolling it back and forth. Work your hands from the middle out to the ends of the rope. If the dough springs back, let it rest for up to 5 minutes before elongating it further. When the rope is about 30 inches long, taper the ends slightly and coat the loaf lightly with flour. Hold one end of the rope between your thumb and forefinger to anchor it and form a snail, working from the inside out and coiling the rope of dough around itself. To complete the look of a snail, pull the outside end of the coil outward and flatten it slightly. Cut a 2-inch slit in the tip and separate the cut into antennae.

If you want to garnish the loaf with sesame or poppy seeds, lightly spray a stream of water into the groove of the coil with a plant sprayer. Drop the seeds in a stream into the moistened groove. It's best to let the loaf rise on parchment paper dusted with cornmeal, because this shape is likely to stick to the peel. Bake the coil when it is slightly underproofed so that it will maintain its definition.

Braid

Divide the dough to be shaped into three equal pieces. (It is hard to shape a braid with pieces of dough that weigh less than 4 ounces each.) Shape each piece of dough into a baguette (see page 36). Then elongate the ropes slightly and taper the ends by pushing down on them as you roll them back and forth. The ropes should all be the same length. Place the ropes side by side, leaving an inch between them. Gather the ropes together at one end and press to seal them. Braid the ropes together into a loaf and press the other ends of the ropes together to seal them. Gently lift the braid onto a cornmeal-dusted peel or pan and let rise. (It's best not to lift a braided loaf after it has risen.) The braid shape is especially nice for challah or semolina bread.

Knot

Shape the dough into a baguette (see page 36). Elongate the baguette slightly so the rope is at least 25 inches long. Roll it lightly in flour, then tie a knot in the middle of the rope. Bring one of the long ends around one side of the knot and tuck it under the loaf, then bring the other end around the other side and tuck it under the loaf. Choose the most attractive side of the knot (the one where the rounded loops protrude) for the top of the loaf. Place the knot on a baking sheet lined with parchment paper, so you won't have to move it when it's ready to be baked. Bake it when it's slightly underproofed so it keeps its definition. (See photograph in color insert.)

Crown or Couronne

Use a piece of dough that weighs at least 12 ounces to make a crown. Shape it into a short baguette (see page 36), but don't taper the ends. To determine the length you need, make the loaf into a donut shape with a 4- to 5-inch center opening. If the two ends don't meet, straighten the rope and roll it under your hands to elongate it further. Form the rope into a donut, overlap the two ends slightly, and press them together to seal, trying not to flatten the seal too much. Just before baking, use scissors to cut one of two patterns into the loaf: To create a spiky effect, make small snips around the entire ring, lifting up the points with the scissors as you cut them. Or make longer cuts (about 2 inches) on the top of the ring, and pull alternating cut pieces of dough in opposite directions to resemble leaves on a branch. Place the crown on a parchment-lined peel or pan to rise.

Epi

An epi is a loaf of bread cut like the top of a blade of wheat. Form the dough into a baguette (see page 36) and let it rise on a well-floured cloth. When the loaf is still

Epi Technique

The correct angle of the scissors for cutting the points on the epi

Pulling the points to alternate sides

The final epi after scoring

slightly underproofed, move it to a baking sheet lined with parchment paper and generously sprinkled with cornmeal. Using sharp scissors, begin at the end of the baguette farthest away from you. Make a shallow 2-inch-long cut on top of the loaf with the point of the flap of dough facing toward you. Lift the cut open and pull the flap of dough to one side. Now make another 2-inch cut in front of the last one. Pull that flap of dough in the opposite direction. Continue to make cuts up the entire baguette, alternately folding the cut dough left and right, until you reach the top. Leave the top bulb-shaped piece straight, like the tip of a shaft of wheat. Bake the loaf immediately.

Fougasse

A plain dough can be shaped and cut into a fougasse or the dough can be filled, then shaped and cut. Use a light white dough such as our French Baguette (page 79) or Focaccia (page 207) for fougasse. Place the dough on a lightly floured surface and pat it into a long narrow rectangle. If you want to fill it, spread a filling such as chopped imported black olives, fresh herbs, or chopped anchovies over the dough, leaving a 1-inch border around the edge. Sprinkle the topping lightly with flour. Fold the dough in thirds like a business letter, the top third down over the

Fougasse Technique

Cutting the opening on a fougasse   Stretching the opening after cutting   The final cut fougasse

middle of the dough and the bottom third over that, completely overlapping the two. Press the three open sides of the fougasse tightly shut.

Let the plain or filled dough rise until doubled in bulk. Then sprinkle a peel or upside-down baking sheet generously with cornmeal and place the fougasse on top, stretching it slightly to make it into a square. Cut a decorative pattern, such as a leaf or a ladder, into the dough with a dough cutter. Stretch the loaf until the cuts form large open holes, then gently slide the fougasse onto a baking stone and bake.

MAKING DECORATIVE PATTERNS AND SCORING

Shape a piece of dough that weighs at least 1 pound into a boule and let it rise until it is still slightly underproofed. Place the loaf on a peel or upside-down baking sheet generously sprinkled with cornmeal. Place a circular cooling rack on top of the loaf and sift or strain flour over the surface. Remove the cooling rack to expose a circular pattern on the top of the loaf. Score the bread along the straight lines that radiate out from the center. Bake, being careful not to spray the loaf when you mist the oven walls, or you will ruin the flour pattern.

Hold a wide chef's knife over the length of a log or a triangular-shaped loaf that is slightly underproofed and sift or strain flour over the top of the bread. Remove the knife and score a series of short cuts across the loaf in the unfloured stripe. Bake the bread immediately.

Allow a round loaf to rise, then score a tic-tac-toe pattern on the top. You can vary the angle of the scored grid, forming square- or diamond-shaped openings.

Dust evenly with flour a 1-pound boule that has just been formed, then press a cake cutter (a ring used to mark portions on a round cake) into the top of the loaf. Press down on the bread firmly enough to make indentations that resemble flower petals. Remove the cake cutter and let the dough rise. Just before baking, dip the rim of a glass in flour and press it down into the middle of the loaf to form the center of the flower.

Saucisson is an attractive cut for log-shaped loaves made with stiffer, denser doughs such as Amy's Rye with Caraway and Mustard Seeds (page 149). Form the dough into a long firm log. Sprinkle the surface evenly with rye or white flour, then score the loaf: Hold a lame or a sharp razor blade perpendicular to the loaf and make a series of slightly diagonal cuts about ¾ inch apart. Let rise and bake normally.

Other Interesting Decorative Patterns and Scoring

Crown Scoring

The angle to hold the scissors for a crown cut

Use shallow snips to make the crown cut.

Saucisson Cut

Hold the blade perpendicular to the loaf for the saucisson.

Tic-Tac-Toe Pattern

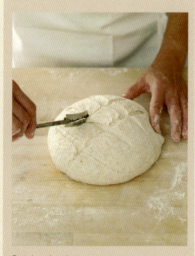

Scoring the tic-tac-toe pattern

Q: How do I determine the proper temperature of ingredients when mixing dough?

A: For our recipes we like the dough to have a temperature of 75° to 77°F when it is fully kneaded. To achieve that, we check the temperature of the various elements that influence the dough—the flour, the air, and the water. Here is a formula that will help you reach the optimum dough temperature. The magic number for us is 225—that is, 75°F multiplied by the three components. Since the flour temperature and room temperature vary depending on the weather, we adjust the temperature of the water, the one variable we can control.

First check the temperature of the flour you'll be using, then check the temperature of your kitchen. If, for example, the flour temperature is 78°F and the room is 80°F, the sum of the two is 158°F. Subtract that from 225°F and you get 67°F, the desired water temperature. The warmth of your hands and the friction caused by kneading will raise the temperature of the dough by three to five degrees, so you should lower the water temperature slightly, to around 63°F, to compensate. If you are using a mixer, be aware that the dough temperature increases by one degree each minute it is mixed on medium speed. After using this formula, check the temperature of the mixed dough with an instant-read thermometer to find out how close you came to our desired result. If biga or poolish is being used cold from the refrigerator, we consider that a fourth element, and the magic number becomes 300 (75 X 4), so you must also check the temperature of that ingredient and subtract it from the magic number.

In the recipes in this book, we have given basic water temperatures that work fine for small batches of dough mixed on moderately temperate days. But if you're making bread on a very hot day, or if you're mixing very large batches of dough, be sure to use the formula given here for each batch of dough.

Q: What do I do if my dough is too wet and looks like heavy pancake batter or porridge?

A: The easiest thing to do is to just throw it out and start again, but think about why that might have happened. Are you sure you weighed/measured all of your ingredients correctly? If so, are you using a lower-protein flour than the recipe specifies? If you are, increase the amount of flour so you'll get dough that is the consistency described in the recipe. Be sure to keep track of the weight of the flour you're adding. If it turns out to be a lot of flour, you may have to adjust some of the other ingredients like the salt to keep the flavor proportions the same. To do this, divide the weight of the salt in the recipe by the original weight of the flour in the recipe to get a percentage number (this is called a baker's percentage); multiply the weight of the flour added by the percentage number to get the extra weight of salt you'll need. For example, say you first used 500 grams of flour, then had to add another 100 grams of flour. The original weight of salt was 10 grams. Ten grams divided by 500 grams is 2 percent (0.02). One hundred grams times 0.02 is 2 grams, so that's the amount of extra salt you'll need to add.

Q: How can I improve the flavor of my bread?

A: Many bread making techniques can improve the flavor of the bread. Of course you should start with good ingredients. Using the best-quality ingredients will make a big difference in the flavor of your bread. Consistently using whole grains and less-refined products, organic flour, fresh nuts, and seasonal produce from a local farmer means your bread will taste that much better. Here are some of the other factors that make a difference.

- **Proper dough hydration:** Making moist dough will improve the flavor of the finished bread. If the dough is too dry, the flour is unable to absorb enough water to become fully hydrated and reach its full flavor potential. Most of our doughs are mixed to achieve a hydration rate of 65 to 75 percent, but wetter doughs, such as Italian ciabatta, can have hydration rates of 80 percent or more. To calculate the hydration rate of a dough, add up the weight of all of the liquids; separately add the weight of all the flours or meals in the dough; divide the weight of the liquids by the weight of the flours. If a dough includes a starter, the weight of the flour and water used to make the starter should also be factored into the formula. In our opinion, the lowest hydration rate that would still result in a workable dough would be 62 percent, but we don't like to work with dough this firm. If you have other bread recipes that you would like to analyze, after determining the hydration rate of the dough, you can adjust the rate by adding or reducing the amount of water to reach the hydration rate you want. Experimentation and experience will tell you the best hydration rate for a specific dough.

- **Proper mixing:** Dough that is made with an autolyse, or rest period, requires less kneading time than dough that is not allowed to rest, so it will be less oxidized by the mixing process. Mixing dough too long, and incorporating too much air into it, destroys the carotenoid pigments in the flour and causes a bleaching effect. This is a common problem in commercial bakeries. The carotenoid pigments in the flour give the dough a fragrant smell, a full flavor, and a crumb with a creamy yellow color. The rest period also lets the gluten in the dough absorb more water with less kneading. And resting makes the dough easier to handle and to shape.

- **Using a ripe sourdough starter, biga, or poolish:** As important as any other factor for developing flavor is the ripeness, or readiness, of the sourdough starter or biga/poolish you mix into the dough. If you're using either a sourdough starter or a sponge starter, be sure it has been allowed to mature fully but is not so old that it doesn't have the strength to leaven the bread properly. As a starter matures it develops organic acids (lactic acid, acetic acid) that make a major contribution to the flavor of bread. A properly matured sourdough starter or sponge starter should have all of the characteristics of ripeness described in Chapter 3.

    If you are making a sponge for a dough that incorporates a sourdough starter, you can determine the sourness of the final dough by the amount of time you age the sponge. For an example of this method, see the recipe for Tangy Twenty-Four-Hour Sourdough on page 129. If you want to make a sourdough bread that is not very tangy, you can use the sponge before it has reached its full sourness. If the same sponge is allowed to mature to a more sour, slightly acidic stage, it will make a tangier, more assertive sourdough bread. The optimum stage is when the sponge tastes slightly sweet with a tangy, slightly sharp aftertaste.

- **Using less yeast and more time for rising:** By reducing the amount of yeast used in standard dough recipes, you can lengthen the fermentation time, allowing the flavors of the other ingredients in the bread to develop and become more pronounced. They will not be masked by a strong taste of yeast. A slower fermentation gives the protein in the flour time to absorb more water, resulting in a loaf with a moister crumb and bread that won't get stale so quickly. Fermentation can be slowed by retarding, or chilling, the dough. Retarding the dough allows more time for the development of organic acids in the dough, which help produce a fuller flavor, a moister texture, and a crunchier crust.

- **Proper fermentation:** To get the best flavor from bread, the fermentation of the dough should be carefully controlled. Try to keep the rising dough at a relatively cool temperature, between 75° and 77°F. Bread dough should be covered when it rises so it stays moist. Let the dough rise as slowly as possible to obtain the fullest flavor from your ingredients.

   If you're working in a cold kitchen, it may be necessary to place the bowl of kneaded dough in a sink filled with warm water to get the dough moving. As long as you keep the dough in the 75° to 77°F range, it's fine.

- **Allow enough time for the first rise:** Make sure to allow the dough to rise completely (it should nearly double) on the first rise. The first rise is most important because most of the flavor development of the dough takes place during that time. Each subsequent rise takes less time and contributes less to the final flavor. (With bread dough that is refrigerated overnight, we consider the first rise to be the rising time before and after it is refrigerated, but before it is shaped.)

- **Browning the crust:** Baking a loaf until the crust has a deep rich brown color will enhance the flavor of the loaf. A dark-crusted loaf of bread has a much fuller flavor than a pale loaf. The reactions between the sugars and amino acids in the dough that result in browning occur only at a temperature above 220°F. As the baking bread reaches this temperature, the crust begins to brown. If the crust is allowed to color fully, the flavor of the caramelized crust will affect the flavor of the whole loaf, because the natural by-products of the sugar–amino acid reaction penetrate inward. Much of the flavor from the crust is transferred to the crumb in the first ten to twenty minutes after the bread is taken from the oven.

STARCH TO SUGAR CONVERSION

Flour is partially made up of starch granules. During fermentation, starch-breaking malt enzymes attack the starch granules, converting them into sugars that the yeast cells use as food.

Q: What factors other than baking time affect crust coloration?

A: Chilling the bread briefly after it has risen, just before baking, will give you a glossier, deeper brown crust. Two factors are involved: First, condensation occurs in the refrigerator, leaving moisture on the crust. The moisture has the same effect as steam in your oven during baking, resulting in a shinier, crisper crust. Second, the greater difference between the dough temperature and the oven temperature after refrigeration causes the bread to brown better. Presumably this is because the yeast action has been slowed down enough to keep the yeast from consuming all of the starch and/or sugar in the dough, allowing those sugars to caramelize in the oven into a golden brown crust.

Sometimes the crust takes a long time to color and never seems to brown enough. If the oven environment is too dry, because steam was not created in the oven or the steam escaped from the oven, the crust will not become as brown as it should and it may have a white, streaky look. Providing adequate moisture around the bread during the first ten minutes of baking is crucial.

Sourdough breads, leavened only with a natural starter, may take longer to brown or may not brown at all because the dough has become too mature and high in acid. The acid-alkaline balance may be off because the dough or the starter fermented for too long, leaving more it acid and less alkaline. (A high-alkaline dough browns better than a dough high in acid.) The yeasts may have consumed all of the starch and sugar in the dough, leaving no sugars to brown or caramelize in the crust.

Salt in the dough may also affect the color of the crust. Dough made without salt will rise relatively quickly because the yeast is not inhibited. Since the fermentation is accelerated, the yeast quickly uses up the supply of starch and sugar in the dough, leaving little natural sugar to color the crust during baking. Dough that is very salty, on the other hand—such as a salt crust used to roast a chicken—won't brown either, because too much salt inhibits browning. The perfect proportion of salt will result in a golden-brown crust (provided the dough has been proofed properly and there is enough moisture in the oven during baking).

Q: I usually mix my dough using warmer water and more yeast than your recipes. What will happen if I modify other recipes by decreasing the yeast and reducing the dough temperature?

A: As the yeast in a dough feeds on starch and sugar, it multiplies. At a lower temperature, this multiplication occurs more slowly than at a higher one. But even with less yeast than in standard recipes, dough that is allowed a long fermentation time will rise as much as yeastier dough once the yeasts build their strength and power. In contrast, if you use a larger amount of yeast or give the dough a warmer rise, the yeast is more quickly exhausted, giving an acidic raw yeast flavor to the bread. And as the dough temperature gets warmer, from 82°F up to 95°F, the yeasts multiply more rapidly and produce gas so the dough rises, but they also give off more sour and unpleasant-smelling by-products that affect the flavor of the bread. That's why we prefer a long, cool fermentation.

Q: How do I convert standard yeast dough recipes to recipes that use a pre-fermented starter?

A: Begin by reducing the amount of yeast by half—but don't use less than one-half teaspoon per pound of flour. Add one and a half cups (340 grams/12.0 ounces) of biga or poolish per one pound of flour and decrease the water in the recipe by a tablespoon for each one and a half cups of pre-ferment added. You may need to add a little more kosher salt, about one-quarter teaspoon per pound (454 grams) of flour, to adjust for the volume of the added pre-ferment.

COMMON PROBLEMS IN BREAD MAKING

The crumb is too dense   The dough was too dry; the dough did not rise enough on the first rise; or the flour used was too strong (that is, too much high-gluten flour).

The crumb is wet and gummy   The dough was too wet and not developed enough through kneading or fermentation; the dough was too cold when it was placed in the oven; or the dough was retarded too long.

The loaf is flat   The dough deflated because it was overproofed; the dough was made too wet, so it spread when rising; or the loaf was shaped too loosely (the skin and the seal of the loaf were not tight enough).

The crust didn't brown or has white streaks   The dough—or the starter—was too mature and too acidic, or there wasn't enough steam in the oven.

The loaf cracked   The dough was not proofed enough or the scored cuts on the loaf were too short or shallow; if the loaf is a rye bread, the dough became highly acidic during the rise, causing the gluten in the dough to break down and the loaf to crack or split before baking. (Rye flour ferments more rapidly than wheat flour, creating acids that break down the weaker gluten structure of rye dough.)

The loaf burst open   The loaf was not proofed enough, and/or it was scored too lightly—or not at all.

The bottom of the bread is dark and the top is too light   The oven heat was uneven, or the loaf was baked too close to the bottom of the oven.

The crust is very thick and tough   The dough was too dry; the dough did not ferment enough on the first rise; there was not enough steam in the oven; or the oven temperature was too low so the bread had to be baked for too long.

The crust is squishy   The loaf was not allowed to brown enough during baking; the bread was not baked long enough after it browned; or the humidity in the air has caused it to soften.

The bread has a big air pocket inside   The dough was not shaped well, or the dough was dry and/or too cold when it went into the oven, creating a pocket under the crust during oven spring.

CLOSING

EATING GOOD BREAD reminds us of why we have devoted our lives to baking. Bread is beautiful, earthy, rich, healthful, humble in its primal simplicity, ancient in its ingredients, satisfying to our bodies, and pleasing to all our senses.

We hope our book will help you enjoy the process of making bread as much as you enjoy eating it.

Good luck and good health!

—AMY AND TOY

Glossary

Ash content A measure of the amount of minerals in a specific flour. A sample of the flour is burned and the ashes, which are composed of minerals, are weighed. Ash content is not considered as important in determining flour quality in America as it is in Europe.

Autolyse The French word for a rest period given to dough during mixing, which allows the gluten in the dough to relax so that the flour can absorb more water. Since kneading time is shortened, the loaves have better flavor because the dough is less oxidized, and they also have a fuller volume.

Baguette The French word for wand or stick, and the name given to a bread shape about three inches wide and twenty-five inches long. Traditional baguettes are made with yeasted white dough and are light and airy with a thin, crisp, golden crust.

Banneton A special basket, often with a linen lining, used for letting dough rise. These baskets work well for soft doughs. Flour is rubbed into the cloth or the grooves of the basket to keep the dough from sticking. The baked loaf has an attractive flour coating and a thicker crust than a loaf risen free-form.

Bâtard A medium-length loaf that is wider in the center and tapered at the tips, often referred to as a French loaf.

Biga The Italian word for a sponge starter made from flour, water, and a tiny bit of yeast. It may be mixed wet or firm and is used to give breads a light, chewy crumb.

Boule The French name for a round ball-shaped loaf. Boule is the root of the word *boulangerie* (bakery). Before the baguette was introduced in France, most loaves were shaped into large or small boules. The person who shaped the bread was the *boulanger* (boule shaper).

Couche The French word for a heavy baker's linen/canvas that is dusted with flour and used to let dough rise. The couche is particularly useful for long, straight loaves like baguettes, ficelles, and bâtards, which are placed side by side on the cloth. The couche cradles the loaves, keeping them straight and preventing them from sticking together.

Crumb The interior of the loaf, also referred to as the *mie*. The crumb is the soft part of the bread, surrounded by the crust.

Elasticity A term describing a dough's ability to spring back when stretched.

Epi A bread shape that looks like the top of a blade of wheat. A long baguette is snipped with scissors and alternating cut sections of dough are pulled in opposite directions to form a decorative pattern.

Extensibility A term used to describe how easily a dough can be stretched once the gluten has been developed through kneading.

Fermentation A bread-making term used to describe the process of dough maturation. Flour and water are mixed with a leavener and allowed to rise and age, resulting in a breakdown of carbohydrates in the dough. The by-products are released in the form of carbon dioxide and alcohol.

Ficelle A slender version of the long, thin baguette loaf. The ficelle is traditionally half the weight of its larger cousin.

Focaccia An Italian flatbread with a dimpled surface. Focaccia can be dressed simply with olive oil and herbs or topped with other ingredients, such as onions, olives, and tomatoes. Focaccia comes from the Latin word *focus*, which means "hearth."

Fougasse A beautiful flat, latticelike bread that originated in the south of France. Some fougasses are filled with ingredients from the Mediterranean, such as black olives, anchovies, or orange flower water. The name comes from the same Latin root as *focaccia*.

Free-form loaf Bread that is shaped and allowed to rise on a flat surface, rather than in a loaf pan, basket, or bread mold that would give it a particular shape.

Gliadin One of the proteins in flour that combines with glutenin to form gluten. It contributes to the extensibility of bread dough.

Gluten The stretchy elastic strands of protein that form when wheat flour is mixed with water and kneaded. The gluten forms a web that traps the carbon dioxide given off by the yeast, causing the dough to rise and creating a network of bubbles in the crumb of the finished loaf.

Glutenin Another protein in wheat flour that combines with the protein gliadin to form gluten. It helps with a dough's strength and elasticity.

Hearth The floor of an oven, usually one made of stone, brick, or cement. Loaves are placed directly on the preheated hearth to bake. A stone hearth can be simulated in a home oven by using a baking stone.

Hydration rate The ratio of water to flour in a dough. See page 260 for instructions on how to determine the hydration rate. In our recipes, the rate is between 65 and 70 percent.

Knead To work a dough by pushing and stretching it in order to develop the gluten in the flour.

Levain The French word for a natural sourdough starter that is made by fermenting a mixture of flour and water until it is ripe enough to leaven bread. The term levain used alone usually refers to a firm, stiff starter that has almost the consistency of dough. (We call the final starter used in our Country Sourdough Boule *levain*; see page 63.) Often the bread made from this starter is also called levain.

Liquid levain The term used for a natural sourdough starter that is made with a high percentage of water relative to the amount of flour.

Mother The word used by some bakers to describe the healthy sourdough starter that is built into the final starter used in various dough recipes. The mother is maintained through regular refreshment with flour and water. When dough is to be made, some of the mother is used to prepare a levain starter or rye sour for the recipe. It is the starter from which all other starters come.

Oven spring The bursting action that occurs when risen dough is placed in a hot oven. When the yeasts get hot, they become very active until they expire at a temperature of 140°F. Their rapid action releases carbon dioxide, which is trapped in the web of gluten in the dough, causing the loaf to "spring up" in the oven, creating a full, well-risen loaf.

Overproof To allow dough to rise too long. Overproofed dough will not rise to its full potential volume in the oven because the yeast supply in the dough has dwindled and the gluten strands have already stretched to their limit, causing the loaf to spread or collapse in the oven's heat.

Pan loaf Bread that is baked in a standard rectangular loaf pan.

Poolish The French name for a wet starter made of flour, water, and a bit of yeast. The poolish is allowed to bubble, rise, and ferment until it nearly triples in volume. When it is ready to use, it will look bubbly and will have tiny folds or creases in the surface where it is just beginning to sink. It should not have completely fallen. Poolish is a sponge starter, similar to biga.

Proof To bring dough to the proper lightness, or to rise. Dough that is fully proofed should have doubled in volume.

Refresh To feed or replenish a starter with flour and water.

Retard To slow the fermentation process of mixed dough. Dough can be placed in a refrigerator or moist retarding chamber to slow the rise, allowing the flavors in the bread to develop more fully over a longer time.

Rise Used interchangeably with "proof" when referring to dough maturation; the action of the dough as it inflates after it is kneaded or shaped into loaves.

Rye sour A sourdough starter made from 100% rye flour and water, used to leaven a batch of dough. If the rye sour is made with salt added it is called a "rye salt sour."

Score To cut or slash the crust of a loaf before baking to create a place for carbon dioxide in the dough to escape. Bread is also scored to give it a more attractive or decorative appearance.

Seam The place where a loaf is sealed after it is shaped. In French it is known as the *clé* (key).

Sourdough bread Any bread made with a natural or wild yeast starter. A sourdough bread can be mild or very tangy depending on the fermentation procedure used. "Pure" sourdough breads are made without the addition of commercial yeast, but tiny quantities of yeast are sometimes used along with a natural starter.

Sourdough starter A mixture of flour, water, and wild yeast that is allowed to ferment and used to leaven bread.

Sponge A mixture of flour, water, and a bit of yeast that is allowed to ferment and is mixed into a dough. In some of our recipes we make a sponge using a portion of the flour, water, and yeast or sourdough starter called for in that specific recipe. This mixture is allowed to ferment for thirty minutes to several hours before it is incorporated into the final dough. In other recipes we use a previously made sponge starter (biga or poolish) that we have maintained.

Sponge starter A starter made from flour, water, and a little bit of yeast that is allowed to ferment until it nearly triples in volume, then begins to crease, fold, and sink slightly on the surface at its peak of ripeness. Biga and poolish are both sponge starters.

Starter Generally, a mixture of flour, water, and some type of leavener—either wild or commercial yeast—that is allowed to ferment and develop to maturity. It is then mixed into bread dough to leaven it, and to improve the flavor, texture, and shelf life of the resulting loaf of bread.

Underproof To keep dough from fully rising or doubling. It is best to bake some breads when they are just slightly underproofed so they get maximum oven spring when they are put into a hot oven.

Mail-Order Sources

Arrowhead Mills Consumer Relations
The Hain Celestial Group
4600 Sleepytime Drive
Boulder, CO 80301
800-434-4246, 7:00 A.M.–5:00 P.M. Mountain Time
www.arrowheadmills.com
A wide variety of stone-ground organic flours (carried by most natural food stores); organic seeds and grains.

Chef's Catalog
www.chefscatalog.com
800-338-3232
Baking stones and peels, KitchenAid mixers, baking pans, and bread molds in a variety of shapes.

Giusto's Specialty Foods
344 Littlefield Avenue
South San Francisco, CA 94080
650-873-6566; 866-972-6879
www.worldpantry.com
Purveyor of high-quality organic flours for over twenty years. Amy's Bread uses their products, as do many of the other respected artisan bread bakers in the United States.

King Arthur Flour, The Baker's Catalogue
58 Billing Farm Road
White River Junction, VT 05001
www.kingarthurflour.com
800-827-6836
Everything for the dedicated baker, including yeast, sourdough starters, proofing baskets and cloths, sheet pans, parchment, and a complete list of excellent flours, both organic and nonorganic; knowledgeable staff, courteous and willing to answer questions about any of their products and services.

Paul's Grains
2475-B 340th Street
Laurel, IA 50141-9513
641-476-3373
www.paulsgrains.com/flours.htm#prodlist
Organic grain farmers who sell their flour online in amounts that are home baker-friendly. Their "Wheat Graham Flour" is a good choice for our recipes that call for "coarse whole wheat flour."

San Francisco Baking Institute (SFBI)
480 Grandview Drive
South San Francisco, CA 94080
650-589-5784
www.sfbi.com
Source for professional grade equipment like bannetons, baker's linen, lames, dough scrapers, and more.

Williams-Sonoma, Inc.
3250 Van Ness Avenue
San Francisco, CA 94109
877-812-6235
www.williams-sonoma.com
High-quality kitchen equipment, including Kitchen-Aid mixers, baking stones, baking pans, circular cooling racks, and other kitchen tools.

Organization

The Bread Bakers Guild of America
670 West Napa Street, Suite B
Sonoma, CA 95476
707-935-1468
www.bbga.org
National nonprofit organization for artisan bread bakers, both professional and nonprofessional. Annual dues are tax-deductible. For more information, see page 9.

Index

Page numbers in *italics* indicate illustrations

A
Acetic acid, 250
Acid-alkaline balance, and crust coloration, 263
Active dry yeast, 50, 250
Aguirre, Dainer, *125*, 125
Alkaline-acid balance, and crust coloration, 263
All-purpose flour, unbleached, 13, 15
Amy's Bread
    at Chelsea Market, 4–5, 46
    in Greenwich Village, 5–6
    in Hell's Kitchen (Ninth Ave.), 2–4
    philosophy of, 7
    pizza toppings, daily, 206
    sandwich ladies at, 211–212, *212*
    staff profiles, 7–8, 46–47, 67, 98, 125, 188–189, 221
    work day/night at, 6–7
Amy's Rye Bread with Caraway and Mustard Seeds, *148*, 149–151
Anaerobic fermentation, 49
Anise, Crispy Bread Sticks with Coriander, Mustard Seeds and, *94*, 95–97
Apricots, Semolina Bread with Sage and, 197–198, *199*, 200
Arrowhead Mills, 15, 269
Artisan Baking Across America (Glezer), 11
"Artisan bread," 9–10
Ascorbic acid solution, 83
Autolyse (resting dough), 25–26, 261

Autumn Pumpkin Bread with Pecans, *233*, 247–249
Avocado and Turkey on Country White Bread, 218, *219*

B
Baguette(s)
    Brie and Tomatoes Vinaigrette on, *217*, 220
    French, *78*, 79–83
    French, Goat Cheese with Black Olive and Roasted Vegetables on a, 215–216, *217*
    of Henri Lovera, 97
    proofing, 83
    proofing, in mold, 39
    scoring, *41*
    shaping, *36*, 36–37
    Wheat, Organic, *100*, 101–104
Baker's linen (couche), 20, 39, 83
Baker's percentage, 260
Baking loaves
    common problems, 264
    loading oven, 40, 42
        oven temperature, 43
    preheating baking stone, 40
    preheating oven, 43
    rotating, 43
    steaming oven, 42–43
Baking sheets, proofing loaves on, 39
Baking stone, 19
    in pizza making, 203
    preheating, 41
    proofing loaves for, 38
    sliding loaves onto, 40, 42

Banneton (proofing basket), 20, 39
Batali, Mario, 203
Bâtard(s)
    Country White (variation), 85–88
    Country White (variation), Turkey and Avocado on, 218, *219*
    Italian Bread, Rustic, Made with Poolish, *84*, 85–88
    Picholine Olive, 179–182, *183*
    Pumpernickel, Chewy (variation), 158, 160
    shaping, *35*, 35–36
    Whole Wheat, with Oats and Pecans (variation), 15
Bell Pepper, Sweet Red, with Black Olive, Rustic, 171–172, *173*, 174
Bianco, Chris, 203
Biga Starter, *53*, 56–57, 58
    in Cinnamon Raisin Bread, *90*, 91–93
    converting standard yeast dough recipes for, 264
    in Focaccia with Fresh Rosemary, 207–208, *209*, 210
    in Onion and Parmesan Bread with Caraway, *162*, 163–165
    in Pumpernickel, Chewy, 157–158, *159*, 160–161
    ripeness of, 261
    in Semolina Bread with Apricots and Sage, 197–198, *199*, 200
    in Semolina Rounds with Black Sesame Seeds, 193–194, *195*, 196
    in Walnut Scallion Bread, Wands of, 175–176, *177*, 178

in Whole Wheat, Course–Grained, with Toasted Walnuts, *108*, 109–111

in Whole Wheat Sandwich Bread with Oats and Pecans, *112*, 113–115

Black Olive
  Goat Cheese with Roasted Vegetables and, on a French Baguette, 215–216, *217*
  with Sweet Red Pepper, Rustic, 171–172, *173*, 174

Black Pepper and Prosciutto Bread, *84*, 89

Black Sesame Seeds, Semolina Rounds with, 193–194, *195*, 196

Bob's Red Mill, 16, 200

Boulangeries, 2

Boule(s)
  Country Sourdough, 120, 121–122, *123*, 124
  Miche, Organic, 139–140, *141*, 142
  Potato Onion Dill Bread, *184*, 185–187
  scoring decorative patterns, 257, *258*
  shaping, *37*, 37
  Teddy Bread, Toy's, *134*, 135–138

Bouley restaurant, 1–2

Bowers, Sharon, 143

Braid shape, 254

Bread, fresh baked
  bagging, 214
  crust, 44
  doneness, testing for, 44
  reheating, 44, 45
  slicing, 45, 218
  storing, 44, 45

Bread: A Baker's Book of Techniques and Recipes (Hamelman), 11

Bread Bakers Guild of America, 9, 269

Bread dough. *See* Bread making

Bread flour, 13, 15
  whole wheat, 14

Bread knife, 45

Bread making. *See also* Equipment and tools; Ingredients
  baking loaves
    common problems, 264
    loading oven, 40, 42, 214
    oven temperature for, 43
    preheating baking stone, 40
    preheating oven, 43
    rotating, 43
    steaming oven, 42–43
  common problems in, 264
  crust
    browning, 262
    coloration of, 44, 262–263
    common problems, 264
    crunchiness, 44
    of milk bread dough, 16
    scoring, 21, 40, *41*, 257, *258*

steaming oven, 43
texture of, 44

dough temperature, optimum, 24, 259, 262

dough temperature, reducing, 263–264

flavor enhancement techniques, 260–262

handmade traditional breads, 8, 10–11

hydration rate in, 24–25, 26, 260

kneading dough
  in electric mixer, 28
  hand kneading, 26, *27*, 28
  skill and strength in, 214
  with special ingredients, 28–29, *29*
  stretch test, 29–30, *30*

mail–order sources for, 269

measuring ingredients, 23–24

physical strength required by, 214

resting dough (autolyse), 25–26, 261

rising dough. *See* Fermentation; Proofing

shaping loaves. *See* Bread shapes

Bread shapes, 214
  baguette, *36*, 36–37
  bâtard, *35*, 35–36
  boule, *37*, 37
  braid, 254
  coil, beehive, or snail, 254
  common problems, 264
  crown (couronne), 255
  decorative patterns and scoring, 257, *258*
  epi, *255*, 255–256
  fougasse, *256*, 256–257
  guidelines for shaping, 253–254
  hand-shaping, 253
  knot, 254–255
  log, 33, *34*
  rolls, *38*, 38
  sunflower, 197

Bread Sticks
  Crispy, with Anise, Coriander, and Mustards Seeds, *94*, 95–97
  Rustic Italian, *84*, 88–89

Bread Twists, Toasty Seeded, *126*, 127–128

Brie and Tomatoes Vinaigrette on Baguette, *217*, 220

Brioche
  Hamburger Buns (variation), 242
  Pan Loaf, *238*, 239–242

Bulgur wheat, substituting for cracked wheat, 138

Buns. *See also* Rolls
  Hamburger, Brioche (variation), 242
  Hot Cross, 46, 243–244, *245*, 246

Butter, 17

C

Cake flour, 14, 15

Cake yeast, compressed, 50–51

Canola oil, 17

Caramel Color, 161
  in Pumpernickel, Chewy, 157–158, *159*, 160–161

Caraway
  Onion and Parmesan Bread with, *162*, 163–165
  in Pumpernickel, Chewy (variation), 161
  Rye, Amy's, with Mustard Seeds and, *148*, 149–151

Carbon dioxide, in bread dough, 49

Carotenoid pigments, 261

Cast-iron skillet, 20

Ceresota/Hecker's flour, 15

Chaffin, David, *67*, 67

Challah, Whole Wheat, 105–107

Chang, Joanne, 11

Cheddar Cheese Sandwich, Grilled New York State, 225–226, *227*

Cheese, 19
  Brie and Tomatoes Vinaigrette on Baguette, *217*, 220
  Goat Cheese with Black Olive and Roasted Vegetables on a French Baguette, 215–216, *217*
  Grilled New York State Cheddar Cheese Sandwich, 225–226, *227*
  Parmesan and Onion Bread with Caraway, *162*, 163–165
  Pizza Crust with Simple Toppings, A Versatile, *202*, 203–206
  Tuna Melt, 213–214

Chef's Catalog, 269

Chelsea Market, 4–5, 46

Chernich, Alice B., 105

Cherry Chocolate Rolls, 231–232, *233*, 234

Chicago sourdough bread, 251

Chocolate Cherry Rolls, 231–232, *233*, 234

Ciabatta, Rustic Italian (variation), 88

Cinnamon Raisin Bread, *90*, 91–93

Cocoa Powder
  in Chocolate Cherry Rolls, 231–232, *233*, 234
  measuring, 234
  in Pumpernickel, Chewy, 157–158, *159*, 160–161

Coffee
  in Chocolate Cherry Rolls, 231–232, *233*, 234
  in Pumpernickel, Chewy, 157–158, *159*, 160–161

Cohen, Irwin, 4

Coil shape, 254

Colicchio, Tom, 2, 109, 149

Coloration, crust, 44, 262–263
Comess, Noel, 11
Compressed cake yeast, 50
Coriander, Crispy Bread Sticks with
    Anise, Mustard Seeds and, *94,*
    95–97
Cornmeal, 16
    coating peel with, 38–39
    medium, 200
Couche (baker's linen), 20, 39, 83
Country Sourdough (variation), 124–125
    in Grilled New York State Cheddar
        Cheese Sandwich, 225–226, *227*
Country Sourdough Boule, 120, 121–
    122, *123,* 124
Country White Bâtard (variation),
    85–88
    Turkey and Avocado on, 218, *219*
Coupe du Monde de la Boulangerie
    (World Cup of Bread Baking), 9
Course–Grained Whole Wheat with
    Toasted Walnuts, *108,* 109–111
Covering dough, 30
Cracked loaf, problem of, 156, 264
Cracked Wheat
    bulgur as substitute for, 138
    soaking, 18, 138
    in Teddy Bread, Toy's, *134,* 135–138
Craft bakeries, 10
Crown (couronne) shape, 255
Crown scoring, 257, *258*
Crust
    browning, 262
    coloration of, 44, 262–263
    common problems, 264
    crunchiness, 44
    of milk bread dough, 16
    scoring, 21, 40, *41,* 257, *258*
    steaming oven, 43
    texture of, 44
    white streaks in, 43, 264
Crust & Crumb (Reinhart), 11
Currants, in Hot Cross Buns, 243–
    244, *245,* 246

D
Decorative patterns, scoring, 40, *41,*
    257, *258*
Dill Potato Onion Bread, *184,*
    185–187
"Dimpling" focaccia dough, 207
Dinner Rolls, Fragrant Whole Wheat,
    116, 117–119
Doneness, testing for, 44
Dough temperature
    controlling, 22, 24, 31
    optimum, 24, 259, 262
    reducing, 263–264
Dupree, Toy Kim, 2
Durum flour, patent, 14, 190
    working with, 196
Durum wheat, 14

E
Eggplant, in Goat Cheese with Black
    Olive and Roasted Vegetables on
    a French Baguette, 215–216, *217*
Eggs, in bread dough, 17
Electric mixer, 20, 28
Epi shape, *255,* 255–256
Equipment and tools
    mail-order sources, 269
    for sourdough breads, 58
    types of, 19–22
Escali Primo scale, 21

F
Fats, in bread dough, 17
Fermentation. *See also* Proofing
    covering dough, 30
    and dough temperature, 24, 48–49,
        262, 263–264
    first rise, 30–31, 262
    long fermentation time, 24, 263–264
    and room temperature, 24, 31
    second rise, 31
    slow, cool rise technique, 24
    slowing/retarding, 31–32, 261
    starch to sugar conversion, 262
    tests of, 31, *32,* 32–33
Ficelle
    proofing in mold, 39
    shaping, 36–37
Field, Carol, 231
Fig and Maple Walnut Bread, 235–
    236, *237*
Flavor enhancement techniques,
    260–262
Flax Seed(s), 18
    soaking, 138, 143
    in Teddy Bread, Toy's, *134,* 135–138
    Whole Grain Spelt, Organic, with
        Sesame and, *133,* 143–146
Flour. *See also* Rye flour; Whole wheat
    flour
    bread, 13, 15
    bread, whole wheat, 14
    cake, 14
    carotenoid pigments in, 261
    durum, patent, 14, 190
    durum, patent, working with, 196
    high–gluten, 13–14
    increasing amount, 259–260
    measuring, 23
    organic, 101
    pastry, 14
    protein content of, 13, 15
    selecting, 12–13
    semolina, 14
    in sourdough starter, 57
    spelt, 146
    storage of, 14
    temperature of, 22, 259
    weighing, 260

Flower petal pattern, 257
Focaccia with Fresh Rosemary, 207–
    208, *209,* 210
Fougasse shape, *256,* 256–257
Freezing bread, 45
French Baguette, *78,* 79–83
    Goat Cheese with Black Olive
        and Roasted Vegetables on a,
        215–216, *217*
French Rye, *152,* 153–156
    Open-Face Mini Smoked Salmon
        Sandwiches on, 228
Fruit, Dried. *See also* Raisin(s)
    Fig and Maple Walnut Bread, 235–
        236, *237*
    in Hot Cross Buns, 243–244, *245,*
        246
    soaking, 18
Full–Flavored Breads. *See* Specialty
    Breads

G
Garbanzo Beans, in Vegetarian
    Hummus on Organic Miche, *222,*
    223–224
Giusto Specialty Foods, 269
Glezer, Maggie, 11
Gluten development, 26
Goat Cheese with Black Olive and
    Roasted Vegetables on a French
    Baguette, 215–216, *217*
Golden Italian Semolina Loaves,
    191–192, *199*
Golden Whole Wheat Bread, *74,*
    75–77
Gold Medal flour, 15
Grande, Jorge, *221,* 221
Grilled New York State Cheddar
    Cheese Sandwich, 225–226, *227*

H
Ham, as pizza topping, 205
Hamburger Buns, Brioche (variation),
    242
Hamelman, Jeffrey, 11
Herbs, fresh and dry, 19
High–gluten flour, 13–14
Hodgson Mill, 75
Honey
    measuring oil and, 111, 119
    in Pumpernickel, Chewy, 157–158,
        159, 160–161
    in Pumpkin Bread, Autumn, with
        Pecans, *233,* 247–249
    as sweetener, 17
    in Walnut Scallion Bread, Wands of,
        175–176, *177,* 178
    in Whole Wheat, Course–Grained,
        with Toasted Walnuts, *108,*
        109–111
    in Whole Wheat Dinner Rolls, Fra-
        grant, *116,* 117–119

in Whole Wheat Sandwich Bread
with Oats and Pecans, *112*,
113–115
Hot Cross Buns, 46, 243–244, *245*, 246
Hummus, Vegetarian, on Organic
Miche, *222*, 223–224
Hydration rate, 24–25, 26, 260

I

Ingredients, 13–19. *See also* Flour;
Water
cornmeal, 16
eggs, 17
fat, 17
liquids, 16
mail–order sources, 269
measuring/weighing, 23–24,
259–260
oats, 16
salt, 17
for sandwiches, 212
specialty, 18–19
sweeteners, 17
temperature of, 22, 259
yeast, 49–51
Instant yeast, 51
Italian Baker, The (Field), 231
Italian Bread(s)
Ciabatta, Rustic (variation), 88
Prosciutto and Black Pepper (variation), *84*, 89
Rustic, *84*, 85–88
Semolina Loaves, Golden, 191–192,
199
Italian Bread Sticks, Rustic (variation),
84, 88–89

J

Jacques, Kendall, *46*, 46

K

King Arthur Flour Company, 15, 20,
21, 52, 75, 105, 124, 161, 269
KitchenAid stationary mixer, 20, 28
Kneading dough
in electric mixer, 28
hand kneading, 26, *27*, 28
skill and strength in, 214
with special ingredients, 28–29, *29*
stretch test, 29–30, *30*
Knives, serrated, 45
Knot shape, 254–255
Kosher salt, 17

L

Lactic acid, 250
Lactobacilli, 250–251
Lahey, Jim, 11, 203
Lame, scoring crust with, 21, 40, *41*
"Lau" (Wen Hong Liu), *98*, 98
Leader, Dan, 11

Leaveners, 48–49. *See also* Biga
Starter; Poolish; Sourdough
Starter(s)
yeast, 49–51
Levain
feeding, 122
Firm, 58, 63
Firm, in Country Sourdough Boule,
122
Firm, in Rye, Amy's, with Caraway
and Mustard Seeds, 149–150
Liquid, *53*, 61, 62
Liquid, in Tangy Twenty-Four-
Hour Sourdough, 129-130
Miche, 58, 64–65
Miche, in Organic Miche, 139–140
Spelt, 58, 68–69
Spelt, in Whole Grain Spelt, Or-
ganic, with Flax and Sesame, 144
Liquid ingredients, 16
Liquid measurements, 23–24
Loading oven, 40, 42, 214
Loaf pans. *See also* Pan Loaves
proofing loaves in, 39
Local Breads (Leader), 11
Log shape, 33, *34*
Lovera, Henri, 97

M

Mackay, Mary, 11
Mackie, Leslie, 10
Mail-order sources, 269
Maltose, 251
Maple syrup, as sweetener, 17
Maple Walnut and Fig Bread, 235–
236, *237*
McDevitt, Kerrie, 46–47, *47*
Measurement
flour, 23
honey and oil, 111, 119
liquid, 23–24
weighing, 24, 259–260
yeast, 51
Measuring cups, liquid, 24
Miche, 5–6
Organic, 139–140, *141*, 142
Organic, Vegetarian Hummus on,
222, 223–224
Miche Levain, 58, 64–65
in Organic Miche, 139–140
Milk, in bread dough, 16
Misting loaves, 42–43
Mixer, electric, 20, 28
Moisture
hydration rate, 24–25, 26, 260
too wet dough, 25, 259–260
water temperature, 16, 22, 259
Molasses
in Bread Sticks, Crispy, with Anise,
Coriander, and Mustard Seeds,
94, 95–97

in Pumpernickel, Chewy, 157–158,
159, 160–161
as sweetener, 17
in Whole Wheat Sandwich Bread
with Oats and Pecans, *112*,
113–115
Mold, baguette, 39
Mondrian restaurant, 109, 120, 149,
190
Mozzarella, Pizza Crust with Simple
Toppings, A Versatile, *202*,
203–206
Murray's Cheese, 5
Mushrooms, as pizza topping, 205
Mustard Seeds
Crispy Bread Sticks with Anise,
Coriander and, *94*, 95–97
Rye, Amy's, with Caraway and,
148, 149–151

N

Nuts
adding, 18
kneading into dough, 28–29
Pecans with Pumpkin Bread,
Autumn, *233*, 247–249
Pecans, Whole Wheat Sandwich
Bread with Oats and, *112*,
113–115
toasting, 111
Walnut Maple and Fig Bread, 235–
236, *237*
Walnut Scallion Bread, Wands of,
175–176, *177*, 178
Walnuts, Toasted, Course–Grained
Whole Wheat with, *108*,
109–111

O

Oats
in Maple Walnut and Fig Bread,
235–236, *237*
rolled, 16
Whole Wheat Sandwich Bread with
Pecans and, *112*, 113–115
Oland, Paula, 11, 125
Olive(s)
Black Olive, Goat Cheese with
Roasted Vegetables and, on a
French Baguette, 215–216, *217*
Black Olive with Sweet Red Pepper,
Rustic, 171–172, *173*, 174
halving, 182
kneading into dough, 28–29
Picholine Olive Bread, 179–182,
183
Picholine Olive Bread, Rare Roast
Beef with Sautéed Onions on,
229
pizza topping, 205
selecting, 18

Olive Oil, 17
   in Bread Sticks, Crispy, with Anise, Coriander, and Mustards Seeds, *94*, 95–97
   in Bread Twists, Toasty Seeded, *126*, 127–128
   in Focaccia with Fresh Rosemary, 207–208, *209*, 210
   in Pizza Crust with Simple Toppings, A Versatile, *202*, 203–206
   with Rosemary Bread, Fresh, 167–168, *169*, 170
   in Tomatoes Vinaigrette and Brie on Baguette, *217*, 220
Onion(s)
   and Parmesan Bread with Caraway, *162*, 163–165
   Potato Dill Bread, *184*, 185–187
   Sautéed, with Rare Roast Beef, on Picholine Olive Bread, 229
Open-Face Mini Smoked Salmon Sandwiches on French Rye, 228
Organic Miche, 139–140, *141*, 142
   Vegetarian Hummus on, *222*, 223–224
Organic Wheat Baguette, *100*, 101–104
Oven
   loading, 40, 42
   preheating, 43
   preheating baking stone, 40
   rotating loaves in, 43
   steaming, 42–43
   temperature of, 43
Oven spring, 19, 33, 42, 43–44
Oven thermometer, 22, 43
Overproofing, 33, 43–44, 83, 264

P
Pan Loaves
   Brioche Pan Loaf, *238*, 239–242
   Cinnamon Raisin Bread, *90*, 91–93
   Country Sourdough (variation), 124–125
   Country Sourdough (variation), in Grilled New York State Cheddar Cheese Sandwich, 225–226, *227*
   Onion and Parmesan Bread with Caraway, *162*, 163–165
   Pumpernickel, Chewy, 157–158, *159*, 160–161
   White, Big Beautiful, 71–72, *73*
   Whole Grain Spelt, Organic, with Flax and Sesame, *133*, 143–146
   Whole Wheat Sandwich Bread with Oats and Pecans, *112*, 113–115
Parchment paper, 21
Parmesan
   and Onion Bread with Caraway, *162*, 163–165

Pizza Crust with Simple Toppings, A Versatile, *202*, 203–206
Pastry flour, 14
Paul's Grains, 138, 269
Pecans
   with Pumpkin Bread, Autumn, *233*, 247–249
   Whole Wheat Sandwich Bread with Oats and, *112*, 113–115
Peel, wooden, 19
   proofing loaves on, 38–39
   sliding loaves onto baking stone, 40, 42
Picholine Olive Bread, 179–182, *183*
   Rare Roast Beef with Sautéed Onions on, 229
Pillsbury flour, 15
Pizza Crust with Simple Toppings, A Versatile, *202*, 203–206
Pizza toppings, suggestions for, 205, 206
Pleasant View Farm, 77
Poilâne, Lionel, 139
Polenta, 16
Ponsford, Craig, 10
Poolish, 52, *53*, 54–55, 58
   in Baguette, French, 78, 79–83
   in Baguette, Wheat, Organic, *100*, 101–104
   in Black Olive with Sweet Red Pepper, Rustic, 171–172, *173*, 174
   in Brioche Pan Loaf, *238*, 239–242
   converting standard yeast dough recipes for, 264
   in Dinner Rolls, Fragrant Whole Wheat, *116*, 117–119
   in Italian Bread, Rustic, *84*, 85–88
   in Picholine Olive Bread, 179–182, *183*
   ripeness of, 261
   in Rosemary Bread, Fresh, with Olive Oil, 167–168, *169*, 170
Poppy Seeds, 18
   Bread Twists, Toasty Seeded, *126*, 127–128
Potato Onion Dill Bread, *184*, 185–187
Pre-ferment. *See* Sourdough Starter
Proofed loaves, refrigerating, 42
Proofing, 31
   baguettes, 39, 83
   on baker's linen (couche), 20, 39, 83
   in banneton (proofing basket), 20, 39
   overproofing, 33, 43–44, 83, 264
   on peel, 38–39, 83
   testing loaves during, 32–33
   underproofing, 33, 264
Proofing basket (banneton), 20, 39
Prosciutto and Black Pepper Bread, *84*, 89

Protein content of flour, 13, 15
Pumpernickel, Chewy, 157–158, *159*, 160–161
Pumpernickel flour, 15, 124, 161
Pumpkin Bread, Autumn, with Pecans, *233*, 247–249

Q
Quick Bread, Maple Walnut and Fig, 235–236, *237*
Quick-rise yeast, 51

R
Raisin(s)
   Cinnamon Bread, *90*, 91–93
   kneading into dough, 28–29
   in Pumpernickel, Chewy, 157–158, *159*, 160–161
   in sourdough starter, 252
   in Whole Wheat Sandwich Bread with Oats and Pecans (variation), 15
Red Pepper, Sweet, with Black Olive, Rustic, 171–172, *173*, 174
Refrigeration of dough
   and crust coloration, 262–263
   and first rise, 262
   proofed "holding" loaves, 42
   for retarding fermentation, 31–32
Refrigeration of sourdough starter, 60, 251
Reinhart, Peter, 11
Resting dough (autolyse), 25–26, 261
Retarding dough (slowing fermentation), 31–32
Rising bread dough. *See* Fermentation; Proofing
Roast Beef, Rare, with Sautéed Onions on Picholine Olive Bread, 229
Rolls
   Challah, Whole Wheat, 105–107
   Chocolate Cherry, 231–232, *233*, 234
   Dinner, Fragrant Whole Wheat, *116*, 117–119
   Hamburger Buns, Brioche (variation), 242
   Hot Cross Buns, 46, 243–244, *245*, 246
   shaping, *38*, 38
Roman, Orlando, *188*, 188
Room temperture, 24, 31, 259
Room thermometer, 22
Rosada, Didier, 11
Rosemary
   Bread, Fresh, with Olive Oil, 167–168, *169*, 170
   Fresh, Focaccia with, 207–208, *209*, 210
Rustic Black Olive with Sweet Red Pepper, 171–172, *173*, 174

Rustic Italian Bread, *84*, 85–88
  Ciabatta (variation), 88
  Prosciutto and Black Pepper
    (variation), *84*, 89
Rustic Italian Bread Sticks, *84*, 88–89
Rye Berries
  cooking, 18, 110
  in Rye with Caraway and Mustard
    Seeds, Amy's, *148*, 149–151
Rye Bread(s), 147–165
  Amy's, with Caraway and Mustard
    Seeds, *148*, 149–151
  French, *152*, 153–156
  French, Open-Face Mini Smoked
    Salmon Sandwiches on, 228
  Onion and Parmesan, with
    Caraway, *162*, 163–165
  Pumpernickel, Chewy, 157–158,
    159, 160–161
Rye flour
  characteristics of, 147
  fermentation, 264
  high-percentage rye dough, 153
  protein content of, 15
  pumpernickel, 15, 124, 161
  in starters, 57, 61
Rye Salt Sour Starter, *53*, 58, 66–67
  in French Rye, 153–154
  in Pumpernickel, Chewy, 157–158
  in Sourdough, Tangy Twenty-Four-
    Hour, 129–130
  in Teddy Bread, Toys, 135
Rye Sourdough Starter, 57, 61, 252
  and Wheat (Miche Levain), 64–65

S
Sage, Semolina Bread with Apricots
    and, 197–198, *199*, 200
Salmon, Smoked, Open-Face Mini
    Sandwiches on French Rye, 228
Salt
  baker's percentage, 260
  and crust color, 263
  kosher salt, substituting for regular
    salt, 17
  Rye Salt Sour Starter, *53*, 58,
    66–67
  and yeast activity, 49
Sandwich Bread, Whole Wheat, with
    Oats and Pecans, *112*, 113–115
Sandwiches, 211–229
  Brie and Tomatoes Vinaigrette on
    Baguette, *217*, 220
  Cheddar Cheese, Grilled New York
    State, 225–226, *227*
  Goat Cheese with Black Olive and
    Roasted Vegetables on a French
    Baguette, 215–216, *217*
  Hummus, Vegetarian, on Organic
    Miche, *222*, 223–224
  ingredients for, 212

Roast Beef, Rare, with Sautéed
    Onions on Picholine Olive Bread,
    229
  Smoked Salmon, Open-Face Mini,
    on French Rye, 228
  Tuna Melt, 213–214
  Turkey and Avocado on Country
    White Bread, 218, *219*
San Francisco Baking Institute (SFBI),
    20, 269
San Francisco-style sourdough bread,
    61, 120, 129, 251
Saucisson cut, 257, *258*
Sausage, as pizza topping, 205
Scale, digital kitchen, 20–21, 24
Scallion Walnut Bread, Wands of,
    175–176, *177*, 178
Scissors, scoring with, 40
Scoring crust, 21, 40, *41*, 257, *258*
Seeded Bread Twists, Toasty, *126*,
    127–128
Seeds, 18. *See also specific seeds*
  garnishing with, 254
  soaking, 138, 143
Semolina Bread(s), 190–200
  with Apricots and Sage, 197–198,
    199, 200
  cornmeal in, 16
  flour for, 14, 190
  Golden Italian Semolina Loaves,
    191–192, *199*
  Rounds with Black Sesame Seeds,
    193–194, *195*, 196
Semolina flour, 14

Sesame Seed(s)
  Black, Semolina Rounds with,
    193–194, *195*, 196
  in Bread Sticks, Crispy, with Anise,
    Coriander, and Mustards Seeds,
    94, 95–97
  in Bread Twists, Toasty Seeded,
    126, 127–128
  in Dinner Rolls, Fragrant Whole
    Wheat, *116*, 117–119
  soaking, 138, 143
  in Teddy Bread, Toy's, *134*, 135–138
  unhulled, 18
  Whole Grain Spelt, Organic, with
    Flax and, *133*, 143–146
Shaping bread dough. *See* Bread shapes
Sheet pans, 21
Silverton, Nancy, 203
Skillet, cast-iron, 20
Slicing bread, 45, 218
"Slow, cool rise" technique, 24
Smoked Salmon, Open-Face Mini,
    Sandwiches on French Rye, 228
Sourdough Bread(s), 120–145
  Country (variation), 124–125
  Country (variation), in Grilled New

York State Cheddar Cheese Sand-
    wich, 225–226, *227*
Country Boule, 120, 121–122, *123*,
    124
crust coloration of, 263
Miche, Organic, 139–140, *141*, 142
mild-flavored, 61
San Francisco-style, 61, 120, 129,
    251
Teddy Bread, Toy's, *134*, 135–138
Toasty Seeded Bread Twists, *126*,
    127–128
Twenty-Four-Hour, Tangy, 129–
    132, *133*
Whole Grain Spelt, Organic, with
    Flax and Sesame, *133*, 143–146
Sourdough Starter(s), 15. *See also*
    Levain
acid-alkaline balance, 263
chemistry of, 250–251
converting standard yeast dough
    recipes for, 264
creating your own, 57, 252–253
dehydrating, 251
feeding (refreshing), 57–58, 60, 251
freezing, 251
longevity of, 251
premade, 52
reactivating, 251
ripeness of, 261
Rye, 57, 61, 252
Rye Salt Sour, *53*, 58, 66–67
  in French Rye, 153–154
  in Pumpernickel, Chewy,
    157–158
  in Teddy Bread, Toy's, 135
  in Twenty-Four-Hour Sour-
    dough, Tangy, 129–130
Rye and Wheat (Miche Levain),
    64–65
sourness, determining, 261
storage of, 60, 251
terminology of, 58
water to flour proportion, 61
White, 59–60, 252
yeast in, 52, 252
Specialty Breads, 166–189. *See also*
    Sweet Specialty Breads
Black Olive with Sweet Red Pepper,
    Rustic, 171–172, *173*, 174
Picholine Olive, 179–182, *183*
Potato Onion Dill, *184*, 185–187
Rosemary, Fresh, with Olive Oil,
    167–168, *169*, 170
Walnut Scallion, Wands of, 175–
    176, *177*, 178
Specialty ingredients, kneading into
    dough, 18–19, *19*
Spelt, Organic Whole Grain, with
    Flax and Sesame, *133*, 143–146
Spelt flour, 146

Spelt Levain, 58, 68–69
  in Organic Whole Grain Spelt with
    Flax and Sesame, 144
Spices, in bread making, 19
Sponge Starter. *See* Biga Starter; Pool-
    ish
Starters. *See also* Biga Starter; Poolish;
    Sourdough Starter(s)
  defined, 51–52
Steaming oven, 42–43
Storage
  bread, 44, 45
  flour, 14
  sourdough starter, 60, 251
  yeast, 50
Sugar, 17, 49
Sullivan, Steve, 11
Sunflower bread shape, 197
Sunflower Seeds, 18
  in Pumpernickel, Chewy, 157–158,
    159, 160–161
Swans Down flour, 15
Sweeteners, in bread making, 17
Sweet Specialty Breads, 230–249. *See
    also* Brioche
  Chocolate Cherry Rolls, 231–232,
    233, 234
  Hot Cross Buns, 46, 243–244, *245*,
    246
  Maple Walnut and Fig, 235–236,
    237
  Pumpkin, Autumn, with Pecans,
    233, 247–249
  yeast in, 49

T
Tahini Sauce, in Vegetarian Hummus
    on Organic Miche, *222*, 223–224
Tangy Twenty-Four Hour Sourdough,
    129–132, *133*
Tapenade, Black Olive, Goat Cheese
    with Roasted Vegetables and, on a
    French Baguette, 215–216, *217*
Team USA, 9
Teddy Bread, Toy's, *134*, 135–138
Temperature. *See also* Dough tem-
    perature
  of baked loaf, 44
  oven, 43
  room, 24, 31, 259
  water, 16, 22, 259
Thermometers, 22
  instant-read digital, 22, 24
Tic-tac-toe pattern, 40, 257, *258*
Timer, digital, 22
Tomatoes
  in Goat Cheese with Black Olive

and Roasted Vegetables on a
    French Baguette, 215–216, *217*
  Vinaigrette and Brie on Baguette,
    217, 220
Tomato sauce, for pizza, 206
Tools. *See* Equipment and tools
Toy's Teddy Bread, *134*, 135–138
Tuna Melt, 213–214
Turkey and Avocado on Country
    White Bread, 218, *219*
Twenty-Four-Hour Sourdough,
    Tangy, 129–130
Twists, Bread, Toasty Seeded, 127–128

U
Unbleached all–purpose flour, 13, 15
Underproofing, 33, 264

V
Vegetables
  in bread dough, 18–19
  Roasted, Goat Cheese with Black
    Olive and, on a French Baguette,
    215–216, *217*
Vegetarian Hummus on Organic
    Miche, *222*, 223–224
Vicuna, Alfredo, 188–189, *189*
Vital wheat gluten, 13–14

W
Walnut(s)
  Maple and Fig Bread, 235–236, *237*
  Scallion Bread, Wands of, 175–176,
    177, 178
  Toasted, Course–Grained Whole
    Wheat with, *108*, 109–111
Walnut Oil, 17
  in Walnut Scallion Bread, Wands of,
    175–176, *177*, 178
Water
  bottled and tap, 16
  hydration rate, 24–25, 26, 260
  mixing dough, 25
  temperature, 16, 22, 259
  too wet dough, 25, 259–260
Water pan, in oven, 42–43
Weighing ingredients, 24, 259–260
Wen Hong Liu ("Lau"), *98*, 98
Wetter dough, 16, 24–25, 26, 260
Wheat Berries
  cooking, 18, 110
  in Dinner Rolls, Fragrant Whole
    Wheat, *116*, 117–119
  storage of, 14
  in Whole Wheat, Course-Grained,
    with Toasted Walnuts, *108*,
    109–111

Wheat bran, 14
Wheat flours, 13
Wheat germ, 14
Wheat and Rye Sourdough Starter
    (Miche Levain), 64–65
White Bread(s)
  Black Olive with Sweet Red Pepper,
    Rustic, 171–172, *173*, 174
  Ciabatta, Rustic Italian (variation),
    88
  Cinnamon Raisin, *90*, 91–93
  Country Bâtard (variation), 85–88
  Country Bâtard (variation), Turkey
    and Avocado on, 218, *219*
  Italian, Rustic, *84*, 85–88
  Pan Loaf, Big Beautiful, 71–72, *73*
  pan loaf, memories of grandparents'
    farm, 77
White Sourdough Starter, 59–60, 252
Whole Foods 365 flour, 15
Whole Grain Spelt, Organic, with
    Flax and Sesame, *133*, 143–146
Whole Wheat Bread(s), 99–119
  aroma of, 104
  Baguette, Organic, *100*, 101–104
  Challah, 105–107
  Course-Grained, with Toasted Wal-
    nuts, *108*, 109–111
  Dinner Rolls, Fragrant, *116*,
    117–119
  Golden, *74*, 75–77
  protein content of, 15
  Sandwich, with Oats and Pecans,
    112, 113–115
Whole wheat flour
  with bran, 124
  bread, 14
  course, 107, 138
  milling of, 14
  organic stone-ground, 14, 75, 101,
    104
  protein content of, 15
Williams, Lynn and Jim, 11
Williams-Sonoma Inc., 269
Window pane stretch test, for kneaded
    dough, 29–30, *30*
World Cup of Bread Baking (*Coupe du
    Monde de la Boulangerie*), 9

Y
Yeast
  consistent results with, 250
  decreasing amount of, 49, 261,
    263–264
  in starter, 52, 252
  in sweet breads, 49
  types of, 49–51